The Home Equity
Sharing Manual

The Home Equity Sharing Manual

David Andrew Sirkin

John Wiley & Sons, Inc.

New York • Chichester • Brisbane • Toronto • Singapore

Library of Congress Cataloging-in-Publication Data:

Sirkin, David Andrew, 1960–
    The home equity sharing manual / by David Andrew Sirkin.
      p.   cm.
    ISBN 0-471-58733-8
    1. Mortgage loans, Equity sharing—United States.   2. House
buying—United States—Case studies.   3. Real estate investment—
United States.   I. Title.
HG2040.15.S57   1994
332.7'22'0973—dc20   94-6190

Printed in the United Sates of America

10 9 8 7 6 5 4 3 2 1

Acknowledgments

The best information in this book is the product of the questions and experiences of my equity sharing clients. I also acknowledge the real estate agents and staff of Property Resource Group who contributed their insights and patience while this book was written. Thanks to Jill Holmquist of Information Finders for her help on research, and to Michael Bittner, CPA, for his willingness to act as a sounding board on tax issues.

Although masculine pronouns are used throughout this book, there is no intent to imply any gender bias.

D.A.S.

Contents

The Home Equity
Sharing Manual

One

Introduction

I first became interested in equity sharing through my own experience. When I arrived in San Francisco in 1984, freshly married, matriculated, and hired, I expected to buy a home. The first few weekends spent touring open houses quickly shattered my illusions. The reality, I discovered, was that neither I nor any of my new colleagues could afford a family home in a nice neighborhood less than an hour from work. Prospects for home ownership were even worse for the less-well-paid nonlawyers in the office, who would need to commute up to two hours to the nearest affordable home. And our home ownership prospects were unlikely to improve; most of the lawyers and staff members who were three to five years our senior had abandoned hope of ever owning a home.

Tempted by tales of a booming San Francisco home market, an out-of-town acquaintance who had money to invest suggested we pool our resources and buy a home together. We would split the down payment, and I would live in the home and make the monthly payments. After five years, we would sell the home and share the profits. The proposal sounded perfect, and my wife and I jumped at the chance. Three months later, we were home owners. Six months later, by way of a newspaper article, I discovered we were equity sharing.

TROUBLE WITH THE AMERICAN DREAM

Almost everyone agrees that owning is better than renting. Over ten years, a $1,000-per-month renter invests the equivalent of $182,946 in the tenancy and has nothing to show for it. If, instead, the renter had spent the $1,000 per month on payments for a $150,000 home, he could have paid down his mortgage $20,541, saved up to $31,000 in income taxes, and had the pride and security of owning a home. If appreciation were only average for the past 40 years, he also would have made a profit of $144,000—a return of 96 percent per year.

But over the past ten years, the benefits of home ownership have slid further out of reach for the average American renter. Although the period ended with a real estate slump, the cost of the median-priced home nationwide increased 68 percent while average income, adjusted for inflation, rose only 13.4 percent. In 1980, the median-priced American home cost 3.66 times the average income; today, that figure is an astounding 5.38 times the average income and is even higher in major cities. Not surprisingly, the percentage of Americans who own homes has dropped for the first time in 50 years. The current rate of home ownership in America ranks behind the rates in Ireland, Spain, Belgium, Greece, Italy, New Zealand, the U.K., Australia, Norway, and Bangladesh!

Sadly, the dream of traditional home ownership is now out of reach for most Americans. A recent survey revealed that a staggering 82 percent of America's 43 million prospective first-time home buyers believed they could not save enough money for a down payment. At a time when the real estate recession should have been an opportunity, median income is $4,000 less than the amount needed to buy a starter home, and fewer than 20 percent of American households can afford the median-priced home in most major metropolitan areas.

Few analysts are forecasting increased affordability during the 1990s. Our economy is engaged in massive restructuring in response to new global competition, a process that is likely to keep wage increases low. At the same time, growth control measures are restricting the supply of new housing, a factor that will ultimately cause prices to rise. Faced with these daunting prospects, young American families are desperately searching for creative new ways to buy their first home. Equity sharing may be their most promising method.

A SOLUTION THAT WORKS

Equity sharing can bridge the widening gap between most American renters and the dream of home ownership. The following three narratives of equity sharing transactions illustrate the benefits of this unique approach to real estate ownership.

Example 1.1   Equity Sharing with "Stranger" Investor

Juan and Celia Moreno had good jobs and owned their home. They fantasized about investing in real estate, and read every "how to" book they could find. But after five years of saving, they had accumulated only $10,000 to invest, not enough for a down payment on any home or investment property in their area. They were particularly frustrated when a house on their block, 12 Adler Circle, came on the market for $150,000, an amount they felt was at least $5,000 less than the home was worth. Janet Williams was also frustrated. After six months of looking, 12 Adler Circle was the first thing she had seen that she really liked. But her $10,000 savings was not enough for the down payment, and she could only qualify for a mortgage of $125,000.

After meeting the frustrated parties at an open house, a real estate agent suggested equity sharing. The Morenos and Janet agreed that each would provide $10,000 toward down payment and closing costs. After five years, the Morenos would get back their $10,000 plus 40 percent of the appreciation. Meanwhile, Janet would make all the monthly payments on a $135,000 mortgage.

Janet's monthly payments, after tax savings, were $753, or $47 less than the $800 she had paid monthly for rent. The Morenos saved $45 per month on their income taxes. After five years, Janet refinanced and paid the Morenos $10,000 plus 40 percent of the appreciation—a total of $16,920. A slump in real estate prices over the final two years of the equity share caused appreciation to be well below the average for any five-year period in the previous 40 years; yet, despite the market slump, the Morenos' return was a satisfying 70 percent over five years, in addition to their $2,700 in tax savings. They avoided paying taxes on this profit by reinvesting their proceeds in another property. Janet now owns her own home.

Example 1.2   Equity Sharing with Seller Investor

Laura Davidson got a great job offer, but there was one hitch: she needed to move from San Francisco to Chicago. This meant selling her townhome. She had purchased it four years before for $150,000, and it was now worth $200,000. She found a comparable residence near her new office for only $125,000, but her excitement was dampened when her accountant told her she would pay $11,121 in income taxes on her gain from the San Francisco sale.

A real estate agent introduced Laura to George and Mary Smith, first-time home buyers with good income and $15,000 in savings. Laura and the Smiths structured a five-year equity share: the Smiths would contribute

(Continued)

(Example Continued)
$14,500 in cash and Laura would contribute $10,000 in home equity and
$500 in cash. The Smiths would make all the monthly payments on a
$180,000 mortgage. After five years, Laura would get back her $10,500
plus 45 percent of the appreciation.

Through equity sharing, Laura owed no income taxes on the sale. Her contribution of $10,500 was more than offset by her tax savings of $11,121; in
fact, she realized $621 *more* than if she had not decided to equity share. She
also saved $69 in income taxes every month. The Smiths' after-tax monthly
payment was $65 less than their rent. After five years, Laura left the equity
share with $23,170. Every penny of this $23,170, plus the $621 and the
$4,140 in tax savings, came to Laura only because of the equity sharing sale.
She reinvested, and continues to defer income taxes and earn a return on this
fund. George and Mary Smith now own their own home.

Example 1.3   Equity Sharing with Parent

Su Wong was $8,000 short on the down payment she needed for a con-
dominium. Her father, Marius, wanted to help but was concerned about de-
pleting his cash reserves. His accountant suggested equity sharing. Marius
had owned his home for 25 years and owed less than $14,000 on his
$40,000 mortgage. By refinancing with a new $23,000 mortgage, he gener-
ated $8,000 for Su's down payment. Although his new mortgage was at the
same interest rate as his old one, the smaller mortgage amount coupled with
the equity sharing tax shelter actually lowered his after-tax monthly payments by $170.

After five years, Su repaid Marius $12,590. He used this amount, to-
gether with the $170 per month he had been saving, to pay off the entire
balance of his new mortgage. This still gained him a small after-tax profit,
which he used to buy Su a new dining room table. Su now owns her own
home—and her own dining room table.

WHAT IS EQUITY SHARING?

Equity sharing is a simple concept. Two parties, an "occupier" and
an "investor," pool resources for a home down payment. They jointly
apply for a mortgage, and both names appear on the deed. For an
agreed number of years, the occupier lives in the home, keeps it up,
and makes all monthly payments. The investor contributes to major
repairs and improvements. At the end of the agreed term, the occupier buys out the investor by repaying the investor's contributions

plus an agreed percentage of the appreciation. If the occupier doesn't want or can't afford the buyout, the property is sold, the two parties get back their contributions, and any profits are shared.

Equity sharing can be a solution to many problem situations. For a would-be homeowner who cannot afford a down payment or cannot quite qualify for a mortgage, equity sharing provides extra down payment funds and loan qualification strength. For a home seller who is looking for top dollar in a slow market or is trying to avoid capital gains taxes, equity sharing provides an army of low-down-payment buyers and a way to defer capital gains taxes indefinitely. For an investor who lacks enough capital to meet the high down payment requirements of investment real estate or is uncomfortable with the risks and management burden of tenant-occupied property, equity sharing provides a small, safe, passive investment with the added bonus of a unique tax shelter. For parents who want to help their children buy their first home, for employers who want to offer the ultimate perk, or for real estate agents who want to double or triple their sales volume, equity sharing provides a solution.

WHY THIS BOOK?

This book on equity sharing is for everyone, from the most unsophisticated first-time buyer to the experienced investor or the seasoned real estate professional. It begins with a full chapter of basics—real estate terms, concepts, and procedures—for first-time home buyers. It then gives a *complete* explanation of equity sharing—not just what should happen, but all the things that might happen, and how and why to prepare for them. Here is a sampling of the book's features:

- A thorough examination of every equity sharing issue—why the issue is significant, *several different ways* to address the issue in the equity sharing documents, and the advantages and disadvantages of each approach, all illustrated with real-life examples.
- A comprehensive and comprehensible presentation of equity sharing tax benefits, with detailed instructions on how to maximize some of the most potent tax shelters currently available.
- Several methods for calculating ownership equity sharing percentages, with step-by-step instructions and worksheets.
- Samples of the most complete and flexible equity sharing legal documents available, annotated with clear explanations and cross-referenced to specific discussions of the same topics in the text.

- An honest and realistic assessment of what can go wrong in equity sharing, and advice on how to minimize risks and resolve problems if they do arise; all of the tools you require to make informed decisions before and during equity sharing.
- A thorough examination of who can benefit from equity sharing and how the potential benefits can be realized.
- Tools and exercises that you can use to determine whether it makes sense to equity share and how equity sharing compares to other alternatives.
- Step-by-step instructions—including sample computations, presentations, advertising, and resources—for finding equity sharing co-owners.
- Separate guides for would-be home buyers, home sellers, investors, parents, employers, and real estate agents.

To those who read this book, an equity sharing agreement will no longer seem like a "black box" full of mysterious words, principles, and rules. Instead, it will be revealed as a collection of well-laid plans, potential problems, and commonsense solutions.

Two

Basics for First-Time Buyers

The process of buying and selling real estate is full of terms and procedures that are completely new to first-time buyers. Unless you first master these basics, you will find it impossible to understand what equity sharing is and how it fits into the real estate universe. This chapter will give you the foundation to become an equity sharing expert.

REAL ESTATE AGENTS

What Agents Do

A real estate agent can give you an overview of the buying process and make you feel secure in the knowledge that an expert will prevent you from making costly mistakes. The agent can help you to select a mortgage loan, prequalify for that loan, and determine how much house you can afford. Using this information, your agent can guide you in deciding the size, configuration, and features you need in a home, and in developing home search criteria.

Your agent can then survey the market for homes that match your criteria. An agent's time and resources allow him to show you more homes than you could find on your own. The agent can access computer databases containing the features of every home available, then prescreen these homes so that you will not waste time looking at homes that don't match. As you shop, the agent can help you evaluate each property by showing you special features, pointing out drawbacks, spotting repair problems, and describing the characteristics of each neighborhood.

When you find a property you like, your agent can prepare a survey of similar homes that were recently sold in the same neighborhood, and help you analyze the survey to determine the price you should offer. He can then prepare a risk-free purchase offer and present the offer to the seller and the seller's real estate agent. During the presentation, your agent's knowledge and experience will increase the chance that the offer will be accepted. If the seller responds with a counteroffer, your agent can help you develop and implement a successful negotiation strategy.

After you strike a deal with the seller contingent on your mortgage approval and property inspection, your agent can help you through the loan application process, set up professional home inspections, and handle any renegotiation of price or terms following inspections. As the transaction progresses, your agent can make sure the seller is complying with the terms of the contract, and facilitate title searches, escrow, and closing.

Given unlimited time and patience for the necessary reading and research, you might successfully buy your first home without an agent, but is that how you should approach one of the largest investments you'll ever make? Buying a home is likely to be as complicated and important as anything you do in your lifetime. There is every reason to get all the expert help you can, especially when the help costs you nothing.

Payment of Agents

One of the best things about using a real estate agent is that you don't have to pay the fee. Your agent is paid by the seller's agent. Here's how it works. A seller enters into a **listing agreement*** or adds his home to the real estate agent's list of available homes and agrees to pay the agent a commission (usually 6 percent of the sale price) if the home sells. The seller's agent advertises the property and usually holds

---

***Bold type** indicates that a definition is given at this occurrence of a term.

weekend open houses. If the buyer has an agent, the seller's agent splits the commission with the buyer's agent.

First-time buyers often wonder how their agent can be loyal to them when he is being paid (indirectly) by the seller. In fact, divided loyalty is rarely a problem for the buyer's agent. He develops a close working relationship with the buyer during the home search and has no working relationship with the seller; in fact, he does not even meet the seller until the day an offer is presented. Moreover, he knows that his key to repeat business and word-of-mouth referrals is the buyer, not the seller, who already has an agent. As long as your agent is not also the seller's agent, you should get loyal and devoted representation.

Selecting an Agent

Buying a home is a major financial and emotional step, and success or failure will rest largely in the hands of your agent. Select an agent just as deliberately as you would a doctor, lawyer, or accountant. Never work with an agent just because he happens to be holding an open house at a home you like. Make a list of candidates based on referrals from friends and family. If you attend an open house or seminar and encounter an agent who seems knowledgeable, add him to your list. Interview your candidates regarding their qualifications, experience, and services. Make sure you check with at least three past-client references for each agent.

You will get the best service and loyalty if you work with one good agent who knows you are loyal in return. You will know your agent is doing a good job if you hear from him regularly, if the advice he gives makes sense, and if you are aware of his hard work on your behalf. If your agent is not giving you the service and attention you want, fire him and find someone else.

WHAT CAN YOU AFFORD?

The Components of Payment

Almost no one pays the full purchase price of real estate in cash. Instead, buyers pay with a combination of two components: (1) a minimum amount of cash, called the **down payment**, and (2) a loan, called a **mortgage**. The maximum price that you personally can pay for a home is controlled by the amount of cash you can raise (your maximum down payment) and the amount you can borrow from lenders (the maximum mortgage amount).

Down Payment Sources

To determine what you can afford, begin by calculating your maximum down payment. Remember this important fact: to reduce the risk that you will abandon the home, most mortgage lenders will require the down payment to be your own money. It can come from bank accounts, retirement funds, or gifts, *but it cannot be borrowed*. When you calculate your maximum down payment, do not include any money you plan to borrow. As we shall see, most lenders count equity sharing funds as down payment cash.

Mortgage Loans

The next step in determining what you can afford is calculating your maximum mortgage amount. A mortgage is a loan **secured by a lien** on the property. This means that if the borrower does not make payments, the lender can force the property to be sold and use the money to repay the loan. The forced sale process is called **foreclosure**. Most mortgage loans are due in monthly payments over 30 to 40 years, but can be repaid sooner if the borrower sells the home or **refinances** by getting a new loan to pay off and replace the old one.

Your maximum mortgage amount is limited by the maximum monthly house payment you can afford. Monthly house payments are often called **PITI**, which stands for mortgage **principal** (the portion of the mortgage payment that actually reduces the amount you owe), mortgage **interest**, **property taxes**, and homeowner's **insurance**. Your maximum PITI will be different for each lender and each loan. The best way to determine your maximum mortgage amount is to shop for your mortgage *before* you shop for you home. After you choose a loan, the lender will set your maximum monthly PITI, loan amount, and home price through a process called **prequalification**.

SEARCH, COMPARE, AND OFFER

Finding the Right Home

After you know what you can afford, develop **home search criteria**: neighborhood, size, features, and price. Asking prices are usually higher than selling prices, especially in a slow market, so set your search price above the amount you actually want to spend. Have your real estate agent make a list of every property on the market that meets your criteria. Include properties that meet most but not all the criteria; you don't want to overlook something special because it doesn't match exactly. Either you or your agent should view every one of these homes. If none seems right, continue your search by having your agent call you immediately each time a new property that meets most of your criteria comes on the market. You may also want to broaden your search criteria, check new neighborhoods, or visit random open houses. It's easy to be mistaken about what you want.

How Much to Offer

When you find a home you like, have your agent provide a **comp survey**, a list of the size, features, and sale price of every similar home recently sold in the same neighborhood. Decide how much to offer based on the survey. Never base your offer on the asking price. If the asking price is much too high, 5 or 10 percent less may still be too much. If the asking price has been reduced for a quick sale, 5 or 10 percent less may insult the seller and end negotiations before they start. Asking price doesn't matter; value matters.

Anatomy of an Offer

Once you determine the value of a property, your real estate agent can prepare a written **purchase offer**—your promise to buy the home if the seller agrees to your terms *and* if the **contingencies** are fulfilled. The contingencies are the requirements and conditions you set that must be satisfied before your promise to buy the home becomes binding. The most common contingencies are:

- Financing contingency—describes the mortgage loan for which you intend to apply, and states that if you are not approved by the lender within a certain number of days, you do not have to buy the home.
- Inspection contingency—gives you the right to have the home inspected by professional inspectors (typically, a termite or structural pest control inspector and a general contractor) within a certain number of days, and states that if you are not satisfied with its condition, you do not have to buy the home.
- Title contingency—gives you time to determine from government records whether the seller really owns the home and whether anyone else might have any interest in it, and states that if you are not satisfied with the seller's ownership, you do not have to buy the home.

Any contingency can be included in an offer. You might require that the seller provide financing (see Appendix B), paint the house to your satisfaction, or rent the house until you are ready to move in. You might delay purchase until you successfully sell your old home or find a new job. You might even condition your offer on the seller's agreement to equity share, or on your ability to find another equity sharing investor.

Your offer and its contingencies will be accepted, rejected, or met with a counteroffer. If and when you and the seller reach an agreement, you make a **good faith deposit** of $500 to $2,000 to show your commitment to the transaction. As more of the contingencies are satisfied, you will be expected to increase the deposited amount.

Some purchase contracts provide for **liquidated damages**. Suppose all the contingencies are satisfied and the buyer still refuses to complete the purchase. A liquidated damages clause guarantees the seller's receiving some or all of the deposit if the buyer doesn't perform, but limits the buyer's losses by preventing the seller from suing for a larger amount.

ESCROW AND CLOSING

Title and Deeds

Title is legal ownership of real estate as shown in government records of ownership. Title is established by a **deed**, the document that represents real estate ownership. You will become the owner of your new home when the seller signs a deed in your name, delivers it to you, and enters it in the government records. At that point, you **hold title** to the property.

Escrow Agents

Most real estate transactions involve an **escrow agent**, a third party who acts as a "neutral zone" between the buyer and buyer's lender and the seller and seller's lender. Escrow agents act on written **escrow instructions** from each of these parties. If a conflict appears in any of the escrow instructions received from either side of the transaction, the escrow agent cannot act until the conflict is resolved.

The escrow agent performs different services for each party. For the buyer, the escrow agent holds the good faith deposit and down payment until **closing**, then delivers the deed and records the transaction in the government records. For the seller, the escrow agent holds the deed until closing, then gives the seller the sale price less any amount the seller owes on his old mortgage. For the buyer's lender, the escrow agent holds the mortgage money until closing, then creates the lender's lien by recording the mortgage in the government records. For the seller's lender, the escrow agent collects the money the seller still owes, then releases the property from the old mortgage lien by recording a release document in the government records.

The Closing Process

The closing process begins at least a week before the actual closing. The escrow agent gathers all the required documents and instructions from all four parties. If there are no conflicts in the instructions, the escrow agent has the seller sign the deed and has the buyer sign the mortgage documents and deposit the down payment. The escrow agent then sends the signed mortgage documents to the new lender for approval, and waits for the lender to return the approved documents plus a check in the amount of the new mortgage. When he has received all the money and all the documents, the money is dispersed, the documents are delivered and recorded, and the closing process ends.

Title Insurance and Closing Costs

In many states, the role of escrow agent is assigned to a **title company**. Title companies also provide **title insurance**, which reimburses the buyer's lender and/or the buyer for any losses suffered if a third party claims an interest in the property.

Closing costs, the expenses of a real estate transaction, generally include:

- Inspection fees;
- Loan fees and points;
- Escrow agent fees;
- Title insurance premiums;
- Government recording fees;
- Real estate agent commissions (paid by the seller);
- Transfer taxes or **stamp fees** (a tax based on a percentage of the sale price).

Local customs vary as to how closing costs are split between the buyer and seller. Often, in addition to his share of closing costs, the buyer must prepay some portion of the insurance or property tax at closing.

WHAT IS EQUITY?

In real estate, **equity** is the difference between property value and mortgage amount:

$$\text{Property value} - \text{Mortgage amount} = \text{Equity}$$

When you first buy a home, your equity is the amount of your down payment. Over time, your equity changes as the property value rises or falls and as the mortgage is paid down.

Three

Basic Equity Sharing Structure

Equity sharing sounds simple. The investor and occupier each contribute to the down payment; the occupier lives in the home, keeps it up, and makes the monthly payments; and the parties share the home appreciation. But closer analysis reveals many complex questions. This is the first of four chapters that will raise and answer these questions. This chapter covers the basics: ownership and possession, financial contributions, repair and improvement, and owners' rights at the end of the equity share.

INTRODUCTION TO THE SAMPLE TRANSACTION

The illustrations and examples of the next four chapters and the sample equity sharing documents in Chapter Ten are based on the equity sharing ownership first introduced in Example 1.2. The property is 3321 Elm Street, San Francisco, and the parties are seller/investor Laura Davidson and occupiers George and Mary Smith. Laura paid $150,000 for 3321 Elm Street four years before the equity share, and owed about $115,000 on her mortgage. The Smiths were renters with accumulated savings of $15,000. The parties agreed on a price of $200,000, and a new $180,000, 40-year adjustable rate mortgage. The Smiths contributed $14,500 cash, and Laura contributed $500 in cash and $10,000 in equity. When we say Laura contributed $10,000 in equity, we mean she received $10,000 less from the sale than she would have without equity sharing. These were the amounts involved in the transaction:

Costs of 3321 Elm Street

Purchase price	$200,000
Closing costs (loan fees, appraisal fees, title insurance, inspections, and escrow fees)	4,000
Attorneys' fees	1,000
Total costs	$205,000

Payment for 3321 Elm Street

New loan	$180,000
Smith cash	14,500
Davidson cash	500
Davidson equity	10,000
Total payment	$205,000

The parties agreed to ownership percentages of 55 percent for the Smiths and 45 percent for Laura. At the end of a five-year term, the Smiths could become sole owners of 3321 Elm Street by repaying Laura's contributions plus 45 percent of the home appreciation. If there was no buyout, the property would be sold, the owner contributions would be returned, and the profits would be split 55 percent (Smiths)/45 percent (Davidson).

In the next few chapters, we will add more details and explain why the parties agreed on these terms. For now, take these facts at face value. Using the Smith–Davidson purchase as a continuing example, this chapter forms a bridge to more detailed discussion by anticipating common questions and answering them in a standard Q-and-A format.

FINANCIAL CONTRIBUTIONS

Q: "Do equity sharing owners share all costs?"

A: Equity sharing owners share the initial costs of buying the property, including the down payment and closing costs. These costs are called *initial capital contributions*. The owners also share the costs of major repairs and improvements; these are called *additional capital contributions*. Initial and additional capital contributions can be shared according to any formula the owners devise, and they are reimbursed before any profits are allocated. Other costs, including mortgage payments, property taxes, insurance premiums, and routine maintenance, are not shared; they are paid by the occupier. Unlike capital contributions, these payments are not reimbursed.

Q: "Which costs are considered initial capital contributions?"

A: The list of costs considered initial capital contributions by the 3321 Elm Street owners, shown in Example 3.1, is typical. Frequently, owners are required to pay some portion of the insurance premium and the property tax when they first purchase the property. These costs are not included as initial capital contributions because they are not part of the purchase costs; rather, they are prepayments of the costs of owning the property. When the equity share involves a seller/investor, the owners must decide whether the seller closing costs will be considered part of the initial capital contribution. **Seller closing costs,** those transaction costs that are customarily paid by sellers, often include sales commissions and transfer taxes (also called "stamps"), but this custom varies from place to place and is always subject to the parties' own negotiations. Including seller closing costs as initial capital contribution causes the occupier to pay extra closing costs just because he happened to equity share with a seller as opposed to another investor. Excluding these costs means that the seller/investor will pay the costs twice: once at the start of the equity share, and again at the time of buyout

---

Example 3.1   Down Payment and Closing Costs, 3321 Elm Street

Down payment	$20,000
Loan points (fee to the lender based on the loan amount—here, 1% of $180,000)	1,800
Other bank fees (including appraisal)	250
Title insurance (for the lender and the owners)	850
Escrow fees	700
Inspection fees	350
Recording and notary fees	50
Attorneys' fees	1,000
Total	$25,000

or sale. Balancing these concerns, we recommend that seller closing costs *not* be considered part of the initial capital contribution.

After the buyer and seller agree which costs are considered initial capital contributions, they must decide how much each owner will contribute. The 3321 Elm Street owners' allocation of initial capital contributions is typical for a buyer/seller equity share. The Smiths made a 5 percent down payment ($10,000) and paid the buyer closing costs ($4,000). The parties split the attorney's fees ($500 each). Laura contributed 5 percent of the purchase price ($10,000) in equity, that is, she received $190,000 in sale proceeds rather than the $200,000 that she would have received if she had not equity shared.

Q: "What if the occupier has little or no down payment?"

A: The lower the occupier's initial capital contribution, the greater the investor's risk. An occupier who makes little or no down payment has little or no equity in the early stages of the equity

---

Example 3.2   Occupier Down Payment and Investor Risk

Suppose the Smiths make no monthly payments and then abandon 3321 Elm Street three months after closing. Losses would include all of the expenses of ownership (mortgage, insurance premiums, property tax, and maintenance), the costs of the recovery process (attorney's fees, arbitration fees, court costs), and any resale expenses (commissions, closing costs). This is how the bottom line would be calculated:

Resale of 3321 Elm Street		$200,000
Less:	Loan repayment (with extra bank fees)	(183,000)
	Costs of resale (6.5% of $200,000)	(13,000)
	Three-months' ownership expenses	(4,602)
	Bank late fees	(102)
	Attorney's fees	(1,500)
	Foreclosure expenses	(1,500)
Total loss		$ (3,704)

Laura would lose $14,204: her initial capital contribution of $10,500 plus the $3,704 overage of expenses. The Smiths would lose their initial capital contribution of $14,500. Suppose the Smiths had made no initial capital contribution. Laura would have lost $28,704: her initial capital contribution of $25,000 plus the overage of $3,704. The Smiths would have lost nothing.

share. This lack of equity increases the likelihood that the occupier will break the promises made to the investor because the occupier has little or nothing to lose. The situation also worsens the consequences to the investor because, if the promises are broken, the investor cannot offset any of his losses with the occupier's equity. Example 3.2 illustrates this problem. An investor who equity shares with an occupier who makes little or no initial capital contribution deserves a very high percentage of the home appreciation in exchange for the high risk. Take special care to investigate the creditworthiness and job stability of the occupier. Require that the occupier contribute to a "reserve fund" if his initial capital contribution is small or nonexistent.

Q: "What about investments after purchase?"

A: Occupiers continue to invest time and money in the property throughout the equity share, but no investment should be reimbursable unless the owners specifically agree in advance to consider it an additional capital contribution. An agreement to make a particular investment reimbursable may be made before or during the equity share, but must always precede the actual investment. This rule ensures that both owners will have control over which investments are reimbursed, and that neither can make bad or inefficient investments at the expense of the other (see Example 3.3).

Example 3.3 Reimbursement without Advance Agreement

Suppose the 3321 Elm Street agreement allowed the Smiths to make any improvements they wanted at their own expense, but stated that they would be reimbursed for the cost of these improvements at the end of the equity share. Mary Smith, who has very peculiar taste in furnishings, decides to have her friend Joan, who just got her contractor's license, install new kitchen cabinets. They choose purple veneer with gold shark's-tooth handles. The cabinets cost $30,000, and the installation is not that bad—for a first attempt.

At buyout time, the home appraises for $225,000. The appraiser is not sure what the kitchen looked like before, so she does not know whether the new cabinets increased the property value. Off the record, she comments that no kitchen cabinets could add $30,000 or more to a property value, and that these poorly installed and ugly cabinets probably lowered the value. This bad investment, over which Laura had no say, will cost her $13,500 (45 percent of $30,000) plus any loss in property value.

Example 3.3 shows the unfairness of making one owner pay for decisions she did not make. Avoid this unfairness by requiring both owners to consent before any expense becomes reimbursable. If you agree on specific additional capital contributions before purchase, include them in the equity sharing agreement. You can find an example of such a provision in section 5.8 of the Equity Sharing and Lease Agreement reproduced in Chapter 10. Otherwise, create a short written agreement confirming that an investment will be considered an additional capital contribution (an example appears later in this chapter). Establish a firm rule that no investment will be reimbursed without a prior *written* agreement.

Q: "Do owners receive interest on money invested after purchase?"
A: Interest on additional capital contributions is not justified where the contribution is made according to ownership share. In that case, the "interest" can be the owners' shares in the property value increase resulting from the contribution. Interest is justified where the contribution is not made by ownership share. In that case, the owners' shares in the property value increase will not be proportional to their contributions, and paying interest can partially equalize the disparity (Example 3.4). *Interest on money invested at the time of purchase (as opposed to afterward) is fatal to equity sharing because it turns the arrangement into a loan for tax purposes and deprives the owners of the tax benefits of equity sharing.*

Example 3.4   Interest on Additional Capital Contributions

Suppose the 3321 Elm Street owners renovate the bathroom at a cost of $10,000. Assume the new bathroom adds $15,000 to the property value, which means the owners made a profit of $5,000, or 50 percent, on their investment. Laura and the Smiths share in this profit according to their ownership percentages (45/55). If they split the cost of the bath 45/55, they would each make a 50 percent profit on their investment. But what if the Smiths paid the entire $10,000 cost of the bath? If they received only 55 percent of the profit (.55 × $5,000 = $2,750), their return would have dropped from 50 percent to 27.5 percent ($2,750/$10,000). At the same time, Laura would make an extra $4,500 even though she invested nothing in the bath. One theoretical way to deal with this unfairness would be to give the entire $5,000 profit to the Smiths. In practice, however, it is not possible to determine that the bathroom added a particular amount to property value. Providing the Smiths with interest on their $10,000 investment is the only practical way to compensate them.

Q: "Is the occupier reimbursed for monthly payments?"

A: The occupier is not usually reimbursed for monthly payments and takes the risk that these payments will vary from month to month or will increase over the equity sharing term. Avoiding these risks is one of the main incentives for an investor to participate in equity sharing rather than purchase rental property. An occupier should be reimbursed when his monthly payment, even after consideration of tax benefits, is substantially higher than rent for similar property. This might be true if the owners borrow a very large portion of the purchase price (90 percent or more), or if the equity share property is located in an area where home prices are relatively high and rents are relatively low. In these situations, the reimbursed portion of the monthly payment is called a *monthly capital contribution*. Most equity sharing owners agree on a fixed monthly capital contribution amount based on the anticipated monthly payments. The agreed amount is binding regardless of what the actual payments turn out to be. This approach provides the occupier some relief from anticipated high monthly payments, but places the risk of increases on his shoulders. Here is how the 3321 Elm Street owners calculated the Smiths' monthly capital contribution:

Step 1: Calculate total monthly payments.

Mortgage interest at 6.25%[a]	$ 938
Mortgage principal reduction[a]	84
Property taxes	202
Insurance	30
Homeowners' association dues	100
Total monthly payment	$1,354

[a] The breakdown of the mortgage payment between principal and interest will change over time. This is the breakdown for the first payment.

Step 2: Calculate after-tax monthly cost.

Tax-deductible interest	$ 938
Tax-deductible property tax	202
Less: Portion lost (due to rent payment to investor)[b]	(220)
Net occupier deduction	$ 920
Anticipated tax savings ($920 × .33[c])	306
After-tax cost ($1,354 − 306)	$1,048

[b] Calculation of the portion of occupier tax deduction lost due to rent payment is explained in Chapter 4.
[c] This calculation assumes a 33 percent tax bracket.

Step 3: Calculate extra monthly payment over equity share term.

After-tax monthly cost	$1,048
Less: Market rental value	(1,000)
"Extra" monthly payment	$ 48
Total over five-year term (60 × $48)	$2,880

Step 4: Discount to present value. The total "extra" monthly payment is discounted to present value because the payments will not be invested all at once. "Discounting" the payment answers this question: How much money would have to be invested today in order to provide enough monthly income to make all of the payments? You need an accountant, a computer, or a fancy calculator to figure this out. Here, using a discount rate of 8 percent, the answer is $594. This becomes the monthly capital contribution.

Some owners calculate monthly capital contribution based on actual rather than projected monthly payments. They subtract the rental value from the occupier's actual after-tax monthly cost. The difference, discounted in some way to reflect the date of contribution, becomes the occupier's monthly capital contribution. This approach is more complicated from an accounting standpoint, and it shifts some of the risk of rising and unpredictable monthly costs to the investor. Most investors will not accept this risk.

OWNERSHIP OF THE EQUITY SHARE PROPERTY

Q: "How is title to the equity share property held?"

A: The deed to equity share property must define the relationship of every owner to every other owner. Often, several types of relationships are involved in a single equity share. This occurs whenever some or all of the owners are married couples. Again, using the Smith–Davidson purchase as an illustration (Example 3.5), we can examine the title term-by-term. The language defines two relationships: (1) that of George and Mary Smith to each other, and (2) that of the Smiths to Laura.

The words "as joint tenants" on the second line of the title statement establish the relationship of George and Mary Smith to each other. A joint tenancy means that if George or Mary dies, the surviving other will automatically own the entire Smith share of 55 percent. Joint tenancy is the most common way for

---

Example 3.5   Title to Equity Share Property

George C. Smith and Mary A. Smith, husband
and wife, as joint tenants as to an undivided 55%
interest, and Laura M. Davidson, an unmarried
woman, as to an undivided 45% interest, all as
tenants in common.

---

related people to hold title to equity share property. It is popular
because it transfers ownership of the property automatically
upon death, without wills or court involvement. The transfer
generally costs nothing and involves no delays or waiting periods.
Nevertheless, married co-owners should ask a real estate lawyer
or escrow agent for the best method of ownership available in
their state.

The last five words in the title statement, "all as tenants in
common," establish the relationship of the Smiths to Laura:
they share a tenancy in common. Holding title in this manner
accomplishes two goals: (1) it protects each owner's interest
from seizure by the creditors of the other owner, and (2) it establishes that if Laura dies, her interest will not automatically
pass to the Smiths. Instead, Laura's interest will pass as provided in her will or, if there is no will, as provided by law. The
situation will be the same if *both* of the Smiths die simultaneously. Tenancy in common is the usual way for unrelated people to hold title to equity share property.

Unmarried domestic partners who purchase as one couple
within an equity share present special problems because they
do not have the benefit of domestic relations laws to govern
their relationship and separation. For this reason, they should
have their own co-ownership agreement. The rights and duties
of each individual within the couple and the disposition of
their jointly held interest if they separate should be clearly
stated.

Q: "Is the equity share a partnership?"
A: Equity sharing owners can form a partnership, but it is not a
good idea. Under certain circumstances, in many states, one
partner can bind the other(s) to an agreement, and one partner's creditors can reach the assets of the other(s). To avoid
these consequences, the equity sharing agreement should explicitly state that partnership is not intended.

OCCUPANCY OF THE EQUITY SHARE PROPERTY

Q: "Can the occupier protect—or lose—the right to occupy?"

A: The equity sharing agreement gives the occupier an exclusive right to occupy. Exclusivity prevents the investor from claiming a right to live in the property with or instead of the occupier.

   The right to occupy is conditional. If the occupier does not fulfill his obligations, including making monthly payments and maintaining the property, his right to occupy is lost.

Q: "Can the occupying owner move out?"

A: The occupier's promise to use the property as a home is often an important factor in convincing the investor to equity share. The investor presumes that an owner-occupier will take better care of the property than a tenant. If the occupier could move out at will, the investor could never be sure that his initial expectation would be fulfilled. For this reason, most equity sharing agreements *require* that the occupier use the property as his principal residence throughout the equity share term. If a job transfer or illness forces the occupier to relocate, and poor market conditions preclude selling, the occupier should be allowed to rent the property with the investor's consent.

Q: "What if the owners intend to rent out the property?"

A: In some equity sharing transactions, the owners plan to rent some or all of the property. The property may have two or more apartments or an "in-law" space; it may be a vacation home that will be rented for some part of the year; or the occupier may expect to move out before the end of the equity sharing term. Under these circumstances, the parties have two options: (1) the occupier can keep the rent, pay the bills, and independently experience any profit or loss, and the investor has no risk and no reward, or (2) both owners can share the income and expenses during any rental.

REPAIR AND IMPROVEMENT

Q: "Are both owners responsible for repairs and improvements?"

A: Most of the responsibilities for maintenance, repair, and improvement of the equity share property fall on the occupier. The occupier must recognize when work is required and arrange to get it done. The investor's only responsibility is to approve of and contribute funds to certain work. The Smith–Davidson equity sharing agreement divides repairs and improvement work into categories and defines which types of work require investor approval and/or contribution (see Example 3.6).

Q: "How does the occupier know when work is necessary?"

A: The occupier is required to conduct regular inspections.

Q: "What does the occupier do if work is necessary?"

A: After discovering a repair problem, the occupier must get at least one bid for the job from a "qualified workman." A qualified workman is someone who holds all licenses legally required for the job and has at least two years' experience in completion of similar work. If the first bid is over $500, the occupier must get at least two more bids. Requiring multiple bids ensures an accurate cost estimate. Accuracy is particularly important in equity sharing because cost will often determine whether the investor must contribute funds. The only time no bids are necessary is when the occupier intends to do the work himself and does not expect reimbursement.

Q: "What if the work is an emergency?"

A: In an emergency, the occupier must get the required bids more quickly, and the bids must provide for quicker completion of the work. Emergencies include malfunctions of the heating, plumbing, electrical, roofing, or foundation systems, or any other dangerous condition.

Q: "What if the investor thinks all the bids are too high?"

A: The occupier might not be seeking the lowest bid because he knows that only a high bid will trigger cost sharing. For this reason, the investor is given a short time to try to get a lower bid before a final bid is selected.

Example 3.6   Categories of Repairs and Improvements

Category 1: Routine maintenance. Work that is needed to maintain the property in a condition that is equivalent to its condition at the start of the equity share, and costs less than $500. Some common examples include landscaping and minor plumbing/electrical repairs. The occupier must pay for this work. Costs are not reimbursed, and investor approval is not required.

Category 2: Occupier damage repair. Work that is needed because of something the occupier did or neglected to do. Deterioration caused by
(Continued)

(Example Continued)
normal wear and tear is not considered occupier damage unless it was worsened by the occupier's failure to perform routine maintenance. Common examples of occupier damage are: pet destruction of flooring, and kitchen fires. The occupier must pay for this work regardless of the amount. Costs are not reimbursed, and investor approval is not required.

Category 3: Necessary repair. Work that is needed to maintain the property in a condition that is equivalent to its condition at the start of the equity share, is not related to occupier damage, and costs more than $500. Roof replacement and painting are common examples. Each owner pays his share of the cost, and both owners are reimbursed. The investor must approve the price of the work, but not the necessity of the repair.

Category 4: Major damage. Necessary repair work that costs more than $5,000, such as repair of catastrophic damage from floods or earthquakes. If the major damage is not covered by insurance or if the insurance will cover less than 75 percent of the repair cost, either owner can force a sale of the property. This provision protects each owner from being forced by the other to pay for repairs he cannot afford. Make sure that the limit you choose for major damage reflects the value and condition of the property and the amount of insurance you carry on it.

Category 5: Discretionary improvement. Work that does not fit into the other categories. Some common examples include room additions and renovations. The investor must preapprove any discretionary improvement if the costs are to be reimbursed. The investor must also approve any discretionary improvement that costs over $1,000, regardless of whether the costs will be reimbursed. With this requirement, the investor maintains control over major changes in the property. The following chart gives a quick-glance summary of the repair and improvement categories:

Type of Repair or Improvement	Definition	Cost Sharing	Shared Decision Making
Routine maintenance	Required upkeep costing less than $500	No	No
Occupier damage	Caused by occupier; not normal wear	No	Yes, if over $500
Necessary repair	Required upkeep costing more than $500	Yes	Yes
Major damage	Required upkeep costing more than $5,000 (or other limit)	Yes, but one owner can force sale of the property unless insurance covers more than 75% of the cost.	
Discretionary improvements	Not required upkeep	Only if owners agree	Yes, if over $1,000 or if cost will be reimbursed

Q: "What happens once a bid is selected?"

A: The occupier signs a written contract with the qualified work-man, each owner contributes his share if necessary, and the work begins immediately. The occupier supervises the work.

Q: "Who is responsible if the work goes poorly?"

A: The occupier must aggressively enforce the owners' rights if the qualified workman does not perform well, and must pursue completion of the work by the original workman or by another qualified workman. A written contract is required because it is very difficult for the occupier to fulfill these responsibilities without one. Any expenses (other than the occupier's time) connected with replacing or suing a bad workman are allocated in the same way as the original cost of the work.

Q: "What if the occupier wants to do work himself?"

A: It is common for homeowners to perform repairs and improvements on their own home, and this is no less true for equity sharing occupiers. Unfortunately, occupier work is the single greatest source of equity sharing disputes (see Example 3.7).

Example 3.7   Occupier as Workman

Suppose Mary Smith, who intends to get her contracting license and go into business with her friend Joan (of the purple cabinets), decides to renovate the 3321 Elm Street guest bathroom. The Smiths and Laura set a budget limit of $10,000. Everyone agrees that each owner will pay the usual prorated share of (1) the cost of materials, estimated at $4,000, and (2) Mary's labor at $15 per hour for an estimated 400 hours. They are all friends by now, so they do not bother with a written contract.

Everything goes well at first. The Smiths pay for all the materials; they plan to bill Laura for her share when the work is finished. Then disaster strikes: a plumbing pipe explodes, damaging the room's framing and fixtures. New materials need to be purchased, but the Smiths are out of money. Mary has already worked over 1,000 hours and has spent $15,000 on materials. The bathroom job has already cost $30,000 and needs to be redone at an additional cost of at least $20,000. The Smiths feel they have worked hard and lived with the mess for months, and they expect Laura to pay her share of the costs. Laura is willing to pay her share of the originally agreed $10,000, but not until a qualified contractor is hired or the bathroom is finished by the Smiths. The parties have a major dispute to resolve.

These are the issues that most frequently cause dispute when the occupier is the workman:

- Quality of workmanship;
- Scope of work;
- Rate of compensation for occupier labor;
- Amount of labor and quantity and quality of materials used;
- Payment schedule or point in time when occupier gets credit for work;
- Responsibility for cost overruns.

The equity sharing agreement should prevent these types of disputes by imposing the following rules for occupier work:

Rule 1: Obtain investor approval. Require investor approval for any big or technical jobs. Major work will affect the investor's equity, and he has a right to know about it even if no contribution or reimbursement is expected.

Rule 2: Request bids for comparison. If the occupier expects reimbursement, require him to get contractor bids for the work, to help establish value. This process protects both owners by ensuring that the value they assign to the work is neither too low nor too high.

Rule 3: Write a contract. Have both owners sign a detailed written contact for the work, to ensure that there will be no misunderstanding or argument about what was agreed (Example 3.8).

Rule 4: Avoid hourly compensation. Because most occupiers are inexperienced, they work more slowly than professionals and are unable to estimate the number of hours required to complete the work. The investor will have no control over the hours spent and will be signing a blank check if he agrees to pay for an unstated number of hours. Reduce the potential for dispute by using a fixed fee for the job rather than hourly compensation for labor.

Rule 5: Limit materials costs. Inexperienced workers frequently waste materials during the learning process. Reduce the potential for dispute by placing a ceiling on materials costs.

Rule 6: Be very specific. State a fixed fee, a fixed completion date, and a fixed compensation schedule in the written contract.

Q: "What if the occupier and the investor disagree about which improvements to make?"

A: Improvements are a highly controversial issue in equity sharing and are generally discussed at length by the parties before they

Example 3.8   Occupier Work Contract

(1) Mary will demolish the existing bathroom, remove debris, reframe with new wood, install tile on the walls and floor (tile sample attached), install new fixtures (photos or model numbers attached), and paint the ceiling and trim ($2,500) (color sample attached).

(2) Mary will be paid $10,000 for the job, in four installments: 25% ($2,500) on signing this agreement, 25% when the job is 25% finished, 25% when the job is 75% finished, and 25% on completion. Each owner will pay his ownership share of these installment amounts.

(3) Mary will finish the job by December 1, 1995.

(4) Mary will be responsible for providing all labor and materials.

(5) If there is any dispute about this agreement, the owners will follow the dispute resolution procedures in their equity sharing agreement.

Occupier	Date	Investor	Date

agree to equity share. Generally, the occupier will want to use his home like any other homeowner, which means having the freedom to introduce any improvement and to demand either cost sharing or reimbursement from the investor. The investor will be afraid of "improvements" that actually lower property value (like the purple cabinets) and of signing a blank check that allows the occupier to spend the investor's money or the investor's equity without the investor's consent.

The equity sharing agreement must balance the occupier's desires and the investor's concerns. If the occupier expects the investor to contribute to the cost of the work, or if the occupier expects to be reimbursed for the cost of the work at the end of the equity share, the improvement will directly affect the investor's return. Consequently, the investor's approval should be required and the investor should be free to withhold that approval. The approval should be in the form of a detailed written agreement describing the scope of work, the cost, and each owner's contribution to cost and/or right to reimbursement.

If the occupier expects neither investor contribution nor reimbursement, the investor takes much less risk. Small improvements without reimbursement have little or no effect on the investor, and the occupier should be allowed to make these at will. Large improvements can *lower* the property value if they are garish or poorly designed or constructed, and the investor should be able to disapprove them if he has a reasonable basis for objection. The agreement must provide a ceiling to determine when an improvement is "small." The Smith–Davidson agreement sets this ceiling at $1,000.

Occupiers often request blanket permission to make improvements at their own expense and be reimbursed only if the property value rises. This arrangement does not work. There is no way to determine whether and how an increase in property value is related to an improvement. Market appreciation could be partially or totally responsible, and the property may have had a potentially higher value without the improvement. An improvement cannot be assumed to be worthwhile just because the property value has increased. Even if this assumption were valid, a fair amount for occupier reimbursement could not be established. The only information available would be the cost of the work, and cost may not be related to value. Poor design decisions and/or workmanship can mean the occupier spent too much, causing cost to be higher than value; conversely, careful spending and luck can cause value to be higher than cost. A fair reimbursement would match the value of the improvement, the amount by which the improvement raised the property value; but no appraiser can tell you an improvement's value. The moral: Stay away from blanket permission for occupier improvements.

Q: "What if the occupier has specific improvements in mind before purchase?"

A: The equity sharing agreement should state which improvements will be made, when they will be made, how they will be funded, and whether costs will be reimbursed. (The model agreement in Chapter 10 contains such a statement.)

CONCLUDING THE EQUITY SHARE

Q: "What happens at the end of the equity share?"

A: Most equity sharing arrangements are intended to last for a specific time period or "term." At the end of the term, the occupier has the right to become sole owner of the property by buying out the investor. If the occupier chooses not to buy out the investor, the investor may buy out the occupier. The equity sharing agreement provides a formula for calculating each owner's buyout price. If neither party wants to buy out the other, the property is sold and the sale proceeds are distributed among the owners.

Q: "How do the owners calculate the buyout price?"

A: The value of each owner's share in the property is called "cotenant equity" and is the sum of the owner's capital contributions and profit share. Cotenant equity is the price for an owner's share in the event of a buyout, or the amount of an owner's proceeds in the event of a sale. To clarify these principles, we can create a financial scenario for 3321 Elm Street and plug in some illustrative figures.

Assume that 3321 Elm Street appreciates in value from $200,000 to $250,000. The owners' initial capital contributions were $14,500 (the Smiths) and $10,500 (Laura). Their additional capital contributions were respectively $3,000 and $2,000. They had also agreed that the Smiths would get credit for $594 in monthly capital contributions. These are the steps to determine each owner's buyout price:

Step 1: Calculate total equity.

Appraised value	$250,000
Less: Cost of sale (6.5%)	(16,250)
Mortgage balance	(175,000)
Total equity	$ 58,750

Step 2: Calculate capital contributions.

Initial capital contributions	$25,000
Additional capital contributions	5,000
Monthly capital contribution	594
Total capital contributions	$30,594

Step 3: Calculate total profit.

Total equity	$58,750
Less: Total capital contributions	(30,594)
Total profit	$28,156

Step 4: Calculate Davidson cotenant equity.

Davidson initial capital contribution	$10,500
Davidson additional capital contribution	2,000
Davidson profit share (45% × $28,156)	12,670
Total Davidson equity	$25,170

Step 5: Calculate Smith cotenant equity.

Smith initial capital contribution	$14,500
Smith additional capital contribution	3,000
Smith monthly capital contribution	594
Smith profit share (55% × $28,156)	15,486
Total Smith equity	$33,580

This relatively simple calculation yields each owner's buyout price. It also approximates the amount each would receive if 3321 Elm Street were sold. Actual proceeds would be different if the sale price were not exactly $250,000 or the costs of sale were not exactly 6.5 percent. Calculating cotenant equity is more difficult if the property value stays the same or goes down. Appendix C explains this process.

Q: "Why subtract 'cost of sale' in a buyout?"
A: Subtracting the approximate seller closing costs, even though these costs will not actually be paid in a buyout, prevents the purchasing owner from paying more in a buyout than the selling owner would receive in a market sale.

Q: "What happens to the mortgage in a buyout?"
A: As part of a buyout, the purchasing owner must either refinance in his own name or convince the original lender to remove the other owner's name from the original mortgage.

Q: "What is the buyout procedure?"
A: The owners begin by establishing the value of the property and calculating the investor's cotenant equity. The occupier then has a specific time period to determine whether he can afford to buy out the investor. Because loan qualification is often a major factor in the occupier's decision to purchase, the time period should be sufficient for the occupier to shop for a loan, submit loan applications, and get a commitment from a lender.

If the occupier decides to complete a buyout, he gives the investor a written notice along with a good faith deposit. An occupier who cannot afford a buyout and is reluctant to move might try to delay sale by giving a false buyout notice. To prevent this tactic, buyout notices should be binding and an owner should face penalties if he fails to complete a buyout after giving a notice. Because the notice is binding, the occupier must be certain he can afford the buyout before giving the notice.

The buyout closes 60 days later. The investor deeds his ownership share to the occupier and receives his cotenant equity in cash. All transaction costs, including bank fees, escrow fees,

---

Example 3.9   Buyout Mortgage Options

Assume 3321 Elm Street is worth $250,000 and the Smiths need $25,170 to buy out Laura. These are their options:

Option 1: Refinance. The Smiths would need to qualify for a large enough loan to pay off the balance of the old loan ($175,000), pay Laura ($25,170), and pay any loan fees associated with the new loan.

Option 2: Keep the existing mortgage. The Smiths would need to convince the lender that they were qualified for the loan on their own and that it could safely release Laura as a borrower. They would also need to have the $25,170 in cash or to be able to borrow that amount from a relative, friend, or "home equity" lender.

---

and recording fees, are paid by the occupier because costs of sale were already subtracted from the investor's proceeds during the calculation of cotenant equity.

If the occupier waives his right to buy out the investor, the investor can buy out the occupier using the same procedure.

The key element of a buyout procedure is strict time deadlines. Buyout deadlines ensure that either a buyout or a sale takes place on or close to the originally scheduled end of the equity sharing term. Keeping the term on schedule is very important if one of the owners is depending on receiving his money on a certain date. In the Smith–Davidson agreement, the occupier's buyout right expires four months before the end of the equity sharing term. Laura, the investor, has 30 days after this expiration to make up her mind. On this schedule, all buyout rights have ended three months before the end of the term, allowing ample time to market the property if both buyout rights are waived.

Q: "What if neither owner wants a buyout?"

A: If both owners waive their buyout rights, the property is offered for sale. Most owners have no difficulty completing the selling process without referring to the equity sharing agreement. But some owners don't agree on pricing strategy, choice of real estate agents, or acceptance of an offer. Disputes frequently stem from differences in owners' motivations to sell (see Example 3.10). To avoid sale disputes and keep the sale process moving forward on schedule, the equity sharing agreement should provide a detailed process for pricing and selling the property. The owners are free to ignore it unless there is a dispute.

Example 3.10   Potential Sale Dispute

Suppose that when they were preparing their equity sharing agreement, the 3321 Elm Street owners had insisted that details of selling the property be left out. They reasoned that everyone would have the same goal—to get as high a sale price as possible—and they felt uncomfortable about being tied down to a mandatory sale procedure.

At the end of the equity share term, the Smiths cannot afford to buy Laura's share. They love the house and the improvements they have made, and they hate the thought of moving. Laura is pregnant and has found her dream house in a Chicago suburb. She is in contract to buy it and needs her money from 3321 Elm Street as soon as possible.

Everyone thinks that 3321 Elm Street is worth between $250,000 and $270,000. The Smiths figure they can wait until a buyer comes along who really appreciates the house, and they don't want to leave one dime on the table. Their price: $269,000 firm. Laura needs a quick sale to get out of her tiny apartment before her baby is born. Her price: $249,000. They compromise at $259,000.

A month passes with no offers. Laura's due date is three months away. She begs the Smiths for a price reduction. They are sympathetic but say they simply cannot afford to take less. Neither party feels that a compromise is possible.

These are the rules that should be followed when the parties have agreed to offer the property for sale:

Rule 1: Begin at appraised value. If you cannot agree on an initial asking price, follow the appraisal rules that appear later in this chapter, and price the property at appraised value.

Rule 2: Avoid controversy on the real estate agent selection. Designation of a particular agent is appropriate if both owners used the same agent for the property's acquisition and were pleased with his services. Otherwise, specify that the agent must have had no previous relationship with either owner. In that way, if you are unable to agree to use a particular owner's agent, neither owner will feel that the other is being favored. Some alternatives to this approach include: a provision for colisting by two agents, one picked by each owner; or short listing periods during which the owners' agents alternate. Be aware, however, that most agents feel that these strategies interfere with the marketing effort.

Rule 3: Set a schedule for mandatory price reduction. Require a reduction of 5 percent each time an asking price has been unchanged for 30 days. Many owners balk at rapid price reductions. They know how much their property is worth and feel that the buyers who are staying away are mistaken as to value or are just cheap. Sometimes, their price is backed up by one or even two appraisals, proving the buyers are wrong. But if a property has had no sales activity for 30 days, it is overpriced. It is unfair for one owner to delay the end of the equity sharing term by being stubborn or unrealistic. A mandatory price reduction program is the most critical element of a sale-related section in an equity sharing agreement. If 3321 Elm Street has been appraised at $250,000, the owners could still have agreed to list it higher. When that strategy failed, they could have relied on their agreement to resolve their price-reduction dispute.

Rule 4: Insist on mandatory acceptance of list price offers. Mandatory price reductions may not be enough to resolve disputes between a motivated and an unmotivated owner. Require that the owners accept any offer at or above list price. Otherwise, an owner who was forced by the agreement to allow a price reduction can prevent a sale by refusing to accept an offer.

Q: "What if the occupier can't afford a buyout but doesn't want to sell?"

A: There are many options besides a buyout or sale. These options are explained in Appendix D.

Example 3.11   Potential Appraisal Dispute

Suppose, again, that at the end of the equity share term, Laura is very anxious to get her money but the Smiths would prefer to continue to live in the home. Thinking that it will save time and money, the owners agree to use just one appraiser. Two weeks later, the appraiser values the property at $250,000. The Smiths strongly disagree with this appraisal and insist on having another one. Laura reluctantly agrees. The Smiths select another appraiser who is an old friend. Two weeks later, the new appraiser values the property at $280,000. Laura thinks this is too high, and she will not agree to average the two appraisals because she questions the impartiality of the second appraiser. On the other hand, she can't afford to wait another two weeks for a third appraisal. The Smiths say they will not pay for any more appraisals and will not agree to a price below $275,000, no matter what additional appraisals say.

Q: "How do the owners determine appraised value?"

A: Establishing property value is the starting point of both buyout and sale. In buyout, the value becomes the basis for determining the buyout price; in sale, it becomes the initial asking price. The equity sharing agreement must have specific and mandatory appraisal provisions.

Here are the most important rules to follow during the appraisal process.

Rule 1: Make the appraiser selection binding. You may jointly select one appraiser, or each owner may select a separate appraiser and average the two appraisals. Either way, you are bound by your selection and cannot insist on repeated appraisals until you get one you like. This approach ensures that there will be no arguments and no delays in the buyout or sale procedures (see Example 3.11).

Rule 2: Set strict time limits. One owner is often more anxious than the other to complete the appraisal process. To avoid delays, provide firm dates for selection of all appraisers and completion of appraisals.

Rule 3: Be sure of the appraiser's qualifications. Set minimum standards for the qualifications of appraisers. Most modern agreements allow appraisals by any licensed appraiser or real estate agent. Many owners prefer to use real estate agents because they are generally less expensive than professional appraisers and no less likely to arrive at an accurate valuation. Require at least two years' local experience.

Rule 4: Insist on impartiality. Disqualify appraisers who have had a prior business or personal relationship with either owner. Each owner should have confidence that the appraisers selected by the other owner will give an honest and impartial opinion of value.

Rule 5: Make cost arrangements clear. Share the cost of joint appraisals; otherwise, have each owner pay his own appraiser.

Q: "What if an owner needs to leave the equity share early?"

A: Each owner wants and needs the security of knowing that the other cannot force a sale before the end of the equity sharing term. The occupier needs this security because moving is traumatic, expensive, and time-consuming. He may also make some nonreimbursable improvements that he expects to be able to enjoy for the full equity sharing term. The investor needs this security for proper financial planning; he does not want to be forced to scramble for an alternate investment at an inopportune time. He also wants to maximize the possibility that he will make money on the equity share and, historically, appreciation is more certain over a longer holding period. To provide security for both owners, most equity sharing agreements do not allow either owner to force an early sale at will.

Unfortunately, circumstances like job loss, job transfers, and illness sometimes require owners to leave the equity share early. Most agreements provide several alternatives for owners in these predicaments. One alternative for the occupier is to rent out the property. The other common alternatives are sale of one owner's share, and early sale of the entire property.

Q: "Under what circumstances can an owner sell his share?"

A: An owner's right to sell must be restricted because of the sale's possible effect on the other owner. Each owner depends on the other's financial strength, stability, judgment, fairness, and willingness to compromise. The agreement must protect each owner from being forced to continue an equity share with a less dependable new owner. But it must afford this protection without prohibiting all transfers.

The model agreement in Chapter Ten permits all transfers to other owners, spouses, and ex-spouses (the latter provision is necessary to accommodate marital separations). Transfers to trusts are also allowed, provided they don't shift control of the property. The common thread in all of these transfers is: responsibility remains on the shoulders of the original owners.

If there will be a new owner who is not a spouse or ex-spouse, whether by sale or gift, the remaining original owner must have an opportunity to reject the newcomer. The model agreement allows rejection on any "reasonable" basis after review of financial information and a personal interview. Some agreements allow rejections only on financial grounds. This arrangement minimizes the likelihood of rejection and makes interviews unnecessary. But it is easy to imagine a prospective owner who is financially qualified but otherwise unsuitable for the responsibilities and interpersonal demands of co-ownership. Laura's evil twin sister Polly, a Chicago commodities trader, is a good example. She is wealthy but known to be a shark. She would not default, but she would make the Smiths' lives absolutely miserable. If Laura decides to raise some cash by selling her equity sharing interest to Polly, the Smiths will need to reject her on nonfinancial grounds.

What counts as a "reasonable" basis for rejecting a new owner? Any grounds for doubting financial qualification, financial stability, honesty, reliability, or cooperation. The judgment must be based on the submitted financial data, credit histories, statements made by personal references, and statements made during the interview. If you cannot point to a specific piece of information or a specific statement as the basis for your doubt, it is probably not reasonable. Where a prospective owner is a member of a legally protected group such as a racial or ethnic minority, take particular care to establish evidence that a rejection was not based on prejudice; otherwise, you may be sued. To force the owners to develop legitimate bases for rejection, the agreement should require that the bases be stated in writing.

If one owner sells his share, the other should have a right to purchase (also called a "right of first refusal") in addition to a right to reject (Example 3.12). The right to purchase may be exercised at asking price or any *lower* price that the seller intends to accept. But if an owner declines to purchase at asking price, he cannot change his mind if a buyer later offers that price or more.

After a new owner has been approved, he is permitted to review the financial information of the remaining owner. It is possible that the financial condition of the remaining owner has deteriorated since the equity share began. The new owner has a right to know that trouble may be ahead.

In some states, partial sale can trigger a property tax increase, which could force the occupier to make higher payments. To prevent unfairness, the agreement should provide that a new investor will pay any increase in property taxes that results from his acquisition.

Example 3.12   Purchase Right on Partial Sale

Assume Laura decides to offer her ownership interest for sale at $25,000. She notifies the Smiths, who can afford to buy but feel the price is too high. They decide to wait until Laura becomes more realistic, and then buy. If Laura gets an offer for $21,000 which she wants to accept, the Smiths will have an opportunity to match it and their strategy will have paid off. But if Laura gets an offer for $26,000, the Smiths will have lost their chance. (If the prospective buyer is someone like Polly, they can still reject her.)

Q: "What if an owner must leave early but can't sell his share?"

A: It makes sense to allow the occupier to force an early sale of the property provided he compensates the investor for financial losses. If the occupier can't or won't live in the property, his obligations are going to be extremely burdensome and it is better for both owners to end the equity share than to risk financial disaster (Example 3.13). The arguments favoring a right to early sale by the occupier do not support allowing an early sale by the investor, who has few ongoing obligations to the equity share. Moreover, although the occupier can pay money to negate the investor's losses, the investor cannot negate the loss of the occupier's home.

In the model agreement, when an occupier forces an early sale, the investor may choose to receive either his cotenant equity or his original investment with interest. If the total sale proceeds are less than the investor's original investment with interest, the occupier must pay the difference. This requirement ensures that the investor will not suffer a financial loss as a result of the occupier's change of mind or bad luck. Before selecting the interest option, the investor should check the income tax impact (Example 3.14).

Common modifications of the early sale provision include lowering the interest rate or limiting the investment-plus-interest option to the first two years of the equity share. Another variation eliminates the investment-plus-interest option where the early

---

Example 3.13   Need for Occupier Early Sale

Suppose that George Smith is transferred to Duluth, Minnesota, at the end of year two of the 3321 Elm Street equity share. Even if the Smiths could rent their home for $1,100 a month, it would not cover all of their monthly payments ($1,354 before tax deductions) plus the cost of hiring someone to fulfill their maintenance and repair responsibilities (probably about $100 per month). If the Elm Street house becomes vacant, they will have to pay a rental commission to get a new tenant and cover the lost rent. Through it all, they will need to continue to perform the bookkeeping and bill paying functions. With all these costs, risks, and time commitments, the odds of a default rise dramatically. All things considered, Laura is better off if the equity share ends than if it continues.

Example 3.14   Investor Compensation on Early Sale

Assume that the 3321 Elm Street property value is $210,000, and that Laura has made two additional capital contributions: $1,000 in month 6 and $1,000 in month 12. Using the steps for calculating the owners' buyout price, shown earlier in this chapter, her cotenant equity is $8,618. If this procedure were followed, Laura would lose money. Her other choice is to receive her $12,500 investment with 12 percent interest.

Davidson initial capital contribution	$10,500
Interest for 2 years (12%)	2,520
Davidson additional capital contribution no. 1	1,000
Interest for 18 months (12%)	180
Davidson additional capital contribution no. 2	1,000
Interest for 12 months (12%)	120
Total	$15,320

After checking with her accountant regarding tax effects, Laura chooses the $15,320. If the total sale proceeds are $21,350, Laura gets $15,320 and the Smiths get the remainder. If the total sale proceeds are $10,000, Laura gets the entire amount and the Smiths owe her another $5,320. Under the agreement, the Smiths could pay in cash or monthly payments over three years.

---

sale is caused by specific events such as job loss, transfer, and illness. The problem with this approach is that the list can never be exhaustive enough to cover all the situations in which the occupier might need to cause an early sale, and the event that actually occurs will probably be the one left off the list. Yet another variation eliminates the investment-plus-interest option where the early sale is caused by any event "beyond the control of occupier." But it is never clear whether a certain event qualifies. For example, if the occupier is offered a better job in another town, has an event occurred that is "beyond the control of occupier?" Should the investor suffer a loss? Avoid potential disputes by requiring that the occupier reimburse any loss from an early sale.

Four

Maximizing Tax Benefits

Equity sharing offers unique income tax benefits. It provides one of the few remaining tax shelters for ordinary income, a method for indefinitely deferring capital gains taxes, and the only way for a home seller to avoid taxes when purchasing a less expensive replacement residence.

After an introduction to real estate tax principles, this chapter explores these equity sharing tax benefits and describes how to structure equity sharing to maximize them. Detailed calculations, simplified for easier presentations, illustrate the various financial effects that may occur under current tax law.

INTRODUCTION TO REAL ESTATE TAXATION

Property Taxes, Transfer Taxes, and Income Taxes

Many first-time buyers confuse the three types of taxes that are commonly discussed in connection with real estate: (1) property taxes, (2) transfer taxes, and (3) income taxes. Property taxes, the annual taxes on the "assessed value" of a property, can be determined on the basis of regular appraisals or the most recent sale price. Transfer taxes are imposed when a property is sold. They are based on the sale price and can be paid by the buyer or the seller, depending on local custom. Income taxes are annual taxes on money earned or gained from any source, including real estate. Equity sharing does not affect the amount or timing of property taxes or transfer taxes, but equity sharing owners must agree on how those tax burdens will be allocated among them. Equity sharing does affect the amount and timing of income taxes, and that effect is the subject of this chapter.

Earnings Taxes and Gains Taxes

It is easier to understand income taxes if you distinguish between earnings and gains. Earnings are the amounts people make from their labor and business operations. Gains are the amounts people make when they sell something at a profit. Example 4.1 lists common items in each category. Some equity sharing tax benefits apply to earnings taxes; others apply to gains taxes.

Example 4.1   Earnings and Gains

Earnings	Gains
Wages	Profit on the sale of stock
Commissions	Profit on the sale of real estate
Fees	
Rents	

Earnings Taxes for Occupiers

Real estate owner-occupiers may deduct mortgage interest and property taxes from their earnings. The mortgage deduction applies to mortgage amounts up to $1,000,000 and is limited to interest payments; the portion of the mortgage payment that reduces the loan balance is not deductible. Mortgage and property tax deductions can be taken against any income, including wages, commissions, and fees. Other home-related expenses, such as insurance, homeowner's association dues, and repair expenses, are not tax-deductible (see Example 4.2).

Example 4.2 is oversimplified, but it illustrates a quick and relatively accurate way to estimate the after-tax cost of home ownership. To get a more accurate result for your situation, fill out an actual tax form or visit your accountant.

Example 4.2   Home Mortgage and Property Tax Deductions

Bill Occupier is an owner-occupier who earns $40,000 per year, has no deductions, and pays 33 percent of his income, or $13,200, in taxes. Bill buys a home and has a $1,300 monthly payment:

Mortgage interest	$ 938
Property taxes	202
Insurance	30
Homeowner's association dues	100
Average repairs	30
Total monthly payment	$ 1,300

Bill's annual deduction will be:

Mortgage interest (938 × 12)	$11,256
Property taxes (202 × 12)	2,424
Total tax deduction	$13,680

Bill's income taxes will now reflect the homeowner's deduction:

Total income	$40,000
Less: Total tax deduction	(13,680)
Remaining taxable income	$26,320
Bill's income taxes (33% of $26,320)	$ 8,700

Bill now saves $4,500 ($13,200 − $8,700) per year on his taxes, or about $375 per month. Each month, when he spends $1,300 on his monthly payments, he saves $375 on taxes. His actual net monthly housing cost is $925 ($1,300 − $375).

Earnings Taxes for Investors

Real estate investors pay income taxes on their real estate earnings, which are calculated by subtracting expenses from rental income. If expenses exceed rental income, there are no earnings and no tax is due when the annual return is filed. Moreover, the investor may be allowed to offset the loss against earnings from other sources, such as more profitable real estate investments or wages. Offsetting the loss means the investor pays less tax on, or "shelters," his other income as shown in Example 4.3.

In determining gain or loss, real estate investors offset rental income against virtually any cost related to the property—mortgage

---

Example 4.3   Tax Shelters

Jane Investor earns $40,000 per year at her job, has no deductions, and pays 33 percent of her income, or $13,200, in taxes. She has purchased and now manages rental property with an annual rental income of $14,400 and annual expenses of $21,060. Her $6,660 annual loss can be deducted against her $40,000 in income:

Total income	$40,000
Less: Total tax deduction	(6,660)
Remaining taxable income	$33,340
Jane's taxes (33% of $33,340)	$11,000

Jane saves $2,200 ($13,200 − $11,000) on her taxes each year because she pays taxes on $33,340 instead of $40,000; she "shelters" $6,660 of her income from taxes.

There is nothing beneficial about a $2,200 tax savings if you must spend $6,660 to get it, but real estate tax rules allow investors to generate tax savings based on "paper" losses, which don't cost the investor anything.

---

interest, property taxes, insurance, homeowner's association dues, repairs, management, and advertising. Investors are also allowed to subtract "depreciation." The concept of depreciation is based on the assumption that buildings (but not land) eventually wear out and must be rebuilt. Each year, the theory goes, a portion of the building's life is used up and the building becomes less valuable. This annual loss of value is part of the cost of operating the building and can therefore be deducted as an expense. Tax law assumes that every residential rental property, regardless of age, has a life of 27.5 years from the date a particular investor first collects rents from it. Consequently, the investor is allowed to deduct 1/27.5 of the value of the building in each of the first 27.5 years he operates it.

Depreciation, unlike other deductible expenses, does not actually cost the investor any money; it is a "paper" loss. It does often cause confusion, however, so a walkthrough, using simple figures, may be helpful. This sample calculation involves a rental condominium purchased for $200,000.

Step 1: Calculate the depreciable value. Depreciation is allowed on buildings but not on land. The owner cannot depreciate the entire $200,000 cost of the property because some portion of that amount

---

Example 4.4   Investor Tax Loss

Rental income	$1,200
Less: Mortgage interest	(938)
Property taxes	(202)
Insurance	(30)
Homeowner's association dues	(100)
Average repairs	(30)
Monthly loss	$ (100)
Depreciation	(455)
Total monthly tax loss	$ (555)

This investor spends $100 per month to generate a tax loss of $555 per month. To an investor like Jane, in Example 4.3, this $555 loss is worth $2,200 in tax savings, or $183 per month. Each month when Jane spends $100 to support the rental property, she saves $183 on taxes she would have paid if she did not own the property. Her after-tax *profit* is $83 per month.

---

represents the cost of the land; instead, the $200,000 cost must be reasonably allocated between land and building, and the depreciation calculation can include only the building cost, closing costs, and the costs of any improvements made to the building. For this example, assume that the building plus the closing costs plus the improvements add up to $150,000.

Step 2: Divide the depreciable value by 27.5.

$$\$150,000/27.5 = \$5,455$$

The owner may subtract $5,455 per year ($455 per month) from the rental income as depreciation expense.

Example 4.4 is oversimplified for illustrative purposes. To get a more accurate result, fill out an actual tax form or visit your accountant. Remember that the amount of tax an investor pays on resale profit is affected by the amount of depreciation he deducts during ownership.

Passive Loss Limitation

Income tax law limits the use of real estate losses as shelters for other income. Here are the basic restrictions and allowances:

- A real estate investor who "actively participates" in management and earns less than $100,000 per year can offset up to $25,000 in losses against other income. The investor actively participates if he is involved in making management decisions about the property.
- A real estate investor who actively participates in management and earns more than $150,000 per year cannot offset any losses against other income.
- A real estate investor who actively participates in management and earns between $100,000 and $150,000 per year can offset less than $25,000 in losses against other income: the amount of allowable offset depends on the income amount.
- If a real estate investor does not actively participate in managing an income property, he can never offset the losses against other income.

Example 4.5   Occupier Gains Taxes

Tom Occupier purchases a condominium for $200,000 and pays $2,000 in the types of closing costs that can be added to basis. Over the next two years, he lives in the property and spends $1,000 on a new deck. Then he sells the property for $250,000 and pays $16,250 in commissions, transfers taxes, and closing costs. These are the effects of his transactions:

Calculation of Proceeds	
Sale price	$250,000
Less: Costs of sale (including commissions and transfer tax)	(16,250)
Net proceeds	$233,750
Calculation of Basis	
Purchase price	$200,000
Closing costs	2,000
New deck	1,000
Total basis	$203,000
Calculation of Gain	
Net proceeds	$233,750
Less: Total basis	(203,000)
Taxable gain	$ 30,750
Amount of tax (33% of $30,750)	$ 10,148

- A real estate investor is always allowed to offset the losses from one property against the income from another.
- Special rules apply to investors who earn their living from real estate. The Internal Revenue Code's Section 469, as amended in 1993, allows certain real estate professionals to deduct unlimited real estate losses against other income.

Jane Investor, in Example 4.3, would not be affected by these rules unless her losses increased from $6,660 per year to over $25,000, or her income increased from $40,000 to over $100,000.

Gains Taxes for Occupiers and Investors

Gains taxes apply to the difference between the proceeds and the basis of real estate. **Proceeds** is the sale price less the costs of sale. **Basis** is the purchase price plus certain closing costs plus the cost of any improvements, but less any depreciation previously deducted. (See Examples 4.5 and 4.6.)

Example 4.6   Investor Gains Taxes

Irene Investor purchases a condominium for $200,000 and pays $3,600 in the types of closing costs that can be added to basis. Over the next two years, she rents out her property and takes $10,920 in depreciation expenses. Then she sells the property for $250,000 and pays $16,250 in commissions, transfer taxes, and closing costs. Her calculations would be:

Calculation of Proceeds	
Sale price	$250,000
Less: Costs of sale (including commissions and transfer tax)	(16,250)
Net proceeds	$233,750
Calculation of Basis	
Purchase price	$200,000
Closing costs	3,600
Less: Depreciation previously taken	(10,920)
Total basis	$192,680
Calculation of Gain	
Net proceeds	$233,750
Less: Total basis	(192,680)
Taxable gain	$ 41,070
Amount of tax (33% of $41,070)	$ 13,553

Tax-Deferred Exchanges—In General

Income tax law provides a way for real estate owners to defer gains taxes. Instead of paying taxes in the year the property is sold, the owner pays them later. The right to pay later allows the owner to use money he would have otherwise sent to the government. Occupiers can use the savings to buy a better home, and investors can use it to invest in new real estate ventures. (See Examples 4.7 and 4.8.)

The U.S. income tax law has strict rules that determine how and when a real estate owner qualifies for deferral. The most basic rule is that deferral is available only when the real estate owner reinvests sale proceeds in other similar real estate. Under the tax law, the owner is *exchanging* one piece of real estate for another, so the deferral process is called a tax-deferred exchange. The rules that apply to occupiers are different from the rules that apply to investors.

Tax-Deferred Exchange Rules for Occupiers

Occupier tax-deferred exchanges are governed by Section 1034 of the Internal Revenue Code, which imposes four main requirements:

1. Both the property sold and the property bought must be the occupier's principal residence.
2. The replacement property must be bought two years before or after the sale.

Example 4.7   Benefits of Deferral for Occupier

Assume the same facts as in Example 4.5. Tom Occupier owes $160,000 on his mortgage.

	Without Deferral	With Deferral
Sale proceeds	$250,000	$250,000
Less: Costs of sale	(16,250)	(16,250)
Loan balance	(160,000)	(160,000)
Income taxes	(10,148)	0
Net proceeds	$ 63,602	$ 73,750

Tom would have an extra $10,148 for the down payment on his new home because of tax deferral. Assuming he had sufficient income to qualify for the mortgage, his new home purchasing power would increase $50,000 with a 20 percent down payment, and $100,000 with a 10 percent down payment.

---

3. Deferral may not be available if the owner has attempted more than one exchange within two years.
4. The property bought must have a value equal to or greater than the net proceeds (sale price less costs of sale) from the property sold; otherwise, the owner can defer tax on only some of the gain.

The Internal Revenue Code's Section 121 is also related to occupier deferrals: owners over 55 are allowed a one-time tax exemption on up to $125,000 in gain from the sale of a principal residence. Many homeowners perform a series of tax-deferred exchanges during the course of their lifetime, then use the exemption after they turn 55. Using this method, they pay no tax on gains in the value of any of the homes they own, unless the total of all the gains exceeds $125,000.

Before attempting a tax-deferred exchange, speak with an accountant. You need professional help to determine whether an exchange is possible, when the new residence must be purchased, and how much the new residence must cost.

Example 4.8   Benefits of Deferral for Investor

Assume the same facts as in Example 4.6. Irene Investor owes $150,000 on her mortgage.

	Without Deferral	With Deferral
Sale proceeds	$250,000	$250,000
Less: Costs of sale	(16,250)	(16,250)
Loan balance	(150,000)	(150,000)
Income taxes	(13,553)	0
Net proceeds	$ 70,197	$ 83,750

Irene would have an extra $13,553 to invest in a new real estate venture because of tax deferral. If she makes a 25 percent down payment, her purchasing power increases $54,000. If her replacement property were to appreciate at the rate of 3 percent per year, these would be the results:

	Without Deferral	With Deferral
New property value	$260,000	$314,000
Appreciation (3% year)	$ 7,800	$ 9,420

Irene would earn an extra $1,620 per year from property appreciation as a result of deferral. This example ignores additional return that she might earn from extra rental income or extra tax benefits during ownership. She earns the extra return by investing the $13,553 she would have sent to the government.

Tax-Deferred Exchange Rules for Investors

Investor tax-deferred exchanges are governed by Section 1031 of the Internal Revenue Code. Investor exchanges are much more complicated than occupier exchanges. Here are some of the many rules that apply:

1. Both the property sold and the property bought must be investment real estate; if the investor has been living in the property sold, he should rent it out for at least one year before attempting an investor exchange.
2. Both the property sold and the property bought should be held by the owner for at least one year.
3. An owner will defer tax on all gain if (a) he receives no cash or personal property in the transaction, (b) the property bought has an equal or greater value than the net proceeds (sale price less costs of sale) from the property sold, and (c) all of the equity from the property sold is invested in the property bought. It is possible to complete a *partially* tax-deferred exchange without meeting all three requirements.

Section 1031 allows two kinds of investor exchanges: (1) simultaneous and (2) delayed. In a simultaneous exchange, the replacement property is bought at exactly the moment when the replaced property is sold. In a delayed exchange, the investor is allowed 45 days after the sale to identify the replacement property, and up to six months after the sale to complete the purchase. The proceeds from the sale must be completely beyond the control of the investor during the six-month delay period. Because other strict and complicated rules apply to delayed exchanges, always consult a professional exchange facilitator or an attorney for help with the process.

MAXIMIZING TAX DEDUCTIONS IN EQUITY SHARING

Section 280A and Fair Rental

Section 280A of the Internal Revenue Code was written specifically for equity sharing owners. Under Section 280A, the occupier can deduct mortgage interest and property taxes, and the investor can deduct depreciation—all on the same property at the same time. To qualify for the depreciation deduction, the investor must collect "fair rental" from the occupier. Investors who don't need deductions because they pay little or no tax, or who can't use deductions because of the passive loss rules, can ignore the fair rental requirement.

The Internal Revenue Code does not define fair rental. The requirement is definitely met when an occupier pays market rent on the investor's share of the property. If the market rental value for the entire property is $1,000 and the investor owns 50 percent market rent for the investor's share would be $500. Many accountants believe that the fair rental requirement can also be satisfied with less than market rent. They argue that landlords often discount rent for good tenants, especially those who manage the property, and an equity sharing investor should be entitled to give the same type of discounts to an occupier. Based on this argument, most equity sharing owners subtract a "good tenant" and/or "management" discount from market rent to arrive at fair market. This discount is valuable because, as we shall see, equity sharing owners maximize tax deductions by minimizing fair rental.

Using the facts from the Smith–Davidson 3321 Elm Street equity share, we can walk through a calculation of fair rental.

Step 1: Calculate market rental value. The best way to calculate market rental value is to ask a real estate agent or research the prices of other similar homes that are available for rent in the area. For this calculation, we will assume the market rental value of 3321 Elm Street is $1,000.

Step 2: Calculate investor percentage of market rental value. Recall that Laura Davidson, our Investor, owns 45% of 3321 Elm Street. This is the portion of the property on which the Smiths must pay fair rental.

$$45\% \times \$1,000 = \$450$$

Step 3: Subtract good tenant and management discounts. There are no rules in the income tax law to determine the allowable amount of good tenant or management discounts. Here, we will use a 10 percent good tenant discount and a $100 management discount.

Market rent	$450
Less: Good tenant discount (10% of $450)	(45)
Management discount	(100)
Fair rental	$305

Using Section 280A

The occupier does not pay fair rental in addition to his mortgage, property taxes, insurance, and homeowner's association dues; rather, he pays fair rental by paying a portion of these expenses "through the investor": the occupier pays the investor the fair rental and the investor uses this money to pay these expenses.

Satisfying the fair rental requirement by paying some expenses through the investor keeps the occupier's total monthly payment as low as possible and maximizes the investor's tax savings. The investor avoids paying taxes on the fair rental by offsetting it, dollar for dollar, with expenses. This leaves the investor a full depreciation deduction without spending any of his own money on expenses.

What exactly are the tax savings involved? Learning that Laura's new job in Chicago pays her $60,000 a year, we can calculate the amount of tax the fair rental arrangement saves her:

Step 1: Calculate depreciation. Assume the 3321 Elm Street building accounted for 75 percent of the total cost of the property. Laura had purchased the property for $150,000, so her depreciable cost for the entire building is 75 percent of $150,000, or $112,500. She now owns 45 percent of the building, so her depreciable basis is 45 percent of $112,500 or $50,625. She can also depreciate her share of closing costs and improvements, which, we will assume, is $2,500.

Example 4.9   Expenses Paid through the Investor

In the Fair Rental example, Laura Davidson uses the $305 she receives from the Smiths as fair rental on 3321 Elm Street to pay homeowner's association dues, insurance, and a portion of the property taxes. The Smiths pay the same total each month, $1,270, with or without fair rental.

	Smiths' Monthly Payment	
	With Fair Rental	Without Fair Rental
Mortgage interest	$ 938	$ 938
Property tax	27	202
Insurance	—	30
Homeowner's association dues	—	100
Fair rental (paid to Davidson)	305	—
Total	$1,270	$1,270

With fair rental, the Smiths pay all of the insurance, all of the homeowner's association dues, and some of the property taxes ($202) through the investor. They pay all of the mortgage and the remainder of the property taxes ($27) directly.

Depreciable cost of building	$50,625
Depreciable closing costs and improvements	2,500
Total depreciable basis	$53,125
Annual depreciation ($53,125/27.5)	$ 1,932
Monthly depreciation ($1,932/12)	$ 161

Step 2: Calculate tax loss.

Monthly fair rental income	$305
Less: Monthly expenses paid by Laura	(305)
Monthly depreciation ($1,932/12)	(161)
Tax Loss	$(161)

Step 3: Calculate tax savings. Laura earns $60,000 a year, has no deductions, and pays 33 percent in taxes. The effect is:

Laura's tax without fair rental arrangement (33% of $60,000)		$19,800
Laura's tax with fair rental arrangement:		
Wage income	$60,000	
Less: Tax loss from equity share	(1,932)	
Taxable income	$(58,068)	
Tax (33% of $58,068)		$19,162
Annual Tax Savings		$ 638
Monthly Tax Savings ($638/12)		$ 53

The $638 tax savings provides an annual return of over 6 percent on Laura's $10,500 investment, in addition to any amount the equity share property appreciates. She will have to repay the tax savings in gains taxes when the equity sharing property is sold, but this payment can be delayed indefinitely through a tax-deferred exchange.

Expenses paid through the investor are not deductible by the occupier. Consequently, the occupier loses tax deductions for any portion of the mortgage interest or property taxes paid this way. In Example 4.9, the Smiths lose a tax deduction of $175 per month because that amount of property tax is paid through Laura. The occupier loses nothing when insurance and homeowner's association dues are paid through the investor because these expenses are not deductible for an occupier even if they are paid directly. To maximize their deductions, co-owners should avoid paying occupier deductible expenses, like mortgage payments and property taxes, through the investor. If there are enough occupier nondeductible expenses, like insurance and homeowner's association dues, to off-set the entire fair rental amount, then the investor should not con-tribute to occupier deductible expenses; if not, the investor should apply the fair rental first to pay occupier nondeductible expenses, then use any balance to pay occupier deductible expenses.

For the Smith–Davidson co-ownership, these would be the neces-sary steps:

Step 1: Calculate total annual occupier rent. For the Smiths, the an-nual occupier rent is $3,660 ($305 × 12).

Step 2: Calculate occupier nondeductible expenses. Here is a list of the 3321 Elm Street annual expenses. For simplicity, mortgage prin-cipal payments have been omitted.

Mortgage interest (occupier deductible)	$11,256
Property tax (occupier deductible)	2,424
Insurance (occupier nondeductible)	360
Homeowner's association dues (occupier nondeductible)	1,200
Total	$15,240

The occupier nondeductible expenses total $1,560.

Example 4.10   Deciding Which Expenses to Pay through the Investor in First Year

Assume the Elm Street equity share began at the end of June 1994. In that year, $1,830 is paid in rent ($305 × 6). Laura would still pay $360 in insurance because that cost is paid in advance for a full year. She would also pay $600 ($100 × 6) in homeowner's association dues, leaving $870 for property taxes ($1,830 − $360 − $600).

Expenses will change over the course of the equity share. If the cost of insurance or homeowner's association dues rises, take advantage of the increases by having the investor pay the increased cost. Because the in-vestor's total expenses cannot exceed the rent, offset every extra dollar the investor spends on these items by a decrease in the amount the in-vestor pays for occupier nondeductible expenses. To avoid accounting dis-asters, make these adjustments at the beginning of each year. Otherwise, the investor's contributions may not equal the occupier rent, or a last-minute adjustment may cause the occupier to face a higher tax bill than expected.

Example 4.11   Annually Adjusting Expenses Paid through the Investor

Suppose that during 1995, the second year of the 3321 Elm Street equity share, insurance cost rises from $360 to $600 per year in June, and homeowner's association dues rise from $100 to $150 per month in February. Because both of these increases came after the first of the year, the owners did not adjust Laura's 1995 expense payments. She continues to pay $360 toward insurance, $100 per month toward dues, and $2,100 toward property tax; the balances of these amounts are paid by the Smiths. For 1996, Laura's payments are adjusted upward so that she pays $600 toward insurance and $150 per month toward dues. These two expenses total $2,400. Because her occupier nondeductible expenses have increased $840, from $1,560 to $2,400, her occupier deductible amount is decreased $840 and she pays $1,260 instead of $2,100 in property tax. This change gives the Smiths an extra $840 in tax deductions, saving them about $23 per month in taxes.

Compare this orderly annual adjustment with the alternative scenario of adjusting payments during the tax year. Beginning in February 1995, Laura pays $150 per month in dues. In April, she pays $1,050 toward property tax ($\frac{1}{2}$ of the $2,100 stated in this agreement). In June, she pays the entirety of the annual insurance, which rose to $600. In November, Laura performs the following calculation:

Total 1995 occupier rent (including December)	$3,660
Less: Insurance contribution	600
First property tax contribution	1,050
Dues contribution (including December)	1,650
Amount needed to offset rent	$ 360

Based on this calculation, Laura contributes $360 to the second installment of property taxes. The Smiths get the check and panic. They were expecting the $1,050 they had always received before. Now they suddenly need to find an extra $690. Avoiding adjustments during the tax year would have prevented this surprise.

Step 3: Determine portion of occupier deductible expenses to be paid by investor. Laura should pay insurance and homeowner's association dues because these expenses are not deductible for the Smiths. But the total of these payments, $1,560, will not entirely offset the $3,660 she collects in rental income. To offset the remaining $2,100, Laura will pay that portion of the property taxes.

When determining which expenses to pay through the investor, remember to consider the first tax year of the equity share. Unless the equity share begins on January 1, the first tax year will be less than a full calendar year. Confirm that the investor will be able to equalize his income and expenses, and the occupier will lose the minimum amount of occupier-deductible expenses, during this partial first year (see Examples 4.10 and 4.11).

Creating a Money Trail

If either of the equity sharing owners has his federal tax return audited, it will be necessary to prove the legitimacy of all the equity sharing tax deductions, using the equity sharing agreement and the canceled checks. The equity sharing agreement should specifically state the occupier's obligation to pay fair rental to the investor. It should also state the amount of fair rental and the way the amount was determined. Then it should recite that it is intended to be a lease as well as a co-ownership agreement, and that the occupier's right to live in the property will be lost if he does not pay rent. This recitation confirms that the investor is truly renting the property to the occupier as required by Section 280A of the Internal Revenue Code. Finally, if should specifically list the *types and amounts* of expenses the investor is required to pay with the rental income. Failing to observe these formalities could result in the investor's depreciation deduction being ruled invalid, in which case the investor would have to pay back taxes, interest, and penalties.

It is also important to have canceled checks, which create proof of payment and establish that the rent and the expenses were paid as required by the agreement. The occupier should write a check for the fair rental to the investor each month. The investor should write checks to the insurance carrier, the homeowner's association, the tax assessor, or the mortgage lender. It is not necessary for the investor to mail or deliver the payments to each payee; in fact, it is probably better to have the investor send the expense checks to the occupier. This approach avoids the confusion and lost checks that seem inevitable when portions of a single payment are made with separate checks in separate envelopes.

TAX-DEFERRED EXCHANGES IN EQUITY SHARING

Income tax law allows both occupiers and investors to exchange their interest in equity share property. Owners are allowed to exchange both into and out of an equity share, provided the equity share is not treated as a partnership for tax purposes.

These are the rules for maintaining exchangeability in an equity share:

Rule 1: Recite in the equity sharing agreement that you do not intend to use partnership tax rules.

Rule 2: Hold title as a tenancy-in-common or joint tenancy, not as a partnership.

Rule 3: Do not file a partnership tax return; report your share of expenses on your own return.

Rule 4: Make sure you meet exchange requirements. An occupier must use the property as a principal residence and replace it with property worth more than his ownership share. An investor must meet all value and equity requirements with his ownership share.

To illustrate the benefits of occupier exchange, assume that 3321 Elm Street appreciates to $250,000, and that cotenant equity is $33,580 for the Smiths and $25,170 for Laura. The calculation required has these steps:

Step 1: Calculate sale proceeds.

Sale price (55% of $250,000)	$135,700
Less: Costs of sale (55% of $16,250)	(8,938)
Net proceeds	$126,762

Step 2: Calculate basis.

Purchase price (55% of $200,000)	$110,000
Buyer closing costs (not including loan fees)	2,700
Improvements	3,000
Total basis	$115,700

Step 3: Calculate taxable gain.

Net proceeds	$126,762
Less: Total basis	(115,700)
Taxable gain	$ 11,062

Step 4: Calculate tax. To keep this illustration simple, we will again assume that the Smiths pay 33 percent of their income in taxes.

33% of $11,062 = $3,650

Recall that the Smiths cotenant equity is $33,580. This is the amount of cash they will have from the sale of 3321 Elm Street. If they complete a tax-deferred exchange, they will have all of this money available for the down payment and closing costs on their new home. If they do not complete a tax-deferred exchange, they will have $29,930 ($33,580 − $3,650) for down payment and closing costs. Here is an example of the new-home prices the Smiths could afford; the prices are approximate and assume closing costs on the new property of about 3 percent. The "5 Percent Down" column assumes the Smiths purchase a new equity share property in an arrangement similar to their co-ownership with Laura.

	20 Percent Down	10 Percent Down	5 Percent Down
Maximum new-home price with no exchange	$130,000	$230,000	$374,000
Maximum new-home price with exchange	$146,000	$258,000	$420,000

The purchase price of the Smiths' new home will also be limited by their capacity for monthly payments. Even so, their purchasing power will be dramatically increased by the exchange.

Step 5: Calculate minimum value of exchange property.

Smith share (55%) of net sale proceeds of
3321 Elm Street ownership = $126,762

The Smiths must buy a new home worth at least $126,762. If they plan to participate in another equity share as 55 percent owners, the new home would need to be worth at least $225,022 ($126,762/.55). If the value of the new home is lower than these minimums, the Smiths will pay some of the tax on their gain. Note that the same analysis would apply whether the Smiths were bought out by Laura or the property were sold.

To illustrate the benefits of an investor exchange, it is easiest to assume that (1) Laura was not a seller/investor, (2) she purchased her 45 percent interest in 3321 Elm Street at the same time as the Smiths, and (3) she made her initial capital contribution of $10,500 in cash.

Step 1: Calculate sale proceeds.

Sale price (45% of $250,000)	$112,500
Less: Costs of sale (45% of $16,250)	(7,313)
Net proceeds	$105,187

Step 2: Calculate basis.

Purchase price (45% of $200,000)	$ 90,000
Buyer closing costs	500
Improvements	2,000
Less: Depreciation taken ($208 × 60)	(12,480)
Total basis	$ 80,020

Step 3: Calculate taxable gain.

Net proceeds	$105,187
Less: Total basis	(80,020)
Taxable gain	$ 25,167

Step 4: Calculate tax. To simplify this calculation, assume that Laura pays 33% of her income in taxes.

$$33\% \text{ of } \$25,167 = \$8,305$$

Recall that Laura's cotenant equity is $25,170; this is the amount of cash she will have from the sale of 3321 Elm Street. If she completes a tax-deferred exchange, she will have all of this money (less exchange costs) available to invest in new income property. If she does not complete a tax-deferred exchange, she will have $16,865 ($25,170 − $8,305) to reinvest.

Step 5: Calculate minimum value of exchange property.

Davidson share (45%) of net sale proceeds of
3321 Elm Street ownership = $105,187

Laura must buy a new investment property worth at least $105,187. If she plans to participate in another equity share as 45 percent owner, the new property would need to be worth at least $233,749 ($105,187/ .45). If the value of the property is lower than these minimum amounts, Laura will pay some (but not all) of the tax.

Step 6: Calculate minimum equity of exchange property.

Net proceeds (from Step 1)	$105,187
Less: Loan balance (45% of $175,000)	(78,150)
Exchange equity	$ 26,487

Laura's down payment on her replacement property would need to be at least $26,487. If her down payment is less than this amount,

even if the value of the property is above the minimum amounts calculated in Step 5, she will pay some of the tax.

Laura's financial benefits are calculated differently if we return to
our original assumption that she is a seller/investor who originally
purchased 3321 Elm Street for $150,000 and lived in it up to the time
of the equity share.

Step 1: Calculate sale proceeds.

Sale price (45% of $250,000)	$112,500
Less: Costs of sale (45% of $16,250)	(7,313)
Net proceeds	$105,187

Step 2: Calculate basis.

Purchase price (45% of $150,000)	$ 67,500
45% of closing costs on original purchase	2,025
45% of seller closing costs from start of equity share	5,850
Buyer closing costs from start of equity share	500
Improvements	2,000
Less: Depreciation taken ($208 × 60)	(12,480)
Total basis	$ 65,395

Step 3: Calculate taxable gain.

Net proceeds	$105,187
Less: Total basis	(65,395)
Taxable gain	$ 39,792

Step 4: Calculate tax. To keep this illustration simple, we will again
assume that Laura pays 33 percent of her income in taxes.

$$33\% \text{ of } \$39,792 = \$13,131$$

Laura's tax is much higher than in the previous calculation because
we have assumed she paid much less for the property (only $150,000)
when she originally purchased it. She is therefore paying taxes on a
much larger profit gained over a longer period of time. This makes tax
deferral even more valuable. If she does not complete a tax-deferred
exchange, she will have only $12,969 ($25,170 − $12,201) to reinvest.

Step 5: Calculate minimum value of exchange property.

Value of 3321 Elm Street ownership (45% of 250,000) = $112,500

Step 6: Calculate minimum equity of exchange property.

Net proceeds (from Step 1)	$105,187
Less: Loan balance (45% of $175,000)	(78,150)
Exchange equity	$ 26,487

These last two steps are the same as in the previous calculation, but there is a very important hidden difference: Laura's basis in her replacement will be lower because she had a lower basis in 3321 Elm Street. This means that when she sells the replacement property, she will have more gain and owe more tax. Fortunately, Laura can continue to defer the tax indefinitely by exchanging her future investment properties.

We must emphasize again that our calculations have been simplified. Before attempting a tax-deferred exchange, any owner should seek the advice of an accountant. This advice is particularly important for investors because the rules governing their exchanges are very technical and complex.

TAX MIRACLE FOR SELLERS WHO EQUITY SHARE

Recall that an occupier may defer gains tax on resale only if the property he buys has a value equal to or greater than the property he sells. A home seller who cannot meet this requirement is said to be "trading down." A seller might be forced into a trading-down situation

---

Example 4.12   Tax Consequences of Trading Down

Assume Laura purchased 3321 Elm Street for $150,000 and paid $3,300 in closing costs. Before she meets the Smiths, a job transfer forces her to sell the property when it is worth $200,000. If she pays 33 percent of her income in taxes and trades down, she could pay tax of $11,121.

Sale price	$200,000	
Less: Costs of sale (6.5%)	(13,000)	
Net proceeds		$187,000
Purchase price	$150,000	
Buyer closing costs	3,300	
Less: Total basis		(153,300)
Taxable gain		$ 33,700
Tax (33% of $33,700)		$ 11,121

Example 4.13   Equity Sharing Tax Deferral While Trading Down

Suppose Laura is moving to an area where home prices are lower, and she does not need or want the kind of home that $200,000 would buy there. If she buys a replacement home for $125,000, she will pay $11,121 in tax and pocket $32,129.

3321 Elm Street sale price	$200,000
Less: Costs of sale (6.5%)	(13,000)
Mortgage balance on 3321 Elm Street	(115,000)
Income tax	(11,121)
Down payment and closing costs on	
new home	(28,750)
Cash remaining	$ 32,129

Now assume Laura equity shares with the Smiths, selling them a 55 percent interest. Because she sold only a 55 percent interest in a $200,000 property, the value of what she sold is only $110,000 and she can accomplish a tax-deferred exchange by purchasing a new home worth $110,000 or more. Her $125,000 home meets this requirement, allowing her to defer the entire $11,121 in tax and pocket $32,750.

New mortgage on 3321 Elm Street	$180,000
Smith down payment	10,000
Less: 3321 Elm Street costs of sale	(13,000)
3321 Elm Street attorney's fees	(500)
Old mortgage balance on 3321 Elm Street	(115,000)
Down payment and closing costs on	
new home	(28,750)
Cash remaining	$ 32,750

Laura actually pockets *more* cash by equity sharing than by selling outright. Her $10,500 initial capital contribution to the 3321 Elm Street equity share is less than her $11,121 tax savings. Moreover, she still owns a 45 percent equity sharing interest, entitling her to a $161 monthly tax deduction plus 45 percent of appreciation. At the end of the equity share term, Laura will be able to complete a tax-deferred exchange of her 3321 Elm Street interest into another *investment* property.

---

because he gets a new job in an area that has lower housing prices, or he needs to lower his monthly payments because of reduced income, or he wants a smaller home because his children have grown and moved away. Unfortunately, trading down can have disastrous tax consequences (see Example 4.12).

Equity sharing allows a seller to defer gains tax on resale even if he trades down. An equity sharing seller sells only a *portion* of his property. He meets tax-deferred exchange requirements if the property he buys has a value equal to or greater than the value of the *portion* he sells. Thus, a seller who sells all of a $200,000 home must buy a $200,000 home to defer tax; but a seller who sells only 55 percent of a $200,000 can defer tax by buying a home worth 55 percent of $200,000 or $110,000 (see Example 4.13).

By equity sharing, a trading-down seller invests the government's money to generate equity sharing tax deductions and profits. A common by-product of this strategy is that the seller pockets extra cash from the sale. The equity share also effectively converts the seller's owner-occupier interest into an investor interest without the one-year waiting period normally required to convert owner-occupied property to investment property. This conversion will later allow the seller to continue to defer gains taxes by exchanging his equity share interest for another investment property.

Five

Calculating Ownership Percentages

Equity sharing ownership percentages determine the share of appreciation that each owner receives at the end of the equity share term. An equity sharing owner with a 45 percent ownership share will receive 45 percent of the increase in value of the equity share property. The amount of appreciation is calculated as follows:

$$\text{Sale price} - \left(\text{Disposition expenses} + \text{Mortgage balances} + \text{Capital contributions} \right) = \text{Appreciation}$$

Using this calculation, we can determine each owner's cotenant equity:

$$\text{Owner's capital contributions} + \left(\text{Owner's ownership percentage} \times \text{Appreciation} \right) = \text{Owner's cotenant equity}$$

There is no set rule or formula for this calculation of equity sharing ownership percentages. When equity sharing first became popular, most ownership percentages matched the owners' contributions to the down payment; for example, an owner who contributed 45 percent of the down payment would become a 45 percent owner. This approach is still popular, but virtually every accountant, lawyer, and real estate agent who assists in equity sharing transactions has a different method of calculating ownership percentages.

In this chapter, we examine three popular methods for determining ownership percentages. After explaining each method through sample calculations, we discuss the method's advantages and disadvantages. The purpose is to provide the tools for equity sharing owners to decide which approach makes the most sense to them. Many owners will want to calculate ownership percentages using all three methods, and then negotiate compromise percentages based on the results.

INTRODUCTION TO SAMPLE TRANSACTIONS

We will use three sample transactions—A, B, and C—in this chapter. In all three, assume all owners pay 33 percent of their income in taxes and have no other deductions. None of the investors owns other real estate or earns more than $100,000 per year. These are the relevant facts for each transaction:

	Trans. A	Trans. B	Trans. C
Price	$200,000	$200,000	$200,000
Down payment	$ 40,000	$ 40,000	$ 20,000
Closing costs	$ 6,000	$ 6,000	$ 6,000
Occupier initial contribution	$ 23,000	$ 5,000	$ 10,000
Investor initial contribution	$ 23,000	$ 41,000	$ 16,000
Planned occupier "sweat equity" improvements	0	$ 3,000	0
Planned investor improvements	0	0	0
Monthly Payments:			
Mortgage interest	$ 933	$ 933	$ 1,050
Property taxes	202	202	202
Insurance	33	33	33
Homeowner's association dues	0	0	100
Total	$ 1,168	$ 1,168	$ 1,385
Market rental value	$ 1,200	$ 1,200	$ 1,000

We will ignore the portion of the monthly mortgage payment that reduces the principal balance. The portions of the monthly payment that are applied to interest and principal change every month throughout the life of a loan. Trying to include this factor in our illustrative calculations of ownership percentages would make the process more complicated than it needs to be for our purposes. In our calculations, we use the amount of interest paid with the initial payment.

PERCENTAGES BASED ON OWNER CONTRIBUTIONS

The first two formulas in this chapter base ownership percentages on contributions to the equity share. These formulas determine the amount of money and/or services each owner invests, and base ownership percentage on each owner's share of the total (see Example 5.1). Ownership percentages must be determined before the equity share begins so that they can be written on the deed and in the equity sharing agreement, becoming the basis for future tax deductions and capital contributions. Because actual contributions can't be known until the end of the equity share, contribution-based approaches focus on planned contributions.

The first contribution-based formula involves the following twelve steps. Here, as throughout the chapter, the facts or results for transactions A, B, and C are given simultaneously.

Step 1: Calculate initial capital contributions.

	Trans. A	Trans. B	Trans. C
Occupier	$23,000	$ 5,000	$10,000
Investor	$23,000	$41,000	$16,000

Step 2: Calculate planned additional capital contributions.

	Trans. A	Trans. B	Trans. C
Occupier	$0	$3,000	$0
Investor	$0	$ 0	$0

Example 5.1   Contribution-Based Model

$$\text{Owner A ownership percentage} = \frac{\text{Planned owner A investments}}{\text{Planned investments of both owners}}$$

Step 3: Add initial and planned additional capital contributions.

	Trans. A	Trans. B	Trans. C
Occupier initial	$23,000	$ 5,000	$10,000
Occupier additional	0	3,000	0
Occupier total	$23,000	$ 8,000	$10,000
Investor initial	$23,000	$41,000	$16,000
Investor additional	$ 0	$ 0	$ 0
Investor total	$23,000	$41,000	$16,000

Step 4: Calculate each owner's percentage of initial and planned additional capital contributions. Percentages are calculated at this point because we need some "working approximations" of ownership percentages for the next few steps.

	Trans. A	Trans. B	Trans. C
Occupier total	$23,000	$ 8,000	$10,000
Investor total	23,000	41,000	16,000
Total of all	$46,000	$49,000	$26,000
Occupier working approximation (%)	50%	16%	39%
Investor working approximation (%)	50%	84%	61%

Step 5: Calculate occupier fair rental.

	Trans. A	Trans. B	Trans. C
Market rental value	$1,200	$1,200	$1,000
Rental value × investor working approximation	600	1,008	610
Less: Good tenant discount (10%)	(60)	(101)	(61)
Management discount	(100)	(100)	(100)
Occupier fair rental	$ 440	$ 807	$ 449

Step 6: Calculate occupier fair rental tax deduction loss. This calculation determines how much of the occupier's mortgage interest and property tax deductions are lost because of the payment of fair rental to the investor. Remember, the investor uses every fair rental dollar to pay property expenses. Fair rental is applied first to pay the occupier's nondeductible expenses, like insurance and homeowner's association dues. Any remaining balance is then applied to the occupier's deductible expenses, mortgage interest, and property taxes.

	Trans. A	Trans. B	Trans. C
Occupier fair rental	$440	$807	$449
Less: Insurance expense	(33)	(33)	(33)
Homeowner's association dues	0	0	(100)
Fair rental tax deduction loss	$407	$726	$316

Step 7: Calculate occupier monthly tax savings.

	Trans. A	Trans. B	Trans. C
Mortgage interest	$933	$933	$1,050
Property tax	202	202	202
Less: Fair rental tax deduction loss	(407)	(726)	(316)
Occupier monthly tax deduction	$728	$409	$ 936
Occupier monthly tax savings (33% of tax deduction)	$240	$135	$ 309

Step 8: Calculate occupier after-tax monthly payment.

	Trans. A	Trans. B	Trans. C
Total payment	$1,168	$1,168	$1,385
Less: Occupier monthly tax savings	(240)	(135)	(309)
After-tax payment	$ 928	$1,033	$1,076

Step 9: Compare after-tax payment with rental value.

	Trans. A	Trans. B	Trans. C
After-tax payment	$ 928	$1,033	$1,076
Rental value	$1,200	$1,200	$1,000

In Transactions A and B, the occupier's after-tax payment is less than the rental value of the property. Under these circumstances, the occupier is not making a monthly capital contribution. In Transaction C, the occupier is making a monthly capital contribution of $76.

Step 10: Determine monthly capital contribution. This step will be necessary only for Transaction C. First, we multiply the monthly capital contribution ($76) by the total number of months in the equity share term (assume 60 months) to give us the total of the monthly capital contribution: $4,560 (60 × 76). Then we discount this total to present value. Discounting answers this question: How much money would have to be invested today in order to provide enough monthly income to make all of the payments? For the answer, you should consult a professional, or use a computer or state-of-the-art calculator. Here, using a discount rate of 7 percent and payment of $76 per month, the answer is $1,067. This becomes the monthly capital contribution.

Step 11: Add all capital contributions.

	Trans. A	Trans. B	Trans. C
Occupier initial	$23,000	$ 5,000	$10,000
Occupier additional	0	3,000	0
Occupier monthly	0	0	1,067
Occupier total	$23,000	$ 8,000	$11,067
Investor initial	$23,000	$41,000	$16,000
Investor additional	0	0	0
Investor total	$23,000	$41,000	$16,000

Step 12: Calculate ownership percentages.

	Trans. A	Trans. B	Trans. C
Occupier total	$23,000	$ 8,000	$11,067
Investor total	23,000	41,000	16,000
Total of all	$46,000	$49,000	$27,067
Occupier percentage	50%	16%	41%
Investor percentage	50%	84%	59%

As mentioned earlier, there is a second alternative formula for calculating contribution-based percentages. This second formula provides a different method of determining the occupier's contribution. In the first formula, we added up the funds that the occupier provided; here, we add up the funds that the investor did not provide. In other words, we compare the amount that the investor has to spend on the equity share investment with the amount he would have spent if he had owned and held the property as rental property. The difference between these two amounts represents the benefit that the occupier has provided to the investor. We consider this benefit to be the occupier's contribution to the equity share.

Steps 1–4: Same as in first formula. These steps are the same because they involve "lump-sum" contributions by both owners to the purchase and improvement of the property. With regard to lump-sum contributions, every dollar paid by the occupier is a dollar saved by the investor, so the owner's initial capital contributions and planned additional capital contributions are the same in both formulas.

Step 5: Calculate investor's negative cash flow. In this step, we calculate the amount (if any) that the investor would have spent each month if he had owned the property alone and rented it out.

	Trans. A	Trans. B	Trans. C
Market rental value	$1,200	$1,200	$1,000
Less: Mortgage interest	(933)	(933)	(1,050)
Property tax	(202)	(202)	(202)
Insurance	(33)	(33)	(33)
Homeowner's association dues	0	0	(100)
Negative cash flow	$ (32)	$ (32)	$ (385)

In Transactions A and B, the investor would not have spent any money on the property each month because rental income exceeded expenses. In Transaction C, the investor would have spent $385 per month.

Step 6: Calculate investor's after-tax monthly cost. This step is necessary only in Transaction C, where the investor would have a monthly cost. The following calculations are made:

Depreciation	
Building value (75% of $200,000)	$150,000
Closing costs	6,000
Total depreciation basis	$156,000
Annual depreciation ($156,000/27.5)	$ 5,673
Monthly depreciation ($5,673/12)	$ 473
Total Monthly Tax Deduction	
Monthly depreciation	$ 473
Negative cash flow	385
Total tax deduction	$ 858
Tax Savings	
33% of $858	$ 284
After-Tax Monthly Cost	
Negative cash flow	$ 385
Less: Tax savings	(284)
After-tax monthly cost	$ 101

We conclude that the occupier is making a monthly capital contribution of $101, because this is the additional amount that the investor would have spent on the property if he were not equity sharing.

Step 7: Determine monthly capital contribution. We again discount the monthly capital contribution to present value using a discount rate of 7 percent. The total amount, $1,418, is the monthly capital contribution in Transaction C. Based on the result of Step 5, there is no monthly capital contribution in Transaction A or Transaction B.

Step 8: Add all capital contributions.

	Trans. A	*Trans. B*	*Trans. C*
Occupier initial	$23,000	$ 5,000	$10,000
Occupier additional	0	3,000	0
Occupier monthly	0	0	1,418
Occupier total	$23,000	$ 8,000	$11,418
Investor initial	$23,000	$41,000	$16,000
Investor additional	0	0	0
Investor total	$23,000	$41,000	$16,000

Step 9: Calculate ownership percentages.

	Trans. A	*Trans. B*	*Trans. C*
Occupier total	$23,000	$ 8,000	$11,418
Investor total	23,000	41,000	16,000
Total of all	$46,000	$49,000	$27,418
Occupier percentage	50%	16%	42%
Investor percentage	50%	84%	58%

PERCENTAGES BASED ON OWNER RETURNS

The third formula in this chapter (Example 5.2) bases ownership percentages on projected investment return. Unlike contribution-based formulas, which reflect notions of fairness and equity, the return-based formula reflects business reality. A prospective equity sharing investor is choosing from a variety of alternative investments, and the occupier must convince him to choose the equity share by making it competitive with those alternatives. To do this, the occupier uses competitive investments to set a target return,

---

Example 5.2   Percentage-Based Model

$$\text{Owner A ownership percentage} = \frac{\text{Owner A target return}}{\text{Total projected appreciation}}$$

projects appreciation of the equity share property, and determines the percentage of this appreciation needed to meet the target return.

The process begins with a survey of returns on comparable alternative investments. All attributes of each alternative are considered, and the following investment features are compared:

- *Liquidity:* Liquidity is the ease with which money can be withdrawn from an investment. Funds invested in equity sharing are nonliquid: the money invested cannot be easily withdrawn during the equity share term. Compare equity sharing to other nonliquid investments like rental real estate, long-term certificates of deposit, or medium-term bonds.
- *Risk:* Risk is the likelihood that some or all of the investment will be lost, or that the investor will not make as much profit as he expects. Equity sharing involves medium-level risk. It is riskier than insured bank deposits and highly rated bonds, and less risky than most stocks and rental real estate.
- *Taxation:* Equity sharing owners can postpone paying income taxes on their profits indefinitely. Tax deferral is not available on certificates of deposit or stocks, but is available on other real estate. Tax deferral is not as valuable as tax exemption, where no tax is ever paid.

The results of the survey and comparison will vary over time. As this book is written, comparable alternative investments are offering 5 to 10 percent returns, and we use a target return of 12 percent per year for the equity share. The target return is expressed in dollars by applying the percentage to the amount of the investment for each year of the equity share term; for example, a 12 percent annual return on a $10,000 investment for five years would be $6,000 (12% × $10,000 × 5).

To determine ownership percentages from target return, we next predict the equity share property's appreciation based on past appreciation of similar properties, planned improvements and repairs, and expected changes to the neighborhood. The length of the equity share term must also be considered. Because real estate values move in two- to five-year cycles, it is difficult to predict appreciation for a term that is less than five years. Appreciation over a shorter term will depend on whether the term happens to fall on the downslope or the upslope of an appreciation cycle. The risk that the term will fall on the downslope should be reflected in a low appreciation projection. Where the term is five years or longer, there is enough time for the market to rebound from a down cycle, and the projection can be conservative without being pessimistic. In this chapter, we will project appreciation of 20 percent over a five-year term. The projected appreciation is expressed in dollars by applying the percentage to the property value, and then subtracting costs. After we have expressed the target return and projected appreciation in dollars, we divide as shown in Example 5.2, to get ownership percentage.

The calculations for percentages based on owner's returns involve the following eight steps:

Step 1: Calculate investor initial capital contribution.

	Trans. A	Trans. B	Trans. C
Investor	$23,000	$41,000	$16,000

Step 2: Calculate investor planned additional capital contributions.

	Trans. A	Trans. B	Trans. C
Investor	$0	$0	$0

Step 3: Add initial and planned additional capital contribution.

	Trans. A	Trans. B	Trans. C
Investor initial	$23,000	$41,000	$16,000
Investor additional	0	0	0
Investor total	$23,000	$41,000	$16,000

Step 4: Determine investor return target.

	Trans. A	Trans. B	Trans. C
Investor total	$23,000	$41,000	$16,000
Multiply by annual return percentage	× 0.12	× 0.12	× 0.12
Annual return	$ 2,760	$ 4,920	$ 1,920
Multiply by years in term	× 5	× 5	× 5
Total return target	$13,800	$24,600	$ 9,600

Step 5: Determine projected appreciation.

	Trans. A	Trans. B	Trans. C
Property value	$200,000	$200,000	$200,000
Multiply by appreciation percentage	× 0.20	× 0.20	× 0.20
Total appreciation	$ 40,000	$ 40,000	$ 40,000

Step 6: Determine projected costs of sale.

	Trans. A	Trans. B	Trans. C
Property value	$200,000	$200,000	$200,000
Total appreciation	40,000	40,000	40,000
Sale price	$240,000	$240,000	$240,000
Multiply by cost of sale percentage	× 0.065	× 0.065	× 0.065
Total costs of sale	$ 15,600	$ 15,600	$ 15,600

Step 7: Subtract costs of sale from appreciation.

	Trans. A	Trans. B	Trans. C
Total appreciation	$40,000	$40,000	$40,000
Less: Total costs of sale	(15,600)	(15,600)	(15,600)
Net appreciation	$24,400	$24,400	$24,400

Step 8: Calculate investor ownership percentage. Using the formula:

$$\frac{\text{Investor ownership}}{\text{percentage}} = \frac{\text{Investor target return}}{\text{Net appreciation}}$$

the results for the three transactions would be:

Transaction A	$13,800/$24,400 =	57 percent
Transaction B	$24,600/$24,400 =	101 percent
Transaction C	$ 9,600/$24,400 =	39 percent

Where this formula yields a percentage that is over 100 percent, as in Transaction B, it is impossible to provide the investor with the target return.

COMPARISON OF APPROACHES

The contribution-based formulas seem intuitively fair: each owner's appreciation share should reflect his relative investment. The return-based formula seems less fair but more realistic: the occupier should offer the investor just enough to entice him to equity share because any less would cause the equity share to fail for lack of a willing investor, and any more will be a waste of the occupier's precious equity and appreciation.

Neither approach consistently favors the occupier or the investor. Our three sample transactions illustrate how the results will vary:

	Ownership Percentages (Occupier/Investor)		
	Trans. A	Trans. B	Trans. C
Contribution-based formula	50/50	16/84	41/59
Alternative contribution-based formula	50/50	16/84	42/58
Return-based formula	43/57	0/100	61/39

In Transaction C, where the mortgage amount is high (90 percent) relative to the price of the property, the return-based approach favors the occupier: the occupier's ownership percentage went from about 40 percent under the contribution-based formulas to 61 percent under the return-based formula. In Transactions A and B, where the owners borrowed 80 percent of the property value, the return-based approach favored the investor. Generally, the higher the down payment percentage, the more the return-based approach will favor the investor. Transaction B, where the investor contributed most of a 20 percent down payment, provides an extreme example of this effect. The return-based approach did not work because the property could not provide the target return. An investor providing most of a 20 percent down payment must be comfortable with an annual return below 12 percent or must expect appreciation above 20 percent. In the end, none of these approaches is necessarily best. The formulas provide a basis for analysis and discussion, and the owners must negotiate their percentages based on their own notions of fairness and accuracy.

Six

Dispute Resolution, Default, and Death

Most equity sharing transactions go basically as planned: the property needs no unforeseen repairs, the market appreciates briskly, none of the owners has any major life changes, and the occupier is ready, willing and able to buy out the investor at the end of the term. But it would be foolish for anyone to proceed with a home purchase or a major investment without preparing for possible problems. This preparation is even more important in equity sharing than in individual purchases. More owners means more people who could die, become ill, or lose their jobs. More owners also means that one person's problems may have a serious effect on several other people.

This chapter is about preparing for the worst. The opening discussion shows how decision making, use of the equity sharing agreement, and dispute resolution are interwoven. Next, it examines the available means of qualifying co-owners, the methods for protecting owners' investments, and the procedures for enforcing the agreement. The chapter ends with a discussion of the consequences of an owner's death.

Throughout the chapter, we use the term "default," with a lower-case "d," to mean the failure of an equity sharing owner to fulfill his obligations to the other owner. As we shall see in the model agreement in Chapter Ten, the equity sharing agreement gives the term "Default," with a capital "D," a narrower and more technical meaning.

DISPUTE RESOLUTION

Avoiding Disputes

Disputes are unpleasant, time-consuming, and expensive. They are also available. Following are a few simple rules that will prevent virtually all equity sharing disputes.

Rule 1: Have both owners help to create the equity sharing agreement. Many equity sharing owners prefer not to participate in creating the agreement. They don't want to invest time and effort in understanding complicated real estate concepts and the special language of equity sharing. They would rather rely on the other owner or a lawyer to prepare the agreement and then review it when it is finished. Often, they never get around to reading it, or they just have time to skim it. If they read it, they don't understand the meaning of many sections, how the parts fit together, and why certain provisions are included. They assume that the only purpose of the agreement is to bind the parties to their promises and that they will master the agreement if a dispute arises.

This relaxed approach is a mistake. Instead, both owners meet with an equity sharing lawyer, initially to discuss the basic issues, and later to review a draft agreement. After completing the initial draft, read it several times to make sure you understand what words mean and why each section is included. Although tedious, this process prepares you to solve problems in an organized, rational manner, through discussions and compromise. First, it forces you to master the concepts and language of equity sharing. When unforeseen circumstances arise and decisions must be made, this mastery will allow you to intelligently analyze the situation, generate several alternative courses of action, understand the consequences of each alternative, and make an enlightened decision. Second, it forces you to reflect on the issues of equity sharing, understand what can go wrong, and mentally prepare to solve problems that might arise. This preparation will eliminate unpleasant surprises and panic reactions.

Third, it forces you to consider each issue from the other owner's point of view and to understand both the rational and the emotional bases of that viewpoint. The resulting empathy makes discussion smoother and easier.

Participating in agreement preparation allows each owner to preview and prepare for future decision making by learning how the other will think and act during the equity share. Incompatible owners can withdraw from the transaction before it is too late. Others can discover the best way to approach issues with their future co-owner and spot behaviors in themselves that might cause problems. Through the agreement negotiation, owners teach themselves how to negotiate, compromise, avoid anger, and transcend impasse.

The value of this rule cannot be overstated. Virtually every co-ownership group seeking help for dispute resolution has no agreement, has a "standard-form" agreement, or has at least one party who did not help prepare the agreement. Co-owners who work on their agreement together rarely have disputes once it is finished. These generalizations are no less true for families and friends than for strangers. If anything, families and friends are *more* likely to have disputes, and the disputes are more emotional and traumatic, angrier, and more difficult to resolve.

Rule 2: If unforeseen circumstances arise, have a meeting before re-reading the agreement. Most owners' first reaction to an equity sharing problem is to consult their agreement, apply it to the problem, and develop an opinion on what solution the agreement requires. The *opinion* then becomes a *position*. Each owner vigorously defends and argues his position, and becomes frustrated and angry if the other owner disagrees. If the owners become convinced that their opposing positions are correct, they are likely to waste time and money on dispute resolution. At best, the process will end with a winner and a loser, and future decisions will be equally contentious.

If a problem arises, have a meeting. Discuss the situation from both owners' viewpoints, develop and analyze some alternative strategies, and make the decision that comes closest to satisfying both owners. Neither owner will get exactly what he wants, and both will feel that they are giving up rights under the agreement. But understanding and compromise will allow continued cooperation and more collective decisions, and both owners will be better off than if each had fought for his rights and one had "won."

Rule 3: Avoid letters and lawyers. When one owner writes a letter to the other, he formalizes dialogue and creates a document that is difficult to reverse. People are more likely to take positions or make demands in writing than in person. Even if they meet after the delivery of a letter, it becomes awkward for the owners to relax and speak freely. Don't write; meet. If meetings don't work, try meditation, where the goal is compromise rather than victory.

Hiring lawyers often worsens co-ownership disputes. Most lawyers are not trained to solve problems or develop compromises; rather, they are trained to present arguments and fight for the best possible result for one side. Moreover, they are used to handling disputes where, unlike in equity sharing, the parties don't need to interact after the fight is over. Without lawyers, and with honest mutual effort, co-owners will resolve a dispute quicker and cheaper, and will be prepared to resolve their next dispute the same way.

Basic Decision Making

Most equity sharing decisions are made informally, often over the telephone. Equity sharing agreements provide formal decision-making procedures in case the owners aren't getting along (see Example 6.1). The model agreement in Chapter Ten requires owner meetings and votes following 14 days' written notice by any owner. An owner who is unable to attend may ask to reschedule or may send his vote in writing. An owner who ignores the meeting loses the chance to vote. The meeting notice states an agenda so that an owner who chooses not to attend or acknowledge the meeting will know what decisions might be made in his absence.

Example 6.1   The Need for a Formal Meeting

Returning to our continuing Smith–Davidson equity share, we learn that Laura sold her interest a year ago to her sister Polly, the Chicago commodities trader whom the Smiths approved because she "seemed nice." Polly needs money for a big pork belly deal she is working on, and she has been trying, unsuccessfully, to get the Smiths to sell 3321 Elm Street early. The Smiths now want to install a spa on their new deck at a cost of $2,000. They do not expect any reimbursement or credit for this expenditure, but because the cost is over $1,000, Polly's approval is required. Polly wants to use frustration over the spa as leverage to get the Smiths to sell, but she knows that she cannot unreasonably withhold her consent. She adopts the tactic of not returning calls. Using the decision-making provisions of their equity sharing agreement, the Smiths call a meeting and place the spa issue on the agenda. When Polly ignores the meeting, they go ahead with the spa.

A frequently perplexing problem in equity sharing arises when one owner is a couple who cannot agree between themselves. The model agreement in Chapter Ten provides that such a couple gets no vote, and the decision of the other owner controls unless it would change the original equity sharing agreement. If Polly had bought Laura's 3321 Elm Street share with her husband Guido, and Guido (who has a cousin in the spa business in San Francisco) wants the Smiths to install a spa, the result of the disagreement between Polly and Guido would be that the spa was approved.

Dispute Resolution Assistance

If owners are unable to resolve a dispute themselves, they need outside help. Traditionally, this help has been provided by courts, with judges or juries hearing the matter and issuing decisions. But this type of dispute resolution has become very expensive and time-consuming. Complex rules and procedures make the system virtually impossible to use without a lawyer, and lawyer's fees for handling even a small trial are over $5,000. The enormous backlog of disputes in most courts delays decisions, sometimes as long as five years.

Most equity sharing owners cannot afford the cost and delay of the court system. Even a short lapse in bill paying or property maintenance would be disastrous, and such lapses are almost inevitable during a court battle. To keep their disputes out of court, owners rely on mediation and arbitration, two alternative dispute resolution methods that avoid litigation.

Mediation

In mediation, an impartial third party attempts to resolve a dispute by developing a consensus between the owners. The mediator uses a combination of alternatives to the owners' positions, creative compromises, and persuasion to arrive at a mutually acceptable solution. The mediator doesn't dwell on past events, doesn't care who is telling the truth, and doesn't determine whether either owner is legally or morally right. These matters are irrelevant because the mediator doesn't issue decisions; his only purpose is to get the owners to agree and move forward.

Mediation works because both owners realize that the alternatives—arbitration or court—are so much more expensive and time-consuming that even the winning party winds up worse off. Frequently, however, only one of the owners wants mediation; the other believes that it will not succeed, that there is no real dispute, or that the dispute will go away if he does nothing. The model agreement in Chapter Ten is designed to get the reluctant owner into mediation. It provides that either owner may initiate the process by selecting a mediator and setting a date. The other gets some leeway to reschedule, but must appear or face legal penalties.

Arbitration

In arbitration, an impartial third party acts as judge and jury. The arbitrator listens to the positions of both sides, reviews the agreement and the law, and issues a binding decision. Unlike a mediator, an arbitrator does determine truth and falsity, and right and wrong. In *binding arbitration*, the parties waive their right to a jury trial and to appeal. Courts recognize the arbitrator's decision as final, and arrange for enforcement by the local sheriff.

Although arbitration is similar to trial, the rules and procedures are more informal than those of a courtroom, and it is possible for an owner to represent himself. Because there is little or no backlog, matters can be heard and resolved with less delay. But arbitration has disadvantages. The arbitrator, unlike a judge or jury, charges for his services, and the parties pay for their lawyers' time *and* the arbitrator's time. The process is cheaper than court only because it is faster. In addition, arbitration's finality means the parties can more easily be bound to bad decisions.

Notwithstanding these drawbacks, the model equity sharing agreement in Chapter Ten requires the owners to submit to binding arbitration any disputes that cannot be resolved through mediation. Either owner is allowed to initiate arbitration. Because the arbitrator's decision will be binding, both owners have input into selection of the arbitrator. The agreement also describes how the costs of arbitration are allocated among the owners.

DEFAULT

The Default Risk

Most equity sharing owners understand the primary risks of the transaction: loss of investment and, for occupiers, loss of home. But these owners are less aware of another major risk: credit blemishes that can prevent them from getting new loans or credit for as long as seven years. These risks are extremely serious and create a high level of mutual dependency among owners. The dependency flows in both directions but weighs more heavily on the investor, who relies on the occupier to fulfill most payment and maintenance duties. The investor must build many levels of default protection into the equity share.

Screening the Occupier

The first level of default protection is careful occupier screening. Because the mortgage lender qualifies the occupier and the investor together, a financially strong investor can compensate for an occupier who is financially weak or has bad credit. As an investor, don't rely on the lender to qualify the occupier; conduct your own investigation, including a review and analysis of financial statements, confirmation of financial information with income tax returns, verification of employment, and verification of savings. A real estate agent or attorney can help you with this qualification process. To confirm the occupier's level of responsibility, obtain a credit report and contact at least two housing references, preferably the occupier's last two landlords.

Staying Informed

The next level of default protection is staying informed. You need to know quickly and reliably if there are any financial or maintenance problems with the equity share. Require that the occupier mail you copies of every bill and payment check associated with the mortgage, property taxes, and insurance. Request notice of any nonpayment or default directly from the mortgage lender. In many localities, you can also request the government records office to notify you if the lender records a notice of default against the property. These measures will ensure that you learn of any nonpayment default immediately.

Conduct inspections of the property at least once a year. The equity sharing agreement should specifically provide for these inspections on a regular basis, following reasonable advance notice. If you do not live near the property, arrange for a friend, or professional inspection service to conduct the inspections.

Both owners also need to protect their property interest and equity against liens that might be recorded against the property. Liens are claims of creditors who might seek to seize the property to satisfy a debt of one of the owners. They can be created voluntarily, as when one of the owners signs a mortgage, or involuntarily, as when an owner refuses to pay a contractor. A lien can result in forced sale of the property, and therefore endangers the owners' investments.

To minimize the risk of liens, record a "Memorandum of Agreement" in the government records. (A sample Memorandum of Agreement is included in Chapter Ten.) This document states that the owners have an equity sharing agreement that restricts the rights of either owner to voluntarily create a lien against the property. Recording the memorandum prevents either owner from becoming subject to a lien that was voluntarily created by the other owner. In addition, conduct annual title searches to ensure that no new liens have been recorded. These searches can be conducted by an attorney or title company at low cost. Finally, where the occupier is having repairs and improvements made to the property at his own expense, the investor can post a "Notice of Nonresponsibility" on the property, to prevent the contractor from placing a lien against the investor's interest if he is not paid by the occupier.

Default Reserve

The next level of default protection is maintaining a default reserve fund—cash that the occupier provides to the investor just as a tenant provides a security deposit to a landlord. The occupier can provide it as a lump sum at the start of the equity share, or gradually, through monthly payments over the course of the first year. The fund can be used to cure small defaults or to initiate dispute resolution without investing additional funds. The smaller the occupier's investment, the greater the chance of a default and the more the investor has to lose. If the occupier is making no down payment, the reserve fund should at least equal three months' mortgage, property tax, insurance, and homeowner's association dues. Allow interest to accumulate on the fund, and return it at the end of the equity share.

Actionable Violation

The next level of default protection is the equity sharing agreement. In the model agreement in Chapter Ten, the minimal level of wrongdoing is called "actionable violation." Owners can "cure" an actionable violation and preclude serious consequences, but failure to cure leads to "default" which has very serious consequences.

There are five types of actionable violations:

1. Failure to follow the equity sharing agreement;
2. Investor interference with the occupier's authorized use of the property;

3. Illegal use of the property by the occupier;
4. Repairs or improvements that do not meet government standards;
5. Any activity that makes the goals of the equity share difficult or impossible to achieve.

When one owner commits an actionable violation, the other may perform any act necessary to correct it. The owner who commits the actionable violation then becomes responsible for all costs and expenses that arise from it. These costs include money spent by the other owner to correct it, and any fines or fees imposed by outside parties like the mortgage lender or the local building department. The model agreement in Chapter Ten also requires a $300 damage payment as compensation for the time involved in correcting the actionable violation and initiating the enforcement process (see Example 6.2).

The enforcement process begins when one owner gives the other a written description of the actionable violation and all actions and payments required to cure it. The recipient must provide evidence of cure within 14 days or the actionable violation becomes a default. The fourth actionable violation cannot be cured and is automatically a default. This rule prevents an owner from continually violating and curing.

The actionable violation process is decisive by necessity. Decisiveness provides a strong deterrent to default. Owners can sometimes be tempted to handle personal misfortunes or disagreements by denial or by failing to fulfill obligations. For example, if George loses his job, he might attempt to avoid embarrassment by making payments late, which might blemish both owners' credit, and delay discussion of the Smiths' financial problems until it is too late to avoid loss of the property. Similarly, if the Smiths are unhappy with Laura's refusal to help renovate a bathroom, they might ignore a leaking pipe, which might cause major wood rot. For the equity share to work, owners need to be encouraged to handle any personal misfortunes or disagreements through discussions and/or mediation, and strongly deterred from failing to fulfill obligations.

The actionable violation process is also quick by necessity. Quickness prevents small acts from causing major losses. Failure to clean rain gutters might cause damage to an entire roof; late loan payments might trigger large late fees. Moreover, an owner never knows whether an actionable violation is a small and isolated oversight or the beginning of a total refusal of the other owner to perform. In the latter case, completing the enforcement process may take months,

---

Example 6.2   Actionable Violation Procedure

Suppose there is a leaking underground water line at 3321 Elm Street. George Smith notices pooling water but takes no action. A week later, a next door neighbor, whose property is downslope of the Smith–Davidson property, complains to George of flooding in his basement and a water-damaged cabinet because of abnormal runoff from the adjacent (3321) land. George gets estimates of $900 to repair the pipe and $200 to replace the cabinet. Because the total cost is over $1,000, the Smiths feel that Laura should pay her ownership percentage of the cost. Laura feels that the high cost resulted from George's negligence in ignoring the problem. They argue, fail to resolve the issue, and the Smiths take no action. Laura's options include:

1. Get the pipe fixed, pay the neighbor, and initiate mediation;
2. Get the pipe fixed, pay the neighbor, and send the Smiths a Notice of Actionable Violation showing they owe her $1,400: $900 for the pipe, $200 for the cabinet, and $300 as damages for the violation.
3. Send a Notice of Actionable Violation requiring the Smiths to get the pipe fixed, pay the neighbor for the cabinet, and pay Laura $300;
4. Do nothing, wait for the neighbor to sue and win, then send a Notice of Actionable Violation requiring the Smiths to get the pipe fixed, pay the neighbor for the court damage award (including any costs and attorney's fees), and pay Laura $300.

The Smiths' options include:

1. Get the pipe fixed, pay the neighbor, and initiate mediation;
2. Get the pipe fixed, pay the neighbor, and send Laura a Notice of Actionable Violation showing she owes them $795: 45 percent of the $1,100 repair cost plus $300 as damages for the violation;
3. Do nothing, wait for the neighbor to sue and win, then send a Notice of Actionable Violation requiring Laura to pay them $795 and pay the neighbor for the court damage award (including any costs and attorney's fees).

On each side, options 1 and 2 are better. By paying for the repair, each owner ensures that no actionable violation is committed, which could result in $300 in damages and possibly a default. Option 1 is better than option 2 because resolving disputes through mediation is less likely to leave the owners' relationship adversarial.

---

during which the enforcing owner bears all the costs of ownership. Quick response minimizes these costs.

Beyond the Actionable Violation

When the guilty owner has been notified of the problem and has had ample opportunity to cure it, quick and decisive action is required to avoid investment loss and credit damage. Follow-up procedures must deter defaults, work quickly and reliably, and not be so harsh that the law will not provide enforcement. In most states, the law will not allow **forfeiture**, an instantaneous loss of an owner's interest without compensation. An agreement that provides that a defaulting owner's interest will automatically pass to the other owner upon default would not be enforceable. Variations on this theme, like a presigned but unrecorded deed, which the nondefaulting owner can record upon default, or a "power of attorney" which the nondefaulting owner can use to sign the property over to himself upon default, have the same problem. The best solution is a procedure called **forced disposition**, which forces the guilty owner to sell his share. Price and terms are set to ensure quick sale, and a damage provision compensates the nondefaulting owner.

Forced Disposition

In a forced disposition, the nondefaulting owner may either buy the defaulting owner's share or force a sale of the entire property. In either case, the defaulting owner's proceeds are reduced by the amount he owes the nondefaulting owner, plus $5,000 in damages. If one owner buys out the other, he may pay for the interest over three years.

As an illustration of the forced disposition procedure, assume the Smiths default halfway through the five-year 3321 Elm Street equity share. This is how the forced disposition would work:

Step 1: Appraise the property. Assume that when the appraisal is completed, the appraised value is $230,000.

Step 2: Calculate total equity.

Appraised value	$230,000
Less: Disposition expenses (6.5%)	(14,950)
Mortgage balance	(178,000)
Total equity	$ 37,050

Step 3: Calculate capital contributions.

Down payment	$20,000
Closing costs	5,000
Monthly contribution	300*
Major repairs	5,000
Total capital contributions	$30,394

Step 4: Calculate total profit.

Total equity	$37,050
Total capital contributions	30,300
Total profit	$ 6,750

Step 5: Calculate defaulting owner's equity.

Smith down payment	$10,000
Smith closing costs	4,500
Smith major repairs	3,000
Smith monthly payments	300
Smith profit share (55% × $6,750)	3,713
Total Smith equity	$21,513

Step 6: Calculate amount owed by defaulting owner.

Unperformed financial obligations	$ 5,500
Uncompleted repairs	900
Unpaid amounts from actionable violation notice	1,500
Interest on amounts advanced by investor	200
Collection and appraisal expenses	1,200
Automatic damages	5,000
Total amount owed	$14,300

Step 7: Calculate buyout price and terms.

Total Smith equity	$21,513
Less: Total amount owed	(14,300)
Buyout price	$ 7,213

*The monthly capital contribution is reduced to reflect the fact that only about half the 60 monthly payments were actually made before the default.

Our agreement allows the investor to make a 25 percent down payment (25 percent of $7,213 is $1,803) and pay the remainder over three years in monthly installments of $150.28.

If Laura chooses not to buy the Smiths' interest on these terms, she can force a sale of 3321 Elm Street. The initial asking price would be the appraised value, but Laura would be entitled to reduce the price 5 percent each 30 days. When the property is sold, Laura would follow Steps 2 through 7 on pages 86–87, except that she would substitute the actual sale price and costs of sale in Step 2. The buyout price in Step 7 would determine the amount of the sale proceeds the Smiths would receive, and Laura would receive the balance.

If the amount of money owed by the defaulting owner exceeds his equity, the model agreement in Chapter Ten requires repayment to the nondefaulting owner over time, with interest. Unfortunately, if the defaulting owner has no assets or moves out of town, it may prove difficult or impossible to collect this debt.

Should the defaulting owner refuse to cooperate with the buyout or sale procedure, the other owner can enforce his rights through binding arbitration. If necessary, the arbitrator can issue an order that a court can enforce through the local sheriff.

Foreclosure

Foreclosure is an alternative way for one owner to force sale of the other's interest following default. Two different types of foreclosures are used in equity sharing. The first type, a "common law" foreclosure, is a process available by law in most but not all states. It requires a court procedure and is usually slower and more expensive than forced disposition. The second type, a "nonjudicial" foreclosure, does not require a court procedure and can be as fast or faster than forced disposition. Moreover, if the nondefaulting owner is the only bidder at the foreclosure sale, he may pay less for the defaulting owner's interest than he would have paid in a forced disposition.

A defaulting owner is only subject to nonjudicial foreclosure if he signs special documents at the beginning of the equity share. The documents are similar to those an owner signs for a mortgage loan, and they provide the same basic rights that a lender has following default on a mortgage. In most equity sharing transactions, only the occupier signs these documents. In a default, the investor determines whether his best strategy is foreclosure or forced sale under the equity sharing agreement. The determination depends on the circumstances of the default, the value of the property, and the financial condition of the occupier, and should be made in consultation with an attorney.

One of the documents, the "equity sharing promissory note," recites a specific amount of money that the occupier owes the investor. Using a specific amount, rather than a reference to the equity that the occupier has at the time of default, is necessary to ensure that the nonjudicial foreclosure can be completed quickly and inexpensively. Because you, as an investor, won't know how much the occupier will owe upon default, estimate the amount. As shown in Example 6.3, include the full mortgage balance, the investor's initial capital contribution, and any automatic damages described in the equity sharing agreement. Make sure the note recites that it is intended to create a debt that includes the mortgage balance but is not in addition to it.

The other document needed to create the nonjudicial foreclosure right may be called an "equity sharing deed of trust" or an "equity sharing mortgage," depending on the state where the property is located. It describes prerequisites to and procedures for public sale of the property, and must be entered in the government records. Some lenders won't allow any additional mortgages or deeds of trust to be recorded against the property. If you plan to use a mortgage or deed of trust, ask your lender if the practice is acceptable.

Eviction

Upon default, the occupier loses his right to occupy, but he may refuse to move out. So long as a defaulting occupier remains in possession, the property is at risk and rental income is lost. For this reason, the investor has the right to evict the occupier. This right can be exercised before or during a forced disposition or foreclosure. The rules governing recovery of possession from an owner-occupier vary from state to state. In some states, unsettled law may make it difficult to evict the occupier until a forced disposition or foreclosure is completed.

Example 6.3   Calculating the Promissory Note Amount

3321 Elm Street mortgage amount	$180,000
Davidson initial capital contribution	10,500
Liquidated damages	5,000
Promissory note amount	$195,500

Bankruptcy

When someone becomes involved in a bankruptcy, all creditors' claims and legal actions against him are frozen and centralized in the bankruptcy court. The court attempts to satisfy as many claims as possible by either selling the assets or creating a payment plan. This process has two important consequences for equity sharing owners: (1) it may be difficult or impossible to enforce equity sharing rights against a bankrupt owner, and (2) a bankrupt owner's interest may be sold by court order, leaving the remaining owner in an equity sharing relationship with someone he has not approved.

The model agreement in Chapter Ten allows the nonbankrupt owner to force a buyout or sale before a bankrupt owner falls behind on his obligations or a new owner is introduced through court-ordered sale. Unfortunately, the nonbankrupt owner must enforce this right in bankruptcy court, and the result is not always predictable. Most bankruptcy courts will enforce buyout and sale rights, provided the property is not discounted from its appraised value and the bankrupt owner is not otherwise penalized. Bankruptcy buyout and sale rights that involve discounts and damages will probably not be enforced. Foreclosure rights in an equity sharing mortgage or deed of trust often work better in bankruptcy than buyout and sale provisions in an equity sharing agreement.

Bankruptcy court proceedings are usually more expensive and slower than binding arbitration. If possible, end the equity share before the bankruptcy begins, even if it means taking a financial loss.

Homestead Rights

Under certain circumstances, homestead rights allow someone in financial trouble to keep his home out of creditors' reach. This could allow a defaulting occupier to own and reside in the equity share property without making payments or fulfilling other obligations. To prevent this unfair result, the equity sharing agreement should provide that the occupier waives his homestead rights. The applicability of homestead rights and the validity of this waiver will vary from state to state.

DEATH

Owner Wills

Death of an equity sharing owner can create significant problems for a surviving owner. If the decedent's assets are tied up in a lengthy court proceeding, it may be difficult or impossible for the surviving owner to enforce the decedent's equity sharing obligations. Payments may be late, maintenance may be ignored, and substantial time and money may be spent fulfilling or enforcing the decedent's responsibilities. Additional problems can arise if many heirs—say, eleven nieces and nephews—inherit small portions of the decedent's interest. Minimize the likelihood of these problems by requiring that all owners prepare wills within six months of beginning the equity share. A will both shortens the probate period and lowers the probability that an interest will be fragmented over many heirs.

Buyout and Sale Rights

The fact that a deceased owner has a will does not completely protect the survivor. The individual who inherits the deceased owner's interest may be financially unqualified or simply unpleasant. To prevent the survivor from being forced to continue an equity share with an unsatisfactory new owner, give him a right to buy out the new owner at appraised value or to force sale of the property. This buyout and sale right should be triggered by any death that causes control of an ownership interest to pass to an outside party. It should also apply to a "conservatorship," a court appointment of someone to take charge of the affairs of another person who is mentally incapacitated. The right should not apply if control of the deceased or incapacitated owner's interest passes to another owner or a spouse.

The timing of the buyout and sale rights is very important. Often, during a lengthy period after a death, it is unclear who will take control of the decedent's assets. The surviving owner's right to trigger a buyout or a sale cannot expire before he learns whether he is comfortable with the new owner. The model agreement in Chapter Ten gives the survivor six months to begin the appraisal process, and one month after appraisal to decide whether to end the equity share. If the survivor triggers a buyout or a sale, no value reductions, penalties, or damages apply unless the deceased owner's estate, his legal heirs, or a new owner have defaulted.

Owner Life Insurance

Life insurance can protect a surviving investor by providing the deceased occupier's beneficiary with money to make monthly payments. This financial cushion lessens the probability that a financially weak new occupier will default before he sells his equity sharing interest or triggers early sale of the property. There should be enough insurance to make payments on the equity sharing property for at least one year, and the beneficiary should be the person who inherits the equity share interest under the occupier's will.

"Mortgage insurance," which pays the mortgage balance if the borrower dies, provides even more protection but is usually more expensive than life insurance that pays one year's monthly payments. If you buy mortgage insurance, make sure it will cover the death of the occupier even if the investor is still alive. Also, provide an alternate method of determining cotenant equity at the end of the equity share term so that repayment of the mortgage with the mortgage insurance increases the occupier's cotenant equity but does not affect the investor's. This will ensure that the deceased occupier's beneficiary, rather than the investor, benefits from the mortgage payoff.

Couples

In many equity sharing groups, either the occupier or the investor (or both) is actually a couple, or subgroup of several people. If a subgroup holds title as joint tenants, each member's interest will pass to the other member of the subgroup upon death, and there will be no effect on the equity share. Any buyout or sale rights in the equity sharing agreement will apply when all of the members of the subgroup die simultaneously, or when the last surviving member dies. If subgroup holds title as tenants-in-common, a deceased member's interest may pass to someone who is not already an owner, and the buyout or sale rights in the agreement will apply.

Seven

Making Equity Sharing Happen— A Home Buyer's Guide

N ow that you understand equity sharing, it's time to act. This chapter will provide the tools a prospective home buyer needs to become an equity sharing occupier. The process is designed to be followed step-by-step, and it includes all of the instructions, language, and forms you need to find a home and an investor. Add some effort and persistence, and you'll be living in your new home in four to six months.

IS EQUITY SHARING FOR ME?

Making equity sharing happen takes significant time and effort. Before beginning the process, it is worthwhile to conduct some self-analysis. Give serious thought to each question on the following home buyer self-analysis checklist, and then answer candidly:

- *Am I willing to stay in one particular home for five years?* Most equity shares have five-year terms and require that the occupier remain in the arrangement for the full term. You forfeit some of your equity as damages if you end the equity share early. If there is any likelihood that you might need or want to move, avoid equity sharing.

- *Are my business and personal circumstances stable?* Life changes can make a wonderful home into a prison. They can also lead to default and loss of investment. No one can predict the future, but if you smell danger (downsizing at your company, for example), avoid equity sharing.

- *Would I feel comfortable discussing anticipated financial troubles with my investor?* The best way to avoid dispute and loss is to discuss trouble early and develop a strategy. If you feel that your finances are no one else's business, avoid equity sharing.

- *Can I share control of my home?* You will need to consult with your investor on major decisions. If you would resent someone else having a say over what you do to your own home, avoid equity sharing.

- *Will I be willing to sell if I can't afford a buyout?* A buyout may be impossible if the property appreciates dramatically, or if your income or creditworthiness decreases. If the investor does not want to continue the equity share, you will be forced to sell. In answering this question, remember that enjoying the home for five years is better than never having lived in it at all. Moreover, if you are forced to sell because a buyout is too expensive, it will mean you have made a substantial profit on your investment.

ASSESSING RESOURCES

Monthly Payment, Loans, and Prequalification

If you decide to equity share, begin by gathering your income records, shopping for mortgages, and determining your loan qualification strength. Use Appendix B as your guide. You will probably refinance at the end of the equity share term, so avoid mortgages with prepayment penalties. In case you can afford to buy out your investor without refinancing, get an assumable loan and ask the lender what it would charge to remove the investor's name at buyout time. Get a prequalification letter from your top three loan choices, to show to prospective sellers and investors.

Down Payment

Determine your down payment resources. Look beyond your bank account to less obvious sources like retirement funds you can borrow and investments you can liquidate. Remember not to allocate all of your resources to down payment and closing costs; you will need cash for moving expenses, minor repairs, furnishing, and decorating, and you should also maintain an emergency reserve.

Potential Investors

Approach friends, relatives, or employers who are potential investors. Explain equity sharing and give them a copy of this book. If any of your contacts are interested, try to reach an agreement about down payment contributions, type and location of home, and equity share term. Other terms, like the ownership percentages and repair and improvement plans, should wait until after you have located the property. Don't worry if you have no potential investors, and don't approach strangers yet. It is easier to find an investor after you have chosen a home and developed an equity sharing plan.

LOCATING THE PROPERTY

Choosing a Real Estate Agent for Equity Sharing

Relatively few agents are familiar with equity sharing, so finding one may be difficult. Begin by asking friends, relatives, and business associates if they know an agent with equity sharing experience. If not, get names of non-equity sharing agents and real estate attorneys, and call them for referrals. Also try the sales managers of the larger real estate brokerage offices in your area. Through this process, assemble a list of equity sharing agents and set up interviews.

Ask the agents about their equity sharing qualifications and experience. In particular, ask how many equity sharing transactions they have handled and whom they represented in those transactions. Determine whether they have successfully represented home buyers whose down payments and price ranges are similar to yours, but who did not have an equity sharing investor lined up in advance. Find out whether they maintain a file or database of possible investors. Make sure the agent will agree to help locate an investor by contacting past clients and sharing the sales commission with any real estate agent who produces an investor. Check the agent's references.

If you can't find an agent with equity sharing experience, look for someone who's interested in learning. Working with an agent who has no equity sharing experience is better than having no agent. Be persistent. Some agents won't be willing to try something new, but you'll eventually find one who is motivated to learn and willing to work as hard as you do. Give him a copy of this book. Once motivated and educated, he will help you find an investor.

Selecting a Property for Equity Sharing

You need to sell prospective investors on the appreciation potential of your property, so look for features that investors find attractive. Find a neighborhood that has recently shown strong appreciation or will be the site of some event or development, like a planned new shopping area, park, or mass transit station, which will make it more desirable. Avoid elements that hinder appreciation, like public housing projects, noisy playgrounds, or major thoroughfares. Pick a house that is less expensive than surrounding properties. Remember that major repairs, additions, or improvements add complexity and risk and might scare investors.

Equity sharing is easiest where the seller is the investor, and certain sellers are more likely to equity share than others. Here is how you can follow the signs of an equity sharing seller:

- Look for property that has been on the market for a long time, but is still overpriced. Have your real estate agent confirm that there have been no recent offers and that the seller is motivated. You can probably convince the seller that equity sharing is the only way for him to participate in future appreciation and ultimately get his price.

- Look for a seller who advertises willingness to accept a low down payment. He may intend to provide seller financing, but you can show him that equity sharing is better.

- Look for a seller who has owned for a long time and has not recently refinanced; he probably has substantial equity. Your real estate agent or title company can check. This seller won't need all of his equity to buy a replacement home, and can afford to equity share.

- Look for a seller who is not purchasing a replacement home or is trading down. Good indications are: a seller of retirement age, mention of relocation, or empty children's bedrooms. Equity sharing can offer this seller extraordinary tax benefits.

DEVELOPING A PROPOSED EQUITY SHARING STRUCTURE

After selecting a property but before making an offer, develop a proposed structure for the equity share. Begin by determining how much capital you will need from an investor. Calculate the total down payment and closing costs, add in the anticipated cost of any planned improvements, and subtract the amount of cash you have.

Next, determine proposed ownership percentages. To use a contribution-based formula (Example 5.1), compare your after-tax monthly costs to the rental value of the home. You can get a good idea of rental value from the classified ads in your local newspaper. Use the comparison to establish monthly contributions, then add these to the initial contributions you already calculated. Divide each owner's contributions into the total, and you will have contribution-based ownership percentages. Alternatively, project appreciation using past appreciation data that your agent can cull from the local Association or Board of Realtors, county tax assessor's office, or census bureau. If none of these sources is available, have the agent give you an opinion based on his experience. Use the appreciation projection to develop return-based ownership percentages (Example 5.2).

CREATING PRESENTATION MATERIALS

Effective presentation materials are essential to successfully locating an investor. The materials will describe you, the property, and the proposed structure, and will demonstrate the benefits of the equity share for the investor. Example 7.1 shows a typical information statement. You would use the statement to solicit and educate potential investors.

These are the components of an effective set of home buyer's presentation materials:

- A description of the property, including size, features, location, price, and photograph;
- A description of you, including a job description, loan prequalification, and down payment resources;
- A summary of the equity sharing proposal, including amount of capital initially required, any additional capital required, term of the investment, rights of the owners at the end of the term, and allocation of appreciation;

- An appreciation projection for the property, with supporting research or documentation;
- A projection of the return to the investor, including any tax benefits.

This sample presentation is designed to raise interest in the equity share, not to provide all of the details. Supplement it with additional information that might be convincing to a particular investor. Perhaps the best kind of supplemental material is the type of comparison demonstrated in Appendix A, in the sections on investor analysis, seller analysis, parent/relative analysis, and employer analysis. Tailor your presentation to your investor by comparing the equity share to that prospective investor's alternatives, and be as specific as you can.

APPROACHING POTENTIAL INVESTORS

After you have created your basic presentation, distribute it to friends, relatives, or employers who are potential investors. It is best to make this distribution in person so that you can explain the material, describe the property in detail, and answer questions.

Example 7.1   Home Buyer's Equity Sharing Statement

PROPOSAL FOR EQUITY SHARING ON 3321 ELM STREET

I.   INTRODUCTION

George and Mary Smith are looking for an equity sharing investor to help them buy a townhome at 3321 Elm Street in San Francisco. They have $15,000 toward the down payment and closing costs, and need another $10,000 to buy the property. They would like to find someone who will invest $10,000 in exchange for 45 percent of the appreciation of the property. The Smiths will pay the mortgage, property tax, and all other monthly costs.

II.   DESCRIPTION OF THE PROPERTY

The property is a two-bedroom, two-bath townhome located on a tree-lined block in San Francisco's Noe Valley neighborhood. The building was built in 1984 and is about 1,500 square feet in size. It has a breathtaking view, a fireplace, a one-car garage, and new carpets. The price is $200,000. [It is a good idea to attach a photograph.]

(Continued)

(Example Continued)

III. ABOUT THE SMITHS

George Smith is an engineer and Mary Smith is a nurse. They both have been at their current jobs for more than five years. They have already prequalified with National Bank for a $180,000 mortgage.

IV. DESCRIPTION OF THE EQUITY SHARE

The total down payment and closing costs will be $25,000. The Smiths will contribute $15,000 of this amount and own 55 percent of the property, and the investor will contribute $10,000 and own 45 percent. The Smiths will make all of the monthly payments and pay for all of the ordinary repairs and maintenance. In five years, the investor will receive $10,000 plus 45 percent of the property appreciation. The arrangement will be described in a detailed equity sharing agreement.

V. PROJECTED APPRECIATION

Despite the recession, Noe Valley property in the $150,000 to $300,000 range has appreciated an average of 25 percent over the past five years. [Attach any supporting documentation you have.] Based on this trend and on the increasing popularity of this neighborhood, we believe that appreciation over the next five years will be at least 25 percent.

VI. PROJECTED INVESTOR PROFIT

If the property appreciates 25 percent over five years, the investor will receive approximately $25,188, which includes the original investment of $10,000 plus profit of $15,188. This profit reflects a return of over 30 percent per year.

Value in 5 years	$250,000
Less: Commissions and costs of sale (6.5%)	(16,250)
Mortgage balance	(175,000)
Down payment and closing costs	(25,000)
Total profit	$ 33,750
Investor share (45%)	$ 15,188
Investor return as annual percentage	30.3%

The investor will be able to defer income taxes on this profit, and can also receive tax deductions during the equity share.

VII. MORE INFORMATION

The information in this proposal is only partially complete, and is open to further negotiation. If you are interested in learning more about it, call George Smith at 555-9220.

EQUITY SHARE PRELIMINARY COMMITMENT

If you find an investor who is willing to commit to the equity share, prepare and sign a document called an "Equity Share Preliminary Commitment" ("the Preliminary Commitment"), which outlines the basic terms of the arrangement (see Example 7.2).

The Preliminary Commitment is important because the occupier and the investor are about to make binding commitments to the seller. They will also incur inspection fees, legal fees, and, in some cases, loan application fees. Perhaps most important, the occupier will suspend his search for other investors. Each party will take these steps in reliance on the other's commitment to equity share. Given the amount at stake, it is both symbolically and legally important that they acknowledge this commitment.

The safest way to acknowledge a commitment to equity share would be to resolve all details and sign a complete agreement. This eliminates any possibility that a disagreement or misunderstanding might scuttle the transaction. But the time and expense involved in preparing a complete agreement would be wasted if the transaction didn't close, and when the investor first commits, there is still a high risk that it *won't* close. Buyer and seller might not agree on price, or physical inspections could reveal significant defects. The Preliminary Commitment is a compromise designed as a quick and inexpensive way to provide security in the early stages of negotiation.

Example 7.2   Sample Preliminary Commitment

EQUITY SHARE PRELIMINARY COMMITMENT

This Equity Share Preliminary Commitment is entered into on May 1, 1993, between George and Mary Smith (the "Occupier") and Simon Smith (the "Investor"). The parties agree as follows:

(1) Occupier and Investor intend to jointly make an offer to purchase 3321 Elm Street, San Francisco, California (the "Property"). They have agreed to offer $190,000 for the Property, but are willing to pay as much as $200,000 if necessary.

(2) The parties agree to contribute up to the following amounts in cash for down payment and closing costs:

Occupier	$15,000
Investor	$10,000

(Continued)

(Example Continued)
If less than $25,000 is required for down payment and closing costs, the parties shall reduce their contributions proportionally.

(3) The parties shall hold title to the property as tenants-in-common in the following percentages (the "Ownership Shares"):

Occupier	55
Investor	45

(4) Occupier shall be entitled to exclusive possession of the property and shall make monthly payments equivalent to the total of the mortgage payments, property taxes, insurance, utilities, and homeowner's association dues. Some of these payments will be made directly, and others will be made as rent to Investor who shall apply the payment to the above expenses. Occupier shall be responsible for the costs of most repairs and improvements.

(5) The term of the equity share will be five years. At the end of the term, Occupier may purchase Investor's interest in the Property for an amount approximately equal to Investor's capital investment plus 45 percent of the net appreciation. If Occupier chooses not to buy out Investor, the Property shall be sold and each party shall be entitled to receive an amount approximately equal to their capital investments plus their Ownership Shares of the net appreciation.

(6) This document shall be superseded by an Equity Sharing and Lease Agreement (the "Final Agreement") to be prepared and signed by the parties before they complete the purchase of the Property. Nevertheless, this document is intended to be binding on the parties until the Final Agreement is completed, and the major terms of this document shall not be materially altered by the Final Agreement unless the parties agree to alter them.

(7) If the parties are unable to successfully negotiate a Final Agreement despite good faith efforts, neither shall make any further effort to purchase the Property, either individually or with another equity sharing cobuyer, for a period of three (3) months, unless this provision is waived in writing.

George C. Smith	DATE
Mary A. Smith	DATE
Simon Smith	DATE

The last paragraph of the Preliminary Commitment prohibits one party from deciding that, although he still wants the property, he would prefer to buy it alone or with a different cobuyer. Suppose the occupier's parents initially decline to equity share, then change their minds after the occupier locates another investor. The occupier would rather equity share with his parents. If the investor who signed the Preliminary Commitment is willing to voluntarily leave the transaction, there is no problem; but if the investor wants to proceed, there will be a dispute about which of the parties has the senior right to buy the property. To avoid this problem, the Preliminary Commitment provides that neither party can reject the other and then attempt to buy the property without him.

I advise against using one Preliminary Commitment for a series of offers on different properties. Using a new form for each offer ensures that there is no misunderstanding about whether a particular property and a particular price are acceptable to the investor. It also reaffirms both parties' commitment to the arrangement before a new purchase offer is made, and allows them to incorporate changes or special arrangements applicable to the new offer.

WRITING AND PRESENTING AN OFFER

Occupier with a Preliminary Commitment

Make your purchase offer in the name of both occupier and investor, and have your agent explain to the seller that it is an equity share. Consider including a contingency requiring completion of an equity sharing agreement as shown in Example 7.3. Placing this clause in your purchase offer will allow you to cancel the transaction if you and your investor are unable to agree to final equity sharing terms.

Example 7.3   Sample Finish Equity Sharing Agreement Contingency

Buyers shall attempt in good faith to negotiate and sign a mutually satisfactory equity sharing agreement within fourteen (14) days of the ratification of this Contract. If Buyers fail to reach such an agreement, they may terminate this Contract by so notifying Seller in writing prior to the expiration of the fourteen (14)-day period. In the event of termination, all of Buyers' deposits shall be promptly refunded in full.

If you can't complete an equity sharing agreement, this language will protect you from liability to the seller and ensure that you recover your good faith deposit. The problem is that it weakens your offer. The seller may see it as a way for you to change your mind. He might miss an opportunity to sell to another buyer during the 14 days, only to learn later that you are backing out. If you include this provision, you risk that the seller will not take your offer seriously or will choose another offer—even at a lower price.

Occupier without a Preliminary Commitment

If your attempts to find an investor have been unsuccessful, don't despair. Your next step is to try to interest the seller in equity sharing. Customize your presentation material for the seller. Delete the section about the property, and expand the section about yourself to include the name of your employer and the amount of your income. Consider adding one or more of the comparisons demonstrated in Appendix A, in the section on seller analysis.

When you prepare your purchase offer, include the requirement that the seller will agree to equity share. A sample clause is shown in Example 7.4. The clause requires that the seller agree to equity share with you as a condition of your purchase offer.

Example 7.4   Sample Seller Equity Share Contingency

Seller agrees to equity share with the Buyer as follows:

(1) Buyer shall make a down payment of $10,000 and shall pay all title insurance costs, escrow fees, and loan fees. Buyer shall pay ½ of the attorneys' fees incurred in preparation of the equity sharing agreement. All such payments shall be considered Buyer's initial capital contribution to the equity share.

(2) Seller shall receive a total of $190,000 in gross sale proceeds, and contribute $10,000 in equity toward the equity share. Seller shall pay ½ of the attorneys' fees incurred in preparation of the equity sharing agreement in cash, and this payment plus the $10,000 in equity shall be Seller's initial capital contribution to the equity share. Seller shall pay all sales commissions and transfer taxes, but these expenses shall not be considered part of Seller's capital contribution.

(3) Seller shall apply jointly with Buyer for the mortgage loan described in Paragraph _____ [refer to loan contingency paragraph elsewhere in purchase contract] of this Contract.

(Continued)

(Example Continued)

(4) The parties shall hold title as tenants-in-common in the following percentages (the "Ownership Shares"):

Buyer	55 percent
Seller	45 percent

(5) Buyer shall be entitled to exclusive possession of the Property and shall make monthly payments equivalent to the total of the mortgage payments, property taxes, insurance, utilities, and homeowner's association dues. Some of these payments will be made directly, and others will be made as rent to Seller, who shall apply the rent payment to the above expenses. Buyer shall be responsible for the costs of most repairs and improvements.

(6) The term of the equity share will be five years. At the end of the term, Buyer may purchase Seller's interest in the Property for an amount approximately equal to Seller's capital contribution plus 45 percent of the net appreciation of the Property above $200,000. If Buyer chooses not to buy out Seller, the Property shall be sold and each party shall be entitled to receive an amount approximately equal to their capital contributions plus their Ownership Shares of the net appreciation.

(7) Buyer and Seller shall attempt in good faith to negotiate and sign a mutually satisfactory equity sharing agreement in accordance with the provisions of this Contract within fourteen (14) days of the ratification of this Contract. If Buyer and Seller fail to reach such an agreement, either may terminate this Contract by so notifying the other in writing prior to the expiration of the fourteen (14)-day period. In the event of termination, all of Buyer's deposits shall be promptly refunded in full.

If the seller is unfamiliar with equity sharing, the offer presentation will be challenging. Be prepared to explain the concept of equity sharing and to answer questions. It frequently helps if your real estate agent meets with the seller's agent in advance, to introduce the plan to use equity sharing. Often, the best you can hope for under these circumstances is to get the seller interested enough to seriously consider the offer, do some research, consult his attorney or accountant, and respond in a few days. Consider leaving the seller a copy of this book to help introduce him to equity sharing, and suggest that he begin by reading Appendix A's section on seller analysis.

Seller Refusal to Equity Share

All is not lost if the seller declines to equity share. You have barely begun to exhaust your investor sources. Rather than abandon negotiations with the seller and risk losing the property, rewrite your offer with a "Find Investor Contingency" (Example 7.5).

This provision gives you 14 days to find an investor, and allows you to escape from the purchase contract and recover your deposit if you fail. Negotiate as long a search period as possible. Don't spend money and time on the physical inspection or loan application process until you find your investor. The provision ensures that you will have ample time to complete these processes afterward.

Unlike the Finish Equity Sharing Agreement Contingency in Example 7.3, this provision is essential protection. Unfortunately, it similarly weakens your offer in the seller's eyes. You can partially mitigate this effect with a 72-Hour Release Contingency as shown in Example 7.6.

This provision protects the seller from losing a new buyer while he is waiting for the original one to satisfy a Find Investor Contingency. It may ultimately force the buyer to give up the property before the 14 days have passed, but it will provide 72 hours for a last-minute effort.

Example 7.5   Sample Find Investor Contingency

Buyer shall attempt in good faith to locate an equity sharing investor within fourteen (14) days of the ratification of this Contract. Seller shall permit Buyer to partially assign his rights under this Contract to the investor. If Buyer locates an investor, or chooses to waive this condition, he shall so notify Seller in writing prior to the expiration of this fourteen (14)-day period. Notwithstanding anything to the contrary in this Contract, all of the time periods stated in paragraphs other than this paragraph shall commence when Buyer provides such notification. If Buyer fails to notify Seller that he has found an investor or waive this provision prior to the expiration of the fourteen (14)-day period, either party may terminate this Contract by so notifying the other in writing. In the event of termination, all of Buyer's deposits shall be promptly refunded in full.

Example 7.6   Sample 72-Hour Release Contingency

If, at any time prior to the satisfaction of Paragraph _____ [refer to "Find Investor" paragraph elsewhere in purchase contract] of this Contract, Seller wishes to accept an offer to purchase the Property from another person, Seller may so notify Buyer in writing. Buyer shall have a period of seventy-two (72) hours from this notification to notify the seller in writing that Buyer removes the condition stated in Paragraph _____ [refer to "Find Investor" paragraph elsewhwere in purchase contract] of this Contract. If Buyer fails to provide such notification, Seller may terminate this Contract. In the event of termination, all of Buyer's deposits shall be promptly refunded in full.

MORE INVESTOR SOURCES

If your early efforts fail, turn to other, more creative ways of locating investors, and don't be timid about reaching out to others for help. Here are some possibilities:

- Contact more relatives and friends, including coworkers. They are by far your best sources for possible investors because, even if they are not interested, they may have other relatives and friends who are. Your presentation materials provide a relatively easy way to test the interest of many people.

- Ask your real estate agent to approach his past clients. Suggest that he mail all of them a copy of your presentation materials, along with a cover letter, and contact the best candidates by telephone. Good candidates include clients who already invest in real estate, and clients who have accumulated a large amount of equity in their homes.

- Ask your agent to share the sales commission with any agent who produces an investor. If he refuses, consider whether you might offer a fee yourself. Once a fee has been established, have your agent telephone all of his contacts—both those who work in the same sales office and those who work in other offices. Follow up with presentation materials, including a description of any fee.

- Enlist the help of the seller's agent, who will be motivated and can contact past clients and other agents. He should also approach the seller, who may have friends who are interested or neighbors who browse his open houses.

- Do an "agent drop," a delivery of your presentation materials to each real estate sales office in your area. Involve your agent or use the telephone book to make a list of all the local offices, map out a course so that you can visit them all efficiently, and take an afternoon to bring a pile of your handouts to each office. If possible, put one of your handouts in each agent's mailbox; otherwise, leave several with the receptionist. Make sure the version of the handout you use describes the fee offered to the agent who produces the investor.

- A "neighbor drop" is another excellent tool for recruiting an investor who is already familiar with the neighborhood and the property,and who is confident that he will be able to keep a close watch on his investment.

- Use classified advertising. Example 7.7 provides a sample ad. The success of classified advertising varies widely according to the type of publication used and the section in which the ad is placed. In addition to the major daily newspapers, consider weekly papers, neighborhood papers, and special-interest papers aimed at businesses and investors. When placing ads in a large daily, stay out of the "Homes for Sale" section; the readers will be other home buyers. Buy space in the "Investment Real Estate" or "Business Opportunity" section instead.

Example 7.7   Sample Buyer Classified Ad for Investor

Investor sought by qualified home buyer for low-risk equity share. $10K needed for part of down payment. Project 30% annual return over 5 years. George 555-9220.

Although some of these steps cost money, we recommend pursuing them all at once. You need to find an investor before the property is sold, and your energies and your agent's level of enthusiasm will be highest during the first two weeks.

QUALIFYING THE INVESTOR

Because the investor won't have major ongoing payment obligations, you don't need to investigate his financial qualifications as closely as he'll need to investigate yours. Get a credit report to make sure he has no credit blemishes that will prevent you from jointly qualifying for a mortgage. Verify his down payment funds and check two personal or business references.

COMPLETING THE PURCHASE

Your purchase contract will probably give you a very short time to complete your physical inspections and equity sharing agreement once you find your investor. As quickly as possible, arrange for the physical inspections. Make an appointment with an equity share attorney for the day after the inspections. This scheduling will allow you to cancel the attorney appointment if the physical inspections go badly, and get a quick start on your equity sharing documents if the inspections go well. In the days before the inspection, submit your mortgage loan applications.

At your first meeting with the attorney, you should provide enough information to prepare draft documents. You can also ask questions and identify issues that you and the investor should discuss before the next meeting with the attorney. That next meeting should be only a few days later; by that time, the attorney should have completed the draft documents so that he can review them with you. If you (or your investor) want to have the documents reviewed by a personal attorney and/or accountant, set up an appointment for that review within two days after your second meeting with the equity share attorney.

Take some time discussing the draft documents with your investor, to make sure you both understand them the same way and to incorporate all of the terms that each of you wants. If the discussions reach an impasse, call the equity sharing attorney for suggestions on how to resolve the dispute. As soon as you agree on changes, transmit them to the attorney so that he can finalize the documents. When they are ready, sign them and remove any related contingency in the purchase contract. Proceed through the remainder of the purchase. Make sure the attorney or your title officer will record the Memorandum of Agreement and the Equity Sharing Deed of Trust (if you are using one) in the government records at the time of closing.

Eight

Making Equity Sharing Happen— A Seller/Investor's Guide

More and more, equity shares are initiated by the investor. This chapter provides step-by-step processes for sellers, investors, and employers to structure equity shares and find qualified occupiers. It includes a broad range of sample language and forms.

IS EQUITY SHARING FOR ME?

To answer that question for yourself, spend some thoughtful time with this investor self-analysis checklist:

- *Can I afford to tie up money for five years?* Although investors are permitted to sell their equity sharing interests, finding a buyer may be difficult. If it is likely that you will need to liquidate before the end of the term, avoid equity sharing.

- *Would I feel comfortable delegating control?* The everyday management of the equity share property will be in the hands of the occupier. If you need to be able to make your own decisions about your investments, avoid equity sharing.
- *Am I willing to consider investment decisions from a homeowner's standpoint?* For the occupier, the equity share property is both a home and an investment, and his primary motivation may not be investment return. For the equity share to run smoothly, you will need to compromise on occasions when quality-of-life concerns clash with investment concerns. If you are unwilling to make this type of compromise, avoid equity sharing.

SELLER PROCEDURES

Minimum Mortgage Amount and Minimum Occupier Down Payment

The loan-to-value ratio (LTV) is a critical factor in determining the rate of return on a real estate investment (see Example 8.1). The higher the LTV, the higher the return.

Example 8.1   Effect of LTV on Return

Compare two hypothetical real estate investments, one with an 80 percent LTV loan, and another with a 90 percent LTV loan. In both, the property appreciates from $200,000 to $250,000 over a five-year term. With the 80 percent loan, return is 14.9 percent; with the 90 percent loan, it is 22.3 percent.

Investment	80% LTV	90% LTV
Down payment	$40,000	$20,000
Original closing costs not including loan fees (1% of $200,000)	2,000	2,000
Loan fees (2% of loan amount)	3,200	3,600
Extra interest on 90% loan (after-tax)	—	4,732
Total investment	$45,200	$30,332
Profit		
Appreciation	$50,000	$50,000
Less: Costs of sale (6.5% of $250,000)	(16,250)	(16,250)
Profit	$33,750	$33,750
Annual Rate of Return		
Profit/Original investment/5 years	14.9%	22.3%

To maximize your equity sharing return, establish a minimum LTV. Have your agent ask a few local lenders what types of LTVs are available for homes in your price range, and set your minimum mortgage amount as high as the loan market will allow. But remember that your risk increases as the occupier's down payment decreases, so require a minimum down payment of at least 3 to 5 percent.

Meeting Your Cash Needs

Once you establish a minimum LTV and occupier down payment, you must confirm that you will end the transaction with enough cash to meet your needs. Take all four of these steps into account as you work toward your bottom line:

Step 1: Calculate cash needed for new home.

> Down payment for replacement residence
> + Closing costs on replacement residence
> + Moving costs
> + Costs of planned repairs and improvements
> + Costs of furnishing and decorating
> Total cash needed for replacement residence

Step 2: Calculate cash needed to repay old mortgage and costs of the sale.

> Balance of old mortgage
> + Any repayment fees charged by lender
> + Sales commission (based on asking price)
> + Transfer tax (based on asking price)
> + Other seller closing costs
> + Cost of any presale repairs and improvements
> Total cash needed for sale

Step 3: Add income tax liability. Determine whether you will qualify for a tax-deferred exchange. If not, calculate your tax on the profit from the sale.

Step 4: Check cash needs against minimum mortgage and down payment. Make sure your minimums equal or exceed the cash you will need. If not, you need to increase either or both of them.

Developing a Proposed Structure

Your proposed equity sharing structure needs to include asking price, mortgage amount, occupier initial capital contribution, term length, and ownership percentages. When choosing a term length, consider the current state of the real estate market and allow enough time for the market to get through its current cycle.

Locating an Occupier

The best way to locate an occupier is to list with a real estate agent who has equity sharing experience. Try to find an agent who has successfully represented equity sharing sellers and maintains a database of equity sharing buyers.

Example 8.2   Sample Equity Sharing Seller Statement

NOE VALLEY EQUITY SHARING OPPORTUNITY

LOCATION:	3321 ELM STREET/27TH
PRICE:	$200,000
DOWN PAYMENT:	$10,000 + Closing Costs
ESTIMATED MONTHLY COSTS:	$1,350
DESCRIPTION:	The property is a two-bedroom, two-bath townhome located on a tree-lined block in San Francisco's Noe Valley neighborhood. The building was built in 1984 and is about 1,500 square feet in size. It has a breathtaking view, a fireplace, a one-car garage, and new carpets.
TERMS:	Buyer and Seller will together apply for a new fixed-rate mortgage of $180,000. Buyer will make a down payment of $10,000, pay all closing costs, and hold title to a 55 percent interest in the property. Seller will pay sales commissions and transfer taxes, and hold title to a 45 percent interest in the property. Buyer will make all of the monthly payments and pay for all of the ordinary repairs and maintenance. Buyer and Seller will split appreciation 55/45 over a five-year term.
MORE INFORMATION:	This statement is intended as an incomplete summary of a possible equity sharing transaction. For more information, contact real estate agent Behrend Eilers at 555-1222.

Your agent should market your property through traditional channels, emphasizing the availability of equity sharing and the low down payment requirement. These are some of the ways in which marketing "with a twist" can focus on the equity sharing opportunity:

- List the property with the **Multiple Listing Service** (MLS), a centralized list of properties for sale that is available to members of your local Association or Board of Realtors. The entry in the MLS should mention that equity sharing is available and state the required down payment and estimated monthly cost. The MLS is only available if you use a real estate agent who is a member.
- Prepare an advertising statement (Example 8.2). Place a photograph of the property at the top of the statement.
- Distribute the advertising statement to agents who call about the MLS listing or visit the property.
- Advertise and conduct weekend open houses for the general public. Emphasize the equity share. Distribute the advertising statement at each open house. (See Example 8.3.)
- Conduct a regional "agent drop" and a local "neighbor drop."

These traditional marketing steps should successfully reach all of the buyers who are actively looking for homes in your price range. But many potential occupiers don't work with an agent or tour open houses because they assume they can't afford to buy. One effective way to reach them is to place a classified advertisement in the "Apartment for Rent" section of your newspaper (Example 8.4).

Qualifying the Occupier

You cannot rely solely on the mortgage lender to assess the qualifications of the occupier. Conduct your own investigation. Add to the purchase contract a contingency requiring the buyer to provide all the

---

Example 8.3   Sample Seller Classified Ad for Buyers

NOE VALLEY. $200,000. Fantastic 2BR
view townhome w/parking. Seller will
equity share w/qualified buyer. $10,000
dn pmt OK. 3321 Elm/27th. Sun. 2–4.
Behrend 555-1222.

Example 8.4   Sample Seller Classified Ad for Renters

$1,350 plus very low down pmt. to OWN a
fantastic Noe Valley 2BR view townhome
with parking. Seller will equity share with
qualified buyer. Behrend 555-1222.

---

necessary information and allowing you to withdraw from the transaction, following your investigation, if the results are unsatisfactory.
A sample clause is shown in Example 8.5.

Completing the Sale

If you are sure you have found the right co-owner and decide to go to
a final sale, include the Seller Equity Share Contingency (Example 7.4) in your purchase contract. Prepare the equity share documentation and complete the transaction according to the instructions in the final section of Chapter Seven.

Example 8.5   Sample Buyer Qualification Contingency

Within five (5) calendar days of mutual execution of this Contract,
Buyer shall provide the following information to Seller:

(1) A copy of Buyer's most recent pay stub;
(2) A copy of Buyer's W-2 form for the most recent tax year;
(3) Copies of Buyer's federal income tax returns for the past two (2)
years;
(4) A completed mortgage loan application form;
(5) A signed statement authorizing Seller to obtain a credit report
on Buyer;
(6) The names and telephone numbers of Buyer's current employer
and last two (2) landlords; and
(7) Bank statements issued within the past thirty (30) days verifying
Buyer's cash assets as stated on Buyer's loan application form.

Seller shall have five (5) calendar days from receipt of the last of these
items to assess Buyer's financial qualifications. If Seller, in his sole
and complete discretion, determines that he is dissatisfied with
Buyer's financial qualifications, Seller may terminate this Agreement
by so notifying Buyer in writing prior to the expiration of this five
(5)-day period.

INVESTOR PROCEDURES

Developing Your Investment Guidelines

The first step for a prospective equity sharing investor is to determine the necessary investment in light of the key factors affecting the investment amount:

- *Risk.* Equity sharing is a relatively conservative investment, but there is still a chance that you might lose some or even all of your investment. When considering a particular investment amount, ask yourself this question: Would a loss of my investment significantly affect my life-style or financial security? If the answer is yes, you are investing too much.
- *Liquidity.* Theoretically, it is possible to sell your equity sharing interest, but you can't count on finding a buyer. Be sure you won't need your investment during the equity share term. Remember to leave yourself enough of a cash reserve for personal and family emergencies, and for equity sharing emergencies like unexpected major repairs.
- *Diversity.* If, even after considering risk and liquidity, you could comfortably invest a large amount, consider the benefits of dividing your investment among two or more equity share properties. By spreading your investment, you avoid having your return dependent on the future of one property and one occupier. Instead, you speculate on the prospects of two or more unrelated properties, making it likely that any misfortune with one will be offset by the success of the other.

After you decide how much you want to invest, determine the target price of the equity share property. (This calculation is easiest if you assume that the occupier will pay all of the closing costs.)

Step 1: Set a minimum down payment and LTV percentage. Keep risk at a reasonable level by requiring at least a 3 to 5 percent down payment from the occupier. Set your minimum LTV at the highest amount that is readily available in your location. Check with some local lenders to determine this amount. For this example, assume a 5 percent down payment and a 90 percent LTV.

Step 2: Determine your investment percentage. Determine the percentage of the total price that your investment will represent by subtracting the occupier down payment percentage and the LTV from 100.

$$100\% - 90\%(\text{LTV}) - 5\% \text{ (occupier down payment)} = 5\%$$

Step 3: Determine target price. Divide your investment amount by your investment percentage to get the target price. For this example, assume a $10,000 investment.

$$\$10,000/.05 = \$200,000$$

After you have determined your investment level and target price, fill in the rest of your equity sharing structure, including the type of property, length of term, and proposed ownership percentages. All of these elements will be subject to renegotiation once the actual property and the occupier are located, but having general guidelines will make your search easier.

Example 8.6   Sample Investor Statement

INVESTOR WILLING TO EQUITY SHARE

Juan and Celia Moreno are interested in investing $10,000 in an equity sharing arrangement. They would like an arrangement with the following terms:

PROPERTY:	A two-bedroom home in good condition in Noe Valley or a similar area.
PRICE:	$200,000.
MORTGAGE:	$180,000 or 90% of the price.
OCCUPIER:	A qualified home buyer who will agree to live in the property for a minimum of five years.
OCCUPIER OBLIGATIONS:	The occupier will contribute $10,000 toward the down payment, make all monthly payments, and pay for all of the ordinary repairs and maintenance.
TERMINATION:	The investors and the occupier will split appreciation 55/45 over a five-year term. At the end of the term, the occupier will either buy out the investor or the property will be sold.

The arrangement will be described in a detailed equity sharing agreement, which will also contain many additional details. For more information, call Celia Moreno at 555-5330.

Finding the Occupier and the Property

You now have two alternative courses of action. The more popular course is to locate an occupier, then let the occupier locate the property. The best way to do this is to prepare a summary of the terms on which you are willing to equity share, and circulate it among local real estate sales offices (see Example 8.6).

Example 8.7   Sample Investor Classified for Buyer Occupier

BUY WITH A LOW DOWN PAYMENT!
Couple wants to invest with qualified
home buyer. Will contribute $10,000
toward down pmt. Celia 555-5330.

In addition to providing this announcement to real estate agents, you may want to place a classified ad (Example 8.7) in the "Homes for Sale" and "Apartments for Rent" sections of the local newspaper.

An alternative course of action is to locate a property before you locate an occupier. This process will take more of your time but will give you more control over property selection. Begin by either enlisting the help of a real estate agent who is experienced with equity sharing, or visiting weekend open houses on your own. When you find a property, develop a proposed structure and advertise for an occupier. When you find a possible occupier, check his financial qualifications, and, if they are satisfactory, prepare a Preliminary Commitment.

DEVELOPING AN EMPLOYER PROGRAM

Employer Contributions

If you are an employer and wish to invest in equity sharing with your employees, you should set two guidelines for your equity sharing contributions: (1) a maximum percentage of purchase price and (2) a maximum dollar amount. The maximum percentage should be no more than 70 percent of the minimum down payment required by local lenders. For example, if local lenders require a 10 percent down payment, limit your contribution to 7 percent. Under these circumstances, the employee's options would include making a 3 percent down payment and getting a 90 percent loan, or making a 13 percent down payment and getting an 80 percent loan. The minimum percentage ensures a reasonable down payment and a reasonably high LTV.

The maximum dollar amount should be based on an employee's salary, so that higher paid employees can receive larger amounts. This approach makes sense because higher paid employees buy more expensive properties, and a small equity sharing contribution won't create a meaningful incentive. If you limit your contribution to 20 percent of an employee's annual salary or a maximum of $15,000, a $50,000 salaried employee could get up to $10,000 as an equity sharing contribution. Assuming a maximum percentage of 7 percent, the employee must buy a home worth at least $142,857 ($10,000/7%) to use this entire amount.

You can vary your equity sharing contribution to create incentives for certain behavior. For example, you might increase the contribution to employees with greater seniority, or to those who purchase homes within a certain radius of the workplace.

Occupier Qualification

Develop underwriting guidelines to ensure that employees do not undertake monthly payment obligations they cannot sustain. The guidelines should include minimum standards for employee credit reports, and minimum debt-to-income ratios.

Term

Allow either party to end the equity share early without penalty. Neither will want to continue if the employee relocates within the company, quits, or is fired. If the employee chooses to end the arrangement early, you should have the senior buyout right. This arrangement prevents the employee from taking advantage of a down cycle in the market to avoid sharing appreciation. For the same reason, limit the frequency with which a specific employee may participate in the equity share program.

Ownership Percentages

The employer should establish a fixed formula for determining ownership percentages based on the relative capital contribution of employer and employee. This formula can be established using the guidelines in Chapter Five.

Nine

Making Equity Sharing Happen— A Real Estate Agent's Guide

This chapter provides real estate agents with tools to increase sales volume by marketing and facilitating equity sharing transactions. A buyer database, listings, a form library, screening of lenders, and cooperation with other agents are especially recommended.

BUILDING A BUYER DATABASE

Recruiting Equity Sharing Home Buyers

Begin your recruiting effort by preparing and distributing a promotional flier directed toward prospective home buyers. You may want to change their order of appearance, but these items should form the content of the flier:

- A summary of your education, licenses, experience, and professional affiliations;

- A brief explanation of equity sharing and the benefits that it offers home buyers;
- A list of the equity sharing services you offer;
- A description of your database and matching service for occupiers and investors;
- A statement that you are currently accepting new home buyers into your program;
- An invitation to call you for an appointment or to attend an informational workshop that you will hold (give details of time and place).

Proofread your flier carefully, and be generous in the number you have printed. A larger initial printing quantity can be cheaper in the long run. When you are ready to distribute the flier, use these tactics:

- Hand it out at weekend open houses;
- Mail copies to past clients;
- Leave stacks of fliers in the lobbies of upscale apartment complexes;
- Post copies on bulletin boards in cafés, malls, laundromats, universities, professional schools, and major employers.

You should also place classified ads in the "Homes for Sale" and "Apartments for Rent" sections of the local newspaper (Example 9.1).

Remember to keep a record of everyone who responds to your advertising efforts, even if the person's financial qualifications are weak. Weak buyers will increase their financial strength over time and could become qualified clients later if you stay in touch with them.

Example 9.1   Agent's Classified Ad for Home Buyers

EQUITY SHARING can allow you to own a home with a very low down payment. R.E. agt. now seeking buyers for equity share program. Free workshop. Call Bill at 555-9922.

Recruiting Equity Sharing Investors

Your recruitment of investors should also start with a promotional flier. Include an example of an investor's return on a hypothetical property through equity sharing. Mail the investor flier to past clients, apartment building owners, and your referral network of accountants and lawyers.

A classified ad is also effective for soliciting investors. Place it in the "Investment Property" or "Business Opportunity" section of the local newspaper (Example 9.2).

In general, it is difficult to solicit new investors without a specific property to describe and promote. The best way to build a database of investors is by gradually generating leads from responses to ads for specific equity sharing opportunities, and through word-of-mouth from satisfied clients. Any time you are advertising a specific equity share, be sure to record the names, addresses, and telephone numbers of all of the investors who respond, even if they are not interested in that particular equity share.

Example 9.2   Agent's Classified Ad for Investors

EQUITY SHARING with a qualified home buyer can yield 20%–40% annual return on small investments at low risk. R.E. agt. currently seeking investors for equity share program. Free workshop. Call Bill at 555-9922.

Constructing a Database

As you generate names of potential occupiers and investors, begin to organize and categorize them. Occupiers should be categorized according to down payment amount, loan qualification strength, and property type. Investors should be categorized according to investment amount and property type. Make sure your records are organized so that you can quickly locate clients who meet specific criteria. A main category of "Buyers with over $10,000 down payments" might have a subcategory of "Can qualify for loans of over $180,000." It will be helpful to have a computer system that is able to generate addressed envelopes. You can then send frequent mailings to your clients to communicate general information and updates as new properties become available.

Creating a database has its own advertising value. Both investors and occupiers will feel that their prospects of finding a suitable co-owner are enhanced by the existence of an extensive database. It establishes your status as a valuable equity sharing resource.

GENERATING LISTINGS

Using Equity Sharing in Farming

"Farming" is a long-term program a real estate agent undertakes to recruit clients. You begin by selecting a specific group or "farm"—usually home owners in a particular neighborhood—on which to focus your recruiting efforts. You then contact the prospects within the "farm" repeatedly over a long time period, both in person and by mail. The contacts are designed to introduce yourself to the prospects and convince them that you are highly skilled, motivated, and familiar with the neighborhood. Hopefully, when one of the prospects decide to sell, he will list his home with you.

Because most neighborhoods are farmed by several competing real estate agents, you need to develop farming tools that distinguish you from your competition. Equity sharing is a proven competitive advantage in farming. These techniques for equity sharing farming are recommended:

- Send your farm an explanation of equity sharing; include examples of hypothetical transactions that demonstrate its benefits.
- Notify your farm that you keep an equity sharing database, and keep them updated on the number of buyers in the database.
- Notify your farm each time you complete an equity sharing transaction; describe the transaction in detail.
- Invite your farm to an equity sharing workshop.
- Send your material to owners of expired listings and for-sale-by-owner (FSBO) properties. Include a specific analysis of how equity sharing could benefit that particular owner.

Using Equity Sharing in Listing Presentations

When you prepare a listing presentation, determine for yourself whether equity sharing could improve the seller's return or increase the salability of the property. If you conclude that equity sharing could be helpful, develop a proposed structure and create comparative calculations that show how equity sharing could benefit the client. Include a basic explanation of equity sharing, a description of your equity sharing experience, examples of past equity sharing transactions, and sample marketing materials that could be adapted for an equity sharing sale of the seller's property.

CREATING A FORM LIBRARY

It will be helpful to have a library of equity sharing forms, clauses, and analyses. Any forms you create should be stored on computer disks for easy introduction of changes or updates. Protect your template carefully between printings, and keep track of your inventory for each printed form. At a minimum, your form library should contain these documents:

- A personal resume, which describes your equity sharing experience, the number of clients in your database, examples of your recent equity sharing transactions, and the availability of references upon request.
- Purchase contract clauses for:
  —Locating an investor for equity sharing;
  —A 72-hour release clause;
  —Seller participation in equity sharing;
  —Completing an equity sharing agreement;
  —Approving the qualifications of the occupier.
- A Preliminary Commitment form.
- Spreadsheets for seller analysis, occupier analysis, and investor analysis.
- Advertising templates for:
  —Marketing listings to equity sharing home buyers;
  —Searching for investors for a specific equity share.
- A list of attorneys and accountants who understand equity sharing.

SCREENING LENDERS

You would be wise to develop a list of lenders who accept equity sharing borrowers and offer loan products that are appropriate for equity sharing. When you are screening to find these mortgage lenders, these are the questions that should drive your search:

- Have they ever heard of equity sharing?
- If so, do they accept applications from equity sharing coborrowers?

- Do they require that coborrowers be related by blood or marriage or must demonstrate a long-term business relationship?
- Will they combine the financial strength of equity sharing borrowers to determine loan qualification?
- Do they require a minimum down payment from the occupier?
- Do they consider an equity share involving a seller to be a refinance rather than a purchase, and, if so, do they apply different loan-to-value ratio (LTV) limitations or underwriting guidelines?
- Do they require a minimum equity sharing term?
- Do they need to approve the equity sharing agreement?

COOPERATING WITH OTHER AGENTS

The most efficient way to build your equity sharing practice is to cooperate with other agents in pairing occupiers and investors. To cooperate effectively, you must agree to share your sales commission with an agent who produces a cobuyer. There is no formula for determining a fair commission split, but it is generally acknowledged that it takes more time and effort to represent the occupier than the investor. We recommend that the occupier's agent receive 75 percent of the commission and the investor's agent receive 25 percent. A common alternative is to split the commission in the same ratio as the buyers split the down payment, but this arrangement may be unfair to the occupier's agent. Usually, the occupier's agent develops a proposed commission split and includes it in marketing materials placed in an MLS listing or distributed by fliers to other agents.

Establish the role and duties of each agent at the outset of the relationship. One agent should be responsible for negotiating with the seller's agents, arranging for inspections, and overseeing the loan application and escrow process. The occupier's agent usually undertakes these responsibilities. The work and commission allocations should be described in a written agreement among all of the agents and brokers involved.

LIABILITY ISSUES

Conflicts of Interest

Prospective equity sharing co-owners have conflicting interests. Presumably, each will try to negotiate capital contributions, ownership shares, and other agreement provisions to his own advantage. The co-owners may disagree about purchase terms, physical inspections, loans, and negotiation strategy. If they choose not to equity share together, they may argue to establish who has a senior right to the purchase contract and the property.

If you act as agent for both co-owners, you must maintain impartiality on any matter in which your clients' interests conflict. You can't represent one client against the other, or do or say anything that favors one client's interests. When the clients negotiate, you must preserve the confidences of each by not revealing his position to the other. The best way to fulfill these responsibilities would be to avoid involvement in discussions or negotiations on conflict issues, but this would mean constantly bowing out of important decisions, a practice that would become frustrating to your clients and might endanger the deal. In the real world of real estate sales, you need to be an active participant and adviser just to hold the transaction together and keep the clients moving forward. The challenge of representing multiple clients in equity sharing is to balance the need to respect the clients' conflicts against the need to help the clients through the transaction.

Here are some practical guidelines for handling equity sharing conflicts of interest:

- Whenever you see that your clients have conflicting interests on a particular issue, point it out by explaining the conflict and the way various possible outcomes would help and hurt each party.
- State your opinion, even if it favors one client's interest over the other's, but point out how the opinion favors one client and fully explain the basis for the opinion.
- Continue to participate in discussions and to attempt to resolve conflicts until it becomes clear that the clients have reached an impasse; then recommend that the clients either continue discussions on their own or visit an equity sharing attorney.
- Disclose potential conflicts *in writing* at the beginning of the transactions, and have the clients sign the disclosure to indicate that they have read and understood it, and agree to have you represent them despite the conflict. Use Example 9.3 as a model; note the clear description of exactly what your role will be, and the implications of the clients' consent.

This disclosure form is not a substitution for any agency disclosure or dual agency forms required by state law. It should be used in addition to such forms.

Example 9.3   Conflict of Interest Disclosure and Consent

This document is intended to advise you of the actual and potential conflicts of interest among individuals in an equity share, and to obtain your written consent to representation despite these conflicts.

During any joint financial undertaking, including the one you are considering, it is likely that each time a decision is made each participant will attempt to maximize his rights and benefits and minimize his duties and burdens. Consequently, the personal and financial interests of the individual participants will frequently conflict. Some examples of potential conflicts in equity sharing include initial investment levels, ownership percentages, ongoing expense obligations, decision-making authority, refinancing or sale, and treatment of default. [*If the investor is not also the seller, add:* A conflict could also arise regarding the conduct of negotiations with the seller, the terms of sale, or the right to purchase the property if both individuals wish to proceed with the purchase but do not want to equity share with each other.]

Where one real estate agent attempts to represent both an investor and an occupier in an equity share, he is representing clients with competing and conflicting interests. While the agent should try to remain neutral in the discussion and resolution of issues involving a conflict among these clients, it is inevitable that the agent will intentionally or unintentionally make statements that favor one client's interest over the other's.

BY SIGNING THIS DOCUMENT, YOU ARE ACKNOWLEDGING THAT YOU HAVE BEEN ADVISED OF AND UNDERSTAND THAT CONFLICTS OF INTEREST EXIST BETWEEN YOU AND THE OTHER PARTICIPANT IN YOUR EQUITY SHARE, THAT YOU ARE BEING REPRESENTED BY A REAL ESTATE AGENT WHO ALSO REPRESENTS THE OTHER PARTICIPANT, AND THAT YOU CONSENT TO THIS REPRESENTATION WITH FULL KNOWLEDGE OF THE CONFLICT.

DATED:_____
                                        Client

DATED:_____
                                        Client

Other Professions

Equity sharing involves elements of real estate, taxation, accounting, and law. It is tempting to try to wear the hats of many different professionals, but this is a dangerous temptation. If you stray outside your area of expertise, you risk providing incorrect advice and being held responsible for the consequences. You may also run afoul of laws that prohibit the practice of law or public accounting without an appropriate license. Protect yourself by following these guidelines:

- On any financial analyses and spreadsheets you prepare, place a disclaimer stating that you are not an attorney or accountant, that the information is not guaranteed to be reliable, and that the reader should verify it with his own professional advisers.
- Know the limits of your knowledge and never be afraid to tell your clients that you do not know the answer to a question.
- Advise your clients, both orally and in writing, to seek legal and accounting advice before closing an equity sharing transaction.
- Find an attorney and an accountant who are familiar with equity sharing, and arrange for permission to call and ask questions on an "as needed" basis. Many professionals will be happy to provide this service without cost, in exchange for client referrals.

Liability Insurance

Some insurance policies that protect against real estate errors and omissions do not provide coverage for transactions involving partnerships and joint ventures. Although equity sharing is not a partnership, you should confirm with your insurance carrier that coverage will not be denied for liability connected to an equity share transaction.

Ten

Annotated Sample Documents

This chapter provides samples of the four documents most commonly used in equity sharing transactions:

1. The Equity Sharing and Lease Agreement—describes the owners' intentions, and answers "what if" questions;
2. The Memorandum of Agreement—entered in the government records to provide notice to outsiders, especially prospective buyers and lenders, that neither of the owners can independently sell the property or borrow money against it;
3. The Equity Sharing Note; and
4. The Equity Sharing Deed of Trust—provide extra security to the investor if the occupier defaults.

Each model document is preceded by an introduction and punctuated by explanatory annotations.

I don't recommend using the sample documents to prepare your own set without professional help. Your documents must fit your transaction. Disputes can be expensive and time-consuming to resolve, and you can't afford missed issues, conflicting paragraphs, or confusing language. Hiring an attorney is inexpensive insurance against potentially costly mistakes.

INTRODUCTION TO THE EQUITY SHARING AND LEASE AGREEMENT

The first purpose of the agreement is to *avoid disputes*. Experience shows that the best way to accomplish this goal is to include step-by-step instructions. Required actions, time frames, and penalties may seem overly restrictive, but remember: no one enforces them except you. So long as you agree, you can ignore them; if you disagree, having them will avoid mental anguish, preserve friendships, and save thousands of dollars in dispute resolution costs. To be safe, whenever you agree to ignore the rules, write down and sign your new arrangement. Having it in writing provides a record of the new arrangement. If you ever disagree about the new plan and have no signed writing, the provisions of the original written agreement will control.

The second purpose of the agreement is to *resolve disputes*. Experience shows that the best way to accomplish this goal is to anticipate unexpected circumstances. Avoid short, simple agreements that assume everything will go fine and everyone will get along; if it doesn't or they don't, each party (or his attorney) will interpret the general language in a way that supports his own position, and some arbitrator, judge, or jury will decide who is more right. This process is complicated, time-consuming, and expensive. At best, the decision is an educated guess less influenced by right and wrong than by which party (or lawyer) is most convincing. Get a thorough agreement that covers every unlikely situation. It will only seem dull and useless until you have a problem.

EQUITY SHARING AND LEASE AGREEMENT FOR 3321 ELM STREET

AGREEMENT CONTENTS*

*Actual page numbers of the document would appear here.

INTRODUCTION

This Agreement is between husband and wife George C. and
Mary A. Smith (collectively "Occupier") and Laura M. Davidson

("Investor") and concerns their equity sharing co-ownership of 3321 Elm Street, San Francisco, California (the "Property").

RECITALS

Occupier and Investor plan to co-own the Property as tenants in common for a term of five (5) years.

Occupier and Investor shall each contribute to the initial acquisition cost of Property and shall share in its appreciation.

Occupier intends to use the Property as a principal residence under the lease provisions of this Agreement.

Investor intends to hold the Property as an investment.

Occupier and Investor now desire to clarify the terms and conditions of their arrangement and reduce them to writing.

In light of their respective goals, Occupier and Investor bind themselves to the provisions of this Agreement and the associated documents which it describes.

[*Annotation.* The "Recitals" summarize the broad intent of the parties. They are useful to an arbitrator, judge, or jury trying to determine the intent of the parties in situations which are not explicitly discussed in the agreement.]

ARTICLE 1—DEFINITIONS

The **bold-type nouns** listed below are defined either at their occurrence or in the Section of this document referred to in parentheses immediately after the term.

Acquisition Escrow means the neutral escrow account used in the transaction in which the Cotenants first become co-owners of the Property.

Acquisition Loan (Section 4.2).

Actionable Death/Conservatorship (Section 7.2).

Actionable Violation (Section 9.7).

Additional Capital Contribution (Section 3.3).

Additional Capital Contribution Interest (Section 3.3).

Additional Capital Contribution Percentage (Section 6.1).

Affected Party (Section 7.2).

Anticipated Work (Section 5.8).

Appraisal Initiation Date (Section 10.1).

Appraised Value means the value as determined under Section 10.1.

Approved Additional Capital Contribution (Section 3.3).

Bankruptcy of a Cotenant (Section 9.8).

Cotenant means Investor or Occupier.

Cotenant Equity (Section 6.1).
Cure (Section 9.7).
Debt Service (Section 4.2).
Default (Section 9.8).
Defaulting Cotenant Equity (Section 9.9).
Discretionary Improvement (Section 5.7).
Disposition Escrow means the neutral escrow account used in the transaction in which either one Cotenant buys the other's interest in the Property or the entire Property is sold.
Disposition Expense (Section 6.1).
Early Sale (Section 7.1).
Effective Date means the date determined under Sections 10.2 and 10.8.
Emergency Items (Section 5.2).
Equity Sharing Deed of Trust (Section 9.6).
Equity Sharing Note (Section 9.6).
Eviction (Section 9.11).
Forced Disposition (Section 9.9).
Foreclosure (Section 9.10).
Governmental Regulations means all applicable laws, ordinances, resolutions, procedures, orders, standards, conditions, approvals, rules, regulations, and the like, of any governmental entity with jurisdiction over the Property.
Homeowner's Association Dues (Section 4.4).
Initial Capital Contribution (Section 3.1).
Initial Capital Contribution Percentage (Section 6.1).
Insurance (Section 4.5).
Major Damage (Section 5.6).
Monthly Capital Contribution (Section 3.2).
Necessary Repair (Section 5.5).
Notice means a writing prepared and transmitted in accordance with Section 10.2.
Occupier Damage (Section 5.4).
Occupier Damage Repair (Section 5.4).
Offering Price (Section 6.4).
Ownership Share (Section 2.1).
Promptly means within three (3) calendar days of the event triggering the requirement to act.
Property Tax (Section 4.3).
Qualified Appraiser (Section 10.1).
Qualified Arbitrator (Section 9.3).
Qualified Mediator (Section 9.2).
Qualified Workman (Section 5.2).
Required Additional Capital Contribution (Section 3.3)

Reserve Fund (Section 9.5).
Routine Maintenance (Section 5.3).
Surviving Cotenant (Section 7.2).
Tenant (Section 2.12).
Termination Value (Section 6.1).
Total Equity (Section 6.1).

ARTICLE 2—TITLE AND POSSESSION

2.1   OWNERSHIP SHARES. The Cotenants will own the following respective undivided percentage interests as tenants-in-common in the entire property (the "Ownership Shares"):

Investor	45%
Occupier	55%

Notwithstanding these ownership interests, all rights, duties and obligations associated with ownership shall be distributed among the Cotenants as provided in this Agreement.

2.2   TITLE. Title to the Property shall be held as follows:

> "George C. Smith and Mary A. Smith, husband and wife, as joint tenants as to an undivided 55% interest, and Laura M. Davidson, an unmarried woman, as to an undivided 45% interest, all as tenants-in-common."

For the purposes of this Agreement and the associated documents to which it refers, (i) George C. and Mary A. Smith, and any voluntary or involuntary successors to either of their interests in the Property, shall be collectively considered a single party known as "Occupier" or one "Cotenant," and (ii) Laura M. Davidson, and any voluntary or involuntary successors to her interest in the Property, shall be collectively considered a single party known as "Investor" or one "Cotenant."

[*Annotation.* Methods of holding title are discussed in Chapter Three. The discussion of successors begins to define the relationship between the owners of the property, anticipating the possibility that, as a result of a sale, gift, death, or some other event, there may well be some new owners during the term of the agreement. For example, Laura could die without a will, and her interest could pass in equal shares to her eleven nieces and nephews. The paragraph establishes that no matter how many owners there are, they will all fall into the category of either "Occupier" or "Investor," and these categories will define their rights and duties. Any new owner or group of owners who obtain their interest from Laura will collectively be "Investor," and any new owner or group of owners who obtain their interest from either George or Mary will collectively be "Occupier." Thus, none of Laura's nieces and nephews will be entitled to move into 3321 Elm Street, but all will become responsible for her obligations to help pay for major repairs.]

2.3 COTENANT'S CONSISTING OF MULTIPLE INDIVIDUALS. Any time a Cotenant consists of more than one individual, the following provisions shall apply:

A. *Joint and Several Liability.* Each individual shall be jointly and severally liable for all obligations and responsibilities of the Cotenant under this Agreement.

B. *Joint Rights.* All rights of the Cotenant under this Agreement shall be deemed jointly held by the individuals comprising the Cotenant. Absent a written agreement or provision of law to the contrary, all such individuals shall be deemed to have equal control of such rights.

C. *Authority.* Any act or omission by one of the individuals shall be deemed the act or omission of the Cotenant. Notwithstanding the preceding statement, however, where any obligation under this Agreement requires the participation of all individuals comprising a Cotenant, the obligation shall not be deemed fulfilled unless and until all such individuals participate.

[*Annotation.* "Cotenant consists of more than one individual" would include married couples like George and Mary, and unmarried domestic partners who purchase together. The term would also include multiple heirs to a deceased owner, like the eleven nieces and nephews who might inherit Laura's 3321 Elm Street interest when she dies. All of these situations present complications in the context of equity sharing.

The first complication concerns responsibilities. Suppose George disappears to Rio with the mailwoman. Could Mary claim that she is responsible for only half the monthly payments on 3321 Elm Street, and that Laura should "go get the rest from George"? The answer is no; under Subsection A, each individual member of a "Cotenant" is personally responsible for 100 percent of its obligations. Mary must make the entire payment and go after George herself.

The second complication concerns rights. Suppose that after Laura's eleven nieces and nephews inherit her interest, one niece (Polly's daughter, Collette) buys out all but the most stubborn of the other relatives and ends up with 91 percent of Laura's interest. Later, the Smiths offer their interest for sale. Does Collette have the right to buy all of the Smiths' interest, 91 percent of the Smiths' interest, or half of the Smiths' interest? The answer is half; under Subsection B, each individual member of a "Cotenant" owns an equal share of its rights. Applied to the right of occupancy, this rule would also mean that, after the Rio incident, Mary would have no more right to live in 3321 Elm Street than George would.

The third complication concerns authority. While George is in Rio, Mary may act on his behalf under Subsection C. But this rule does not apply to matters that specifically require participation of both individual members of a "Cotenant," like signing papers in connection with a sale.]

2.4   TRANSFEREES AND SUCCESSORS. For the purposes of this Section only, the term "transferee" shall be deemed to include any successor, assign, or personal representative of any individual holding an interest in the Property. Each "transferee" of an interest in the Property, whether voluntary or involuntary, shall immediately be deemed to assume all obligations and liabilities of the individual whose interest they obtained. Such "transferee" shall Promptly execute this Agreement and failure to do so shall constitute an Actionable Violation. Nothing in this Section or in this Agreement shall be interpreted to alter a former Property interest holder's obligations, responsibilities, or liabilities under this Agreement up to and including the date of any transfer.

2.5   MARRIAGE OR REMARRIAGE OF COTENANT. Should a Cotenant marry or remarry while this Agreement remains in effect, that Cotenant shall immediately cause his/her new spouse to either (i) execute this Agreement thereby agreeing to be bound by all of its terms, or (ii) execute a recordable quitclaim deed in favor of the Cotenant whom he/she will be marrying.

[*Annotation.* In some states, including California, a new spouse may argue that he or she accumulated ownership in real estate over the course of a marriage even if the other spouse acquired the property before the marriage. As a result of this potential problem, title insurers will sometimes refuse to insure a sale by a married seller without his or her spouse's signature, even though the title is held by only the selling spouse.

For example, suppose Laura marries Dave during the equity share, but continues to own her 45 percent of 3321 Elm Street in her own name. Later, when the Smiths buy out her interest, the title insurer may require Dave's signature even though Laura never deeded any of 3321 Elm Street over to him. The necessity of Dave's signature does not present a problem if Dave is willing to sign. But what if Dave and Laura have separated and Dave has disappeared or refuses to sign? The sale could be delayed indefinitely, causing damage to both Laura and the Smiths. This section attempts to avoid this potential problem. It requires that, before the marriage, Dave signs either the agreement (which will later require him to cooperate in the Smiths' buyout) or a "quitclaim" deed, which will prevent Dave's signature from being required later.]

2.6   ASSIGNMENT AND DELEGATION. Except as specifically provided in this Agreement, no Cotenant shall have the right to assign any of his rights or to delegate any of his duties under this Agreement without the written consent of the other Cotenant.

2.7   PARTNERSHIP NOT INTENDED. The Cotenants do not intend to create a partnership, joint venture, or subdivision, but to describe terms and conditions upon which they shall hold undivided interests in the Property as tenants-in-common.

[*Annotation.* See Chapter Three.]

2.8   INCOME TAX DECLARATIONS. Pursuant to Section 761 of the Internal Revenue Code of 1986, as amended, the Cotenants elect out of subchapter K of chapter 1 of that Code and agree to report their respective shares of the items of income, deductions, and credits associated with ownership of the Property in a manner consistent with that election. Occupier shall treat the Property as a personal residence for tax purposes and may claim all tax benefits for deductible payments made by him/her under this Agreement. Investor shall treat the Property as residential rental property for tax purposes, and may claim all tax benefits for the amount by which deductible payments made by him/her under this Agreement plus allowable depreciation exceeds rent collected from Occupier. Both Cotenants agree to cooperate in the event the other undertakes a tax-deferred exchange upon disposition of their interest in the Property pursuant to Internal Revenue Code Section 1031 or 1034.

[*Annotation.* This section lays the groundwork for future tax reporting on the property. The first sentence eliminates the need for the owners to file partnership tax returns and preserves the right of the owners to defer income taxes on resale by exchanging their share of 3321 Elm Street for another property. The next two sentences establish the roles of the parties as Occupier and Investor and will support their use of the special equity sharing tax deductions. The last sentence anticipates the possibility that one party might need the other's signature on documents in order to accomplish a tax-deferred exchange as explained in Chapter Four.]

2.9   PARTITION. While each of the Cotenants recognizes that they may have a right to seek partition of the Property pursuant to California law, they also recognize that such action is likely to have negative consequences for the other Cotenant. Accordingly, each Cotenant agrees to waive his/her right to seek partition or sale in lieu of partition.

[*Annotation.* "Partition" of co-owned property under California law is analogous to the dissolution of a partnership or marriage. When a court grants a "partition," it sells the co-owned property and divides the proceeds among the owners. The problem with the right to seek a court-ordered "partition" is that it allows any owner to force a sale of the property. For example, if Laura lost her job and needed money to pay her bills, she could seek a partition and, if successful, force the Smiths to move. This right would undercut the provisions of the agreement, which restrict one owner's right to force a sale. To avoid this problem, equity sharing owners in California generally waive the right to seek a "partition."]

2.10   OWNERSHIP RIGHTS RESTRICTIONS. This Agreement alone shall govern all rights with respect to the ownership, use, possession, enjoyment, management, and disposition of the Property, and each Cotenant relinquishes all common law or statutory rights which he/she might otherwise have as an owner of the Property except the right to assert a common law lien. Except as specifically provided in this Agreement, no Cotenant:

(i)   Is authorized to act as agent for or on behalf of any other Cotenant;

(ii)   Perform any act which would be binding on any other Cotenant;

(iii)   Create personal liability for any other Cotenant;

(iv)   Incur any debt or obligation related to the Property;

(v)   Cause any interest in the Property to be assigned, transferred, pledged, or encumbered; or

(vi)   Cause any joint claims of the Cotenants to be assigned, transferred, pledged, or released.

[*Annotation.* The first part of this section clarifies the owners' intention that the agreement govern all aspects of their ownership. They do not intend, for example, for Laura to have a legal right to live in the property just because she is a legal owner. Otherwise, she could claim a right to live in the house instead of or together with the Smiths. The same sentence preserves the owner's right to "assert a common law lien." In the event an owner is not fulfilling his/her promises under the agreement, this right provides one of many enforcement mechanisms. Use of the right is discussed in a later annotation.]

2.11   RIGHT TO OCCUPY. Both Cotenants expressly relinquish all rights to occupy the Property which might otherwise arise preemptively or by operation of law as a result of their ownership interests in the Property. Occupier shall have the exclusive right to occupy the Property for so long as Occupier continues to adhere to the terms and conditions of this Agreement. This right is derived solely from the provisions of this Agreement which shall be considered Occupier's lease. Investor may terminate the lease in the event of a Default by Occupier. Occupier recognizes that his/her right to occupy the Property may be terminated notwithstanding his/her ownership interest in the Property.

[*Annotation.* See Chapter Three.]

2.12   DUTY TO OCCUPY. So long as Occupier shall have the exclusive right to occupy the Property under this Agreement, he/she shall use the Property as his/her principal residence unless Investor otherwise consents. Occupier must request such consent in advance and in writing. Investor shall respond to the request Promptly and shall not unreasonably withhold consent. If Occupier rents the Property to another person (a "Tenant") under this Section: (i) Occupier's duties or responsibilities under this Agreement shall not change, (ii) Occupier shall be entitled to all of the rent collected from the Tenant, (iii) Occupier shall be responsible for all costs associated with rental including but not limited to rent collection costs, eviction, and solicitation of new tenants in the event of vacancy, and (iv) Income tax deductions shall be allocated so that Investor does not suffer negative tax consequences as a result of the change in occupancy.

[*Annotation.* See Chapter Three.]

2.13   INSPECTION. Investor may enter the Property under the following circumstances:

A. *Routine Inspection.* Investor may perform an inspection of the Property on up to one (1) occasion every three (3) months following twenty-four (24) hours' advance Notice.

B. *Actionable Violation.* Investor may enter the Property as necessary to perform any act required to negate any Actionable

Violation which has already been the subject of a Notice of Actionable Violation.

[*Annotation.* See Chapter Six.]

ARTICLE 3—CAPITAL CONTRIBUTIONS

[*Annotation.* See Chapter Three.]

3.1 INITIAL CAPITAL CONTRIBUTIONS. Each Cotenant's "Initial Capital Contribution" is the amount he/she contributed toward the down payment, loan points and fees, appraisal fees, inspection fees, attorney's fees, title insurance costs, processing fees, notarization fees, escrow fees, and recording fees. Initial Capital Contribution shall not include payments for hazard insurance, property taxes, sales commissions, or transfer tax even if they are made directly from an acquisition escrow account. The Cotenant's Initial Capital Contributions are as follows:

A. *Investor Contribution.* Investor's Initial Capital Contribution was TEN THOUSAND AND 00/100 DOLLARS ($10,000.00) in retained equity and FIVE HUNDRED AND 00/100 DOLLARS ($500.00) in cash.

B. *Occupier Contribution.* Occupier's Initial Capital Contribution was FOURTEEN THOUSAND FIVE HUNDRED AND 00/100 DOLLARS ($14,500.00) in cash.

3.2 MONTHLY CAPITAL CONTRIBUTION. Only if Occupier makes all Regular Monthly Payments required by Article 4, he/she shall be presumed to have made an additional "Monthly Capital Contribution" in the total amount of FIVE HUNDRED NINETY FOUR AND 00/100 DOLLARS ($594.00). This presumed amount shall not be increased even if Occupier's actual Regular Monthly Payments are greater than anticipated.

3.3 ADDITIONAL CAPITAL CONTRIBUTION.

A. *Definition.* "Additional Capital Contribution" means a contribution of funds, goods, services, labor, or effort used in connection with the Property which is either (i) explicitly called a "Required Additional Capital Contribution" in this Agreement, or (ii) explicitly approved by both Cotenants in advance in writing (an "Approved Additional Capital Contribution"). For any Approved Additional Capital Contribution not made entirely in cash, the approval writing shall state the agreed value of the portion of the Approved Additional Capital Contribution to be provided by each Cotenant.

B. *Improper Contributions.* No Cotenant shall be reimbursed in any manner for a contribution of funds, goods, services, labor, or effort which is not an Additional Capital Contribution.

C. *Contribution Allocation.* Unless otherwise agreed in advance in writing, all Additional Capital Contributions shall be allocated by Ownership Share.

D. *Contribution Notice and Response.* Either Cotenant may prepare a Notice requesting fulfillment of an Additional Capital Contribution obligation. The Notice shall describe the basis for the obligation which, as provided in Subsection 3.3 A, shall be either an explicit requirement of this Agreement or another writing previously signed by both Cotenants. The Notice shall also state precise and reasonable instructions for satisfying the obligation, including a due date for any cash payment which is no sooner than seven (7) days from the Effective Date of the Notice. Any Notice not meeting all of the requirements of the two preceding sentences shall be invalid. If the Notice is valid, each Cotenant shall satisfy the obligation in accordance with the instructions stated in the Notice.

E. *Additional Capital Contribution Interest.* "Additional Capital Contribution Interest" shall be simple interest on the cash amount or agreed value of a particular Additional Capital Contribution from the date the contribution is made until the close of the Disposition Escrow at an annual rate of six percent (6%). Cotenants shall be entitled to Additional Capital Contribution Interest only when the Cotenants agree in writing in advance either that (i) a particular Additional Capital Contributions shall not be allocated by Ownership Share or (ii) that payment of interest is warranted for some other reason. Other than as provided in this Subsection, Cotenants shall not be entitled to interest on Additional Capital Contributions.

ARTICLE 4—REGULAR MONTHLY PAYMENTS

[*Annotation.* This article establishes that the Smiths are responsible for paying all of the routine monthly costs of owning the property. To maximize tax benefits for both owners, some of these costs are paid "through" Laura as discussed in Chapter Four. In a situation where the investor does not want or cannot use the tax benefits, no provision for occupier rent is necessary. If occupier rent is eliminated, the "Investor Contribution" sections can also be deleted.]

4.1   OCCUPIER RENT. Pursuant to Internal Revenue Code Section 280A, Occupier shall pay rent to Investor in the amount of THREE HUNDRED FIVE AND 00/100 DOLLARS ($305.00) per month. The rental amount has been calculated as follows:

Fair market rental value of entire Property	$1,000.00
Fair market rental value of Investor's share (45%)	450.00
Less: Good tenant reduction (10%)	(45.00)
Management Credit	(100.00)
Net rent	$ 305.00

Occupier shall pay rent on the first day of each and every month commencing July 1, 1994.

4.2   DEBT SERVICE. Occupier shall be individually and solely responsible for all interest and principal payments associated with the ONE HUNDRED EIGHTY THOUSAND AND 00/100 DOLLARS ($180,000.00) loan from National Bank used to purchase the Property (the "Acquisition Loan"). Occupier shall make these payments on or before the date they are due and perform all other obligations required by the note and deed of trust associated with the Acquisition Loan in a timely fashion. Occupier shall prevent negative amortization by making monthly payments in an amount sufficient to pay all outstanding interest due as of the date of the latest monthly statement received from the lender. After each payment is made, Occupier shall Promptly mail a copy of the monthly Acquisition Loan statement and payment check to Investor.

4.3   PROPERTY TAX. "Property Tax" shall include all property taxes, bonds, and government assessments associated with ownership of the Property regardless of the date such obligations originated. Property Tax shall be paid as follows:

A. *Investor Contribution.*

(i)   *First Year.* During calendar year 1994, Investor shall contribute EIGHT HUNDRED SEVENTY AND 00/100 DOLLARS ($870.00) toward Property Tax. Investor shall make this contribution by depositing one half ($\frac{1}{2}$) of this amount in the Acquisition Escrow, and providing to Occupier a check for one half ($\frac{1}{2}$) of this amount payable to the County of San Francisco on or before October 1, 1994.

(ii) *Other Years.* During each full calendar year of co-ownership, Investor shall contribute TWO THOUSAND ONE HUNDRED AND 00/100 DOLLARS ($2,100.00) toward Property Tax. Investor shall make this contribution by providing to Occupier a check for one half ($\frac{1}{2}$) of this amount payable to the County of San Francisco on or before April 1 and October 1 of each such year. During the final year of co-ownership, the Investor Contribution to Property Tax shall be prorated to the closing date of the Disposition Escrow.

B. *Occupier Duties.* Occupier shall be individually and solely responsible for all Property Tax payments not made by Investor Contribution. Occupier shall deposit the initial Property Tax payment (above the Investor Contribution) in the Acquisition Escrow, and deliver the full amount of any subsequent Property Tax payment (including any Investor Contribution) to the county of San Francisco on or before the date it is due. After each payment is made, Occupier shall Promptly mail a copy of the Property Tax bill and payment checks to Investor.

4.4 HOMEOWNER'S ASSOCIATION DUES. "Homeowner's Association Dues" shall include all payments to the Elm Street Homeowner's Association which are required of owners of the Property, including but not limited to Regular Assessments, Property Tax Assessments, and Special Assessments. Notwithstanding the preceding sentence, however, "Homeowner's Association Dues" shall not include any Special Assessment which (i) is levied for specific repairs or capital improvements and (ii) exceeds the sum of ONE THOUSAND AND 00/100 DOLLARS ($1,000.00). Special Assessments meeting these two criteria shall be deemed Necessary Repairs. Homeowner's Association Dues shall be paid as follows:

A. *Investor Contribution.* Investor shall contribute ONE HUNDRED AND 00/100 DOLLARS ($100.00) per month toward Homeowner's Association Dues. Investor shall make this contribution by providing to Occupier a check for this amount payable to the Elm Street Homeowner's Association on or before the first day of each month.

B. *Occupier Duties.* Occupier shall be individually and solely responsible for all Homeowner's Association Dues payments not made by Investor Contribution. Occupier shall deliver the full amount of any Homeowner's Association Dues payment (including any Investor Contribution) to the Elm Street Homeowner's Association on or before the date it is due.

[*Annotation.* Large homeowner's association assessments earmarked for repairs or improvement to the association's common areas are excluded from the definition of homeowner's association dues because they are more like capital contributions than monthly expenses.

Defining them as necessary repairs makes them "required" capital contributions, which means that both owners must contribute.]

4.5   INSURANCE.

A. *Definition.* "Insurance" shall include all insurance coverage related to the Property regardless of whether it is obtained by one Cotenant, both Cotenants, or a homeowner's association.

B. *Casualty Requirements.* To the extent such coverage is not obtained by a homeowner's association, the Cotenants shall obtain coverage for casualty losses to the Property and to all personal property jointly owned by the Cotenants. Such insurance shall include coverage for all risks customarily covered by a homeowner's insurance policy in San Francisco County at the time of policy inception, including earth movement. Policy limits shall be adequate for restoration of the Property to its pre-loss value and replacement of all co-owned personal property.

C. *Liability Requirements.* To the extent such coverage is not obtained by a homeowner's association, the Cotenants shall obtain coverage for comprehensive public liability incident to the ownership and use of the Property for all individuals comprising Cotenants. Policy limits shall be at least FIVE HUNDRED THOUSAND DOLLARS ($500,000) per occurrence.

D. *Named Insureds.* All Insurance policies obtained by the Cotenants shall list all individuals comprising Cotenants as named insureds.

E. *Premiums.* Premiums for Insurance policies obtained by the Cotenants shall be paid as follows:

(i)   *Investor Contribution.* Investor shall contribute THREE HUNDRED SIXTY AND 00/100 DOLLARS ($360.00) per year toward Insurance. Investor shall initially make this contribution by depositing the full amount in the Acquisition Escrow, and subsequently by providing to Occupier a check for this amount payable to the Insurance carrier on or before May 1 of each year. Any reimbursed overpayment of Insurance premiums paid by Investor shall be Promptly returned to Investor.

(ii)   *Occupier Contribution.* Occupier shall be individually and solely responsible for all Insurance payments not made by Investor Contribution. Occupier shall deliver the full amount of any Insurance payment (including any Investor Contribution) to the Insurance carrier on or before the date it is due.

F. *Procurement.* Occupier shall be individually and solely responsible for obtaining all Insurance required by this Section.

G. *Proceeds.*

(i) *Damage to Property.* Insurance proceeds intended by the carrier as compensation for the cost of repair of particular damage to the Property shall be applied to repair such damage unless, pursuant to Section 5.6, the Cotenants do not repair such damage.

(ii) *Damage to Personal Property.* Insurance proceeds intended by the carrier as compensation for the cost of repair of particular personal property jointly owned by the Cotenants shall be applied to repair such property. Insurance proceeds intended by the carrier as compensation for the cost of repair of personal property owned by one Cotenant shall be paid to that Cotenant.

(iii) *Loss of Use.* Insurance proceeds intended by the carrier as compensation for loss of use of the Property shall be paid to Occupier unless Occupier's right to occupy the Property has been terminated, in which case such proceeds shall be paid to Investor.

[*Annotation.* Like most property owners, equity sharing owners need two types of insurance: casualty and liability. Casualty insurance pays for repair or replacement if the property is damaged by a fire or other covered event. There should be enough casualty insurance to rebuild if the house is destroyed. The value of the land does not need to be insured.

Liability insurance covers the owners if they are sued by someone else in connection with the property. There should be enough liability insurance to protect the owners against all foreseeable liabilities. A $500,000 limit is common, but a higher limit is necessary where small children live on the property. The children's visiting friends might be injured, and children's injuries tend to be very expensive.

For a home (like 3321 Elm Street) that is part of a complex governed by a homeowner's association, the association generally carries both casualty and liability insurance, but the insurance carried by the association is not adequate for individual owners. The owners need to supplement the association coverage without duplicating it. An insurance agent can help owners decide what additional insurance they need. The equity sharing agreement limits the occupier's responsibility to obtaining only the supplemental insurance.

The agreement requires that all owners be named as insureds in all policies. In the casualty policy, naming both owners ensures that any proceeds checks will be made payable to all owners. This prevents any single owner from misappropriating the money. Frequently, the checks will be made payable to the lender for the same reason. In the liability policy, naming both owners ensures that there will be coverage no matter which owner is sued.]

4.6 REALLOCATION OF INVESTOR CONTRIBUTION. Not later than January 31 of each year, the Cotenants shall adjust the amounts of Investor Contribution for Homeowner's Association Dues or Insurance to correspond with any changes in the cost of these items. Any adjustment shall cause a corresponding adjustment in the amount of Investor Contribution for Property Tax such that the total Investor Contribution for Homeowner's Association Dues, Insurance, and Property Tax in any calendar year equals the annual Occupier Rent of THREE THOUSAND SIX HUNDRED SIXTY AND 00/100 DOLLARS ($3,660.00).

4.7 OTHER UTILITIES AND SERVICES. Occupier shall be individually and solely responsible for the cost of all other utilities and services to the Property including but not limited to electricity, natural gas, water, sewer, and refuse removal. Occupier shall pay such costs on or before the date payment is due.

ARTICLE 5—MAINTENANCE, REPAIR, AND IMPROVEMENT

5.1 GENERAL CLEANING. Occupier shall keep the Property free from debris and in a neat, clean, and sanitary condition at all times.

5.2 ADMINISTRATION OF WORK. Occupier shall arrange for and supervise all maintenance, repair, or improvement of the Property as follows:

A. *Inspection and Initiation.* Occupier shall regularly inspect the Property for damage, deterioration, and malfunction, and shall initiate correction efforts as described below.

B. *Emergency Items.* "Emergency Items" shall include malfunctions of the HVAC, plumbing, electrical, roofing, or foundation systems, or any other condition within or upon the Property that immediately endangers the integrity of the Property, or the safety or health of the public, Occupier, or Occupier's relatives, guests, tenants, or subtenants.

C. *Obtaining Bids.* Occupier shall obtain a bid for any task of maintenance, repair, or improvement from a Qualified Workman. A "Qualified Workman" shall include any person who holds all licenses legally required for the task and has at least two (2) years' experience completing similar tasks. If the bid exceeds ONE THOUSAND AND 00/100 DOLLARS ($1,000), Occupier shall Promptly obtain bids for the same task from two (2) other Qualified Workmen. Occupier shall obtain all required bids (i) within seven (7) calendar days of discovery of an Emergency Item or (ii) within thirty (30) calendar days of discovery of any other damage, deterioration, and malfunction. A bid shall be disqualified unless it provides a completion date (a) for Emergency Items, within thirty (30) calendar days of commencement of work, and (b) for any other damage, deterioration, and malfunction, within ninety (90) calendar days of commencement of work.

D. *Bid Selection.* If Occupier obtains any bids of ONE THOUSAND AND 00/100 DOLLARS ($1,000) or less from Qualified Workmen, he/she shall unilaterally select from among such bids. If Occupier does not obtain any such bids, he/she shall Promptly discuss all bids with Investor. If Investor is dissatisfied with the bids, he/she shall have up to seven (7) calendar days from presentation of the bids to obtain additional bids. If Investor obtains any bids of ONE THOUSAND AND 00/100 DOLLARS ($1,000) or less from Qualified Workmen, Occupier shall unilaterally select from among such bids. If neither party obtains any such bids, they shall agree on a bid selection prior to commencing work.

E. *Arrangement and Supervision.* Upon bid selection, Occupier shall (i) Promptly enter into a written contract based on the selected bid and describing the scope of work, price, payment schedule, and completion date, (ii) arrange for access by the Qualified Workman to the work area, (iii) inspect the completed work, and (iv) arrange for payment upon satisfactory completion.

F. *Breach of Construction Contracts.* In the event a Qualified Workman fails to perform all of his/her contractual obligations, Occupier shall use reasonable efforts to (i) accomplish completion of the work as close to the contractual completion date as possible, and (ii) pursue all available legal remedies arising from the breach. Any costs associated with these efforts shall be allocated among the Cotenants in the same way as the costs of the underlying work.

G. *Occupier Labor.* Occupier may not complete maintenance, repair, or improvement work himself/herself unless such work is either (i) of a type customarily completed by a homeowner without contracting skill or experience, or (ii) preapproved in writing by Investor. If Investor is required to contribute to the cost of the work under this Agreement and/or if Occupier's labor shall be an Additional Capital Contribution, Occupier must (a) obtain bids as required by Subsection 5.2 C and (b) enter into a written contract with Investor describing the scope of work, price, payment schedule, completion date, and specific conditions under which Occupier receives Additional Capital Contribution credit for his/her labor.

5.3 ROUTINE MAINTENANCE. "Routine Maintenance" shall include any task of maintenance, repair, or improvement which (i) is required to maintain the Property in a condition equivalent to its condition on the Effective Date of this Agreement and (ii) can be completed by a Qualified Workman for a cost of ONE THOUSAND AND 00/100 DOLLARS ($1,000) or less. Occupier shall be individually and solely responsible for the cost of all Routine Maintenance.

5.4 OCCUPIER DAMAGE REPAIR. "Occupier Damage Repair" shall include any task of maintenance, repair, or improvement which (i) is required to maintain the Property in a condition equivalent to its condition on the Effective Date of this Agreement and (ii) would not have been then necessary but for Occupier Damage. "Occupier Damage" means damage, deterioration, and malfunction caused or accelerated by willful or negligent acts or omissions (other than normal usage but including failure to perform Routine Maintenance) by Occupier or Occupier's relatives, guests, pets, tenants, or subtenants. Occupier shall be individually and solely responsible for the cost of all Occupier Damage Repair.

5.5 NECESSARY REPAIR. "Necessary Repair" shall include any task of maintenance, repair, or improvement which (i) is required to maintain the Property in a condition equivalent to its condition on the Effective Date of this Agreement, (ii) cannot be completed by a Qualified Workman for a cost of ONE THOUSAND AND 00/100 DOLLARS ($1,000.00) or less, and (iii) is not related to Occupier Damage Repair. "Necessary Repair" shall also include certain Special Assessments of the Elm Street Homeowner's Association as described in Section 4.4. The cost of Necessary Repairs shall be a Required Additional Capital Contribution.

5.6 MAJOR DAMAGE. "Major Damage" shall include any Necessary Repair which cannot be completed by a Qualified Workman for a cost of FIVE THOUSAND AND 00/100 DOLLARS ($5,000.00) or less. As soon as possible after any event causing Major Damage to the Property, Occupier shall (a) proceed as required by Subsections 5.2 A–C, and

(b) determine the amount of insurance available for repair. If the available insurance is sufficient to pay at least seventy-five percent (75%) of the cost of repair, Occupier shall proceed with the repair as provided in Subsections 5.2 E–G, and the remaining twenty five percent (25%) of the cost of repair shall be a Required Additional Capital Contribution. If not, the Property shall be sold as provided in Section 6.4. In such event, the Offering Date shall be the first (1st) business day after the determination that available insurance is not sufficient to pay at least seventy-five percent (75%) of the cost of repair, and the amount of insurance proceeds (if any) shall be added to the Termination Value for the purpose of determining Cotenant Equity.

[*Annotation.* The purpose of this section is to set an upper limit on owner liability for repair costs. A limit is important so that neither owner is forced into default by an expense he/she cannot afford. The owners are always free to waive the limits if they both can afford the work. Make sure that the limit reflects the value and condition of the property.]

5.7 DISCRETIONARY IMPROVEMENTS. "Discretionary Improvements" shall include any task of maintenance, repair, or improvement which is not Routine Maintenance, Occupier Damage Repair, or Necessary Repair. Any Cotenant may undertake a Discretionary Improvement at his/her own expense provided such expense (i) does not exceed ONE THOUSAND AND 00/100 DOLLARS ($1,000.00) and (ii) is not an Additional Capital Contribution. Any other Discretionary Improvement must be approved by both Cotenants, in advance, in a writing that states the scope of work, price, payment schedule, completion date, amount and date of each Cotenant's contribution, and whether the contributions are Approved Additional Capital Contributions. Approval of a Discretionary Improvement that does not involve an Additional Capital Contribution may not be unreasonably withheld.

5.8 ANTICIPATED WORK. The Cotenants have agreed on the following terms and conditions regarding certain maintenance, repair, or improvement. To the extent this Section conflicts with other Sections of this Article, this Section shall control. Contributions described in this Section are Required Additional Capital Contributions.

A. *Roof Repair.* No later than October 15, 1994, the Cotenants shall retain Ken's Roofing Company to repair the roof of the Property at a cost of ONE THOUSAND AND 00/100 DOLLARS ($1,000.00). The Cotenants shall contribute their respective Ownership Shares of this amount in cash by providing checks for one half (½) of their shares to Ken's Roofing Company on or before October 15, 1994, and additional such checks Promptly upon completion of the roof repair.

B. *Rear Deck.* No later than June 15, 1995, Occupier shall construct a deck in the rear yard of the Property according to the specifications on Exhibit A to this Agreement. The deck shall comply with all Governmental Regulations and be constructed in a good and workmanlike manner. Occupier shall be responsible for obtaining all labor and materials, and for paying any costs of labor and materials that exceed Investor's cash contribution. The Cotenants shall assume a cost of ONE THOUSAND AND 00/100 DOLLARS ($1,000.00) for the deck, and this assumption shall be binding regardless of the actual cost or value of labor and materials. The Cotenants shall be credited with contributions to this assumed cost as follows:

(i) *Investor Contribution.* Investor shall be credited the amount of FOUR HUNDRED FIFTY AND 00/100 DOLLARS ($450.00), which Investor shall contribute by providing a check in this amount to Occupier Promptly upon request.

(ii) *Occupier Contribution.* Occupier shall be credited the amount of FIVE HUNDRED FIFTY AND 00/100 DOLLARS ($550.00) for all expenditures and labor regardless of actual cost or value. Occupier shall not receive any portion of this credit until the deck has been completed according to the specifications on Exhibit A.

[*Annotation.* This section provides two examples of ways to include planned, pre-agreed work in an equity sharing agreement. The roof work provision demonstrates how problems revealed during a pre-purchase inspection should be handled. The important points to cover are the scope of work, time frame, and cost.

The deck provision demonstrates how "sweat equity" can be handled. Note that the Smiths take the risk of unforeseen problems and cost overruns. This is only fair; they have chosen to undertake the work and have provided the timing and cost estimates on which Laura based her decision to participate. If the job goes poorly, the Smiths are always free to ask Laura for additional funds or reimbursement credit, but she is free to refuse.

The document described as "Exhibit A" is the plans and specifications for the deck and includes a drawing of how the house will look when the deck is completed. For any large projects, a drawing is needed to establish the scope of work. A document like Exhibit A should also include a description of the materials and construction method that will be used. Exhibit A to this Agreement has not been included in this book.]

5.9   REGULATORY COMPLIANCE. All maintenance, repair, or improvement work shall comply with Governmental Regulations and all requirements imposed by any homeowner's associations or adjacent owners with a legal or contractual right to impose such requirements on the Property.

ARTICLE 6—DISPOSITION AT TERM

[*Annotation.* See Chapter Three and Appendix C.]

6.1   COTENANT EQUITY.

A. *Additional Definitions.* The following terms shall be used in this Section:

(i)   *Termination Value.* "Termination Value" shall be either (i) the sale price in the event the entire Property is sold to a non-Cotenant or (ii) the Appraised Value in all other circumstances.

(ii) *Disposition Expense.* "Disposition Expense" shall be either (i) six and one half percent (6.5%) of the Appraised Value in the event one Cotenant purchases the other's interest or (ii) the actual sales commissions, transfer tax, and customary seller closing costs in the event the entire Property is sold to a non-Cotenant.

(iii) *Total Equity.* "Total Equity" is the Termination Value less the Disposition Expense less the outstanding balance of the Acquisition Loan.

(iv) *Additional Capital Contribution Percentage.* Each Cotenant's "Additional Capital Contribution Percentage" shall be that Cotenant's total Additional Capital Contribution plus any Additional Capital Contribution Interest due to that Cotenant, divided by the total Additional Capital Contribution of both Cotenants plus any Additional Capital Contribution Interest due to either of them.

(v)   *Initial Capital Contribution Percentage.* "Initial Capital Contribution Percentage" shall be:

Occupier	58%
Investor	42%

B. *Calculation of Cotenant Equity.* "Cotenant Equity" shall be calculated as follows:

(i)   *Additional Capital Contribution.* The Cotenants shall compare

Item (a)—total Equity, to

Item (b)—the total Additional Capital Contribution including any Additional Capital Contribution Interest.

If Item (a) is greater, each Cotenant's Cotenant Equity shall include the full amount of the Cotenant's Additional Capital Contributions including any Additional Capital Contribution Interest. If Item (b) is greater, each Cotenant's Cotenant Equity shall be the Cotenant's Additional Capital Contribution Percentage of Total Equity and nothing more.

(ii) *Monthly Capital Contribution.* The Cotenants shall subtract Item (b) from Item (a), then compare

Item (c)—the difference between Item (b) and Item (a), to

Item (d)—Occupier's Monthly Capital Contribution.

If Item (c) is greater, Occupier's Cotenant Equity shall include the full amount of Occupier's Monthly Capital Contribution. If Item (d) is greater, Occupier's Cotenant Equity shall include the full amount of Item (c).

(iii) *Initial Capital Contribution.* The Cotenants shall subtract Item (d) from Item (c), then compare

Item (e)—the difference between Item (d) and Item (c), to

Item (f)—the total Initial Capital Contribution.

If Item (e) is greater, each Cotenant's Cotenant Equity shall include his/her Initial Capital Contribution. If Item (f) is greater, each Cotenant's Cotenant Equity shall include the Cotenant's Initial Capital Contribution Percentage of Item (e).

(iv) *Appreciation.* The Cotenants shall subtract Item (f) from Item (e). Each Cotenant's Cotenant Equity shall include his/her Ownership Share of the difference between Item (e) and Item (f).

6.2   DISPOSITION VALUATION. Not later than fifty-four (54) months from the Effective Date of this Agreement, the Cotenants shall initiate determination of the Appraised Value of the Property pursuant to Section 10.1.

6.3   COTENANT RIGHT TO PURCHASE.

A. *Occupier Notification.* Not later than fifty-six (56) months from the Effective Date of this Agreement, Occupier shall provide Notice to Investor of his/her intent to purchase Investor's interest in the Property (a "Notice of Intent to Purchase").

Occupier waives his/her right to purchase if the Notice of Intent to Purchase is not given in time. The Notice of Intent to Purchase shall be binding, and failure to timely complete the purchase as provided in this Section shall be an Actionable Violation.

B. *Investor Notification.* If Occupier waives his/her right to purchase, not later than fifty-seven (57) months from the Effective Date of this Agreement, Investor shall provide Notice to Occupier of his/her intent to purchase Occupier's interest in the Property (a "Notice of Intent to Purchase"). Investor waives his/her right to purchase if the Notice of Intent to Purchase is not given in time. The Notice of Intent to Purchase shall be binding, and failure to timely complete the purchase as provided in this Section shall be an Actionable Violation.

C. *Good Faith Deposit.* Within five (5) calendar days of the Effective Date of the Notice of Intent to Purchase, the purchasing Cotenant shall deposit ONE THOUSAND AND 00/100 DOLLARS ($1,000.00) in the Disposition Escrow.

D. *Cotenant Purchase Date.* The "Cotenant Purchase Date" shall be the first business day that occurs after the lapse of sixty (60) days from the Effective Date of the Notice of Intent to Purchase.

E. *Loan Assumption or Refinancing.* On or prior to the Cotenant Purchase Date, for the Acquisition Loan, the purchasing Cotenant shall either (i) provide full repayment or (ii) arrange to have the nonpurchasing Cotenant fully released as a borrower. The purchasing Cotenant shall be individually and solely responsible for any associated costs.

F. *Cash Payment and Transfer.* On or prior to the Cotenant Purchase Date, the following shall be deposited into the Disposition Escrow:

(i) *Purchasing Cotenant.* The purchasing Cotenant shall deposit the nonpurchasing Cotenant's Cotenant Equity in cash (less the Good Faith Deposit).

(ii) *Nonpurchasing Cotenant.* The nonpurchasing Cotenant shall sign and deposit (a) a fully executed grant deed conveying his/her interest in the Property to the purchasing Cotenant, (b) escrow instructions in accordance with the terms of this Agreement, and (c) all signed documents necessary to fulfill the requirements of this Agreement.

Release of funds and title recordation shall occur on the Cotenant Purchase Date. If Investor is the purchasing Cotenant, Occupier's right to occupy the Property shall terminate on that date.

G. *Transaction Costs.* Except as otherwise provided in this Agreement, the purchasing Cotenant shall be individually and solely responsible for any costs associated with a Cotenant purchase under this Section.

6.4   SALE AT TERM.

A. *Offering Date.* The "Offering Date" shall be the first business day that occurs after the lapse of fifty-seven (57) months from the Effective Date of this Agreement. If Occupier and Investor both waive their purchase rights under the preceding Section, the Property shall be offered for sale beginning on the Offering Date.

B. *Offering Price.* The "Offering Price" shall be the price at which the Property is offered for sale at any particular time. The Offering Price on the Offering Date shall be the Appraised Value of the Property. If the Property is not subject to a ratified purchase contract on the thirtieth (30th) day that a particular Offering Price has been in effect, the Offering Price shall be reduced five percent (5%).

C. *Listing of Property.* Beginning on or prior to the Offering Date and continuing until the Property is sold, the Cotenants shall list the Property for sale with a licensed real estate agent who is a member of the local Multiple Listing Service. Unless otherwise agreed by the Cotenants, the Property shall be listed (i) for periods of sixty (60) days, (ii) with a sales commission of six percent (6%), and (iii) by Mr. Behrend Eilers of XYZ Realtors or, if Mr. Eilers is unwilling or unable to list the Property, by a real estate agent who has had no prior business or personal relationship with either Cotenant.

D. *Acceptance of Offers.* The Cotenants shall accept any purchase offer that (i) is at or above the Offering Price, (ii) yields all proceeds to seller in cash, (iii) provides for close of escrow within sixty (60) days, and (iv) contains no contingencies or demands that are not in accordance with local custom. In the event multiple offers simultaneously meet this requirement, the Cotenants shall select the most advantageous offer.

E. *Close of Escrow.* On or prior to the date specified in the purchase contract for close of escrow, the Cotenants shall sign and deposit into the Disposition Escrow (i) a fully executed grant deed conveying the Property to the buyer, (ii) escrow instructions in accordance with the terms of this Agreement, and (iii) all signed documents necessary to fulfill the requirements of this Agreement. Occupier's right to occupy the Property shall end on the date of close of escrow.

F. *Distribution of Proceeds.* Sale proceeds shall be used to retire all outstanding obligations secured by the Property and pay all Disposition Expense. From any remaining balance, each Cotenant shall receive his/her Cotenant Equity.

ARTICLE 7—EARLY DISPOSITION

7.1   EARLY SALE. Under the terms of this Section, Occupier may cause the Property to be offered for sale before the Offering Date (an "Early Sale"). Except as specifically provided elsewhere in this Agreement, Investor shall not cause the Property to be offered for sale before the Offering Date.

A. *Notice of Early Sale.* If Occupier desires Early Sale, he/she shall provide Notice of such desire to Investor (the "Notice of Early Sale").

B. *Valuation.* Not later than five (5) calendar days from the Effective Date of the Notice of Early Sale, the Cotenants shall initiate determination of the Appraised Value of the Property pursuant to Section 10.1.

C. *Early Sale Offering Date.* The "Early Sale Offering Date" shall be the first (1st) business day that occurs after determination of Appraised Value. The Property shall be offered for sale beginning on the Early Sale Offering Date.

D. *Sale Procedure.* The Cotenants shall follow the procedures described in Subsections 6.4 B–F, substituting the term "Early Sale Offering Date" for the term "Offering Date."

E. *Early Sale Damages.* The Cotenants agree that Investor's damages in the event of an Early Sale by Occupier will be difficult to ascertain, and agree that Investor shall be entitled to liquidated damages. Investor shall have a choice of accepting either liquidated damages or his/her Cotenant Equity. The amount of liquidated damages shall be equal to Investor's Initial and Additional Capital Contributions plus simple interest on the Contributions at the rate of twelve percent (12%) per annum from the date of the Contribution until the date of Early Sale. This amount is a reasonable estimate of Investor's Damages in the event of an Early Sale by Occupier. Investor shall receive liquidated damages in cash prior to any distribution to Occupier. If the Total Equity is insufficient to fully pay liquidated damages, Occupier shall execute a note payable to Investor in the amount of the shortfall at an interest rate of eight percent (8%) fully amortized over three (3) years and payable in monthly installments.

[*Annotation.* See Chapter Three.]

7.2 DISPOSITION ON DEATH AND CONSERVATORSHIP.

A. *Actionable Death.* An "Actionable Death/Conservatorship" is any death or appointment of conservator which would cause control over any interest in the Property to pass to a person who is not (i) already a Cotenant or one of the individuals comprising a Cotenant or (ii) married to a Cotenant.

B. *Affected Parties.* An "Affected Party" is (i) any of the individuals comprising the Cotenant whose interest has been affected by the Actionable Death/Conservatorship, (ii) any individual who inherited an interest in the Property through the Actionable Death/Conservatorship, and (iii) any conservator, executor, administrator, or court with control over an interest in the Property because of the Actionable Death/Conservatorship.

C. *Surviving Cotenant.* A "Surviving Cotenant" is a Cotenant not comprised of any individual who is an Affected Party.

D. *Valuation.* Any Surviving Cotenant may initiate determination of the Appraised Value of the Property pursuant to Section 10.1 within one hundred eighty (180) calendar days of learning that a particular event was an Actionable Death/Conservatorship. A Surviving Cotenant waives all rights under this Section if determination of Appraised Value is not initiated in time.

E. *Notice of Death/Conservatorship Disposition.* A "Notice of Death/Conservatorship Disposition" is a Notice by any Surviving Cotenant of intent to (i) purchase the remainder of the Property or (ii) cause the Property to be sold. Not later than thirty (30) calendar days from the first determination of Appraised Value resulting from a particular death or conservatorship. Notice of Death/Conservatorship Disposition must be provided to all Affected Parties whose identities are reasonably discoutrable by the Surviving Cotenant. A Surviving Cotenant waives all rights under this Section if the Notice of Death/Conservatorship Disposition is not provided to all Affected Parties in time.

F. *Cotenant Purchase.* If the Notice of Death/Conservatorship Disposition states intent to purchase the remainder of the Property, the Cotenants shall follow the procedures described in Subsections 6.3 C–G substituting the term "Notice of Death/Conservatorship Disposition" for the term "Notice of Intent to Purchase." A Notice of Death/Conservatorship Disposition that states intent to purchase shall be binding, and failure to timely complete the purchase as provided in Subsections 6.3 C–G shall be an Actionable Violation.

G. *Sale.* If the Notice of Death/Conservatorship Disposition states intent to cause the Property to be sold, the Cotenants shall follow the procedures described in Section 6.4 except that the "Offering Date" shall be the first (1st) business day after the Effective Date of the Notice of Death/Conservatorship Disposition.

[*Annotation.* See Chapter Six.]

7.3 COTENANT WILLS. Within ninety (90) days of the Effective Date of this Agreement, each Cotenant shall create a document specifying the disposition of his/her interest in the Property in the event of his/her death. No Cotenant shall specify that his/her interest passes to more than two (2) individuals.

[*Annotation.* See Chapter Six.]

ARTICLE 8—OTHER TRANSFERS OF PARTIAL INTERESTS

[*Annotation.* See Chapter Three.]

8.1 GENERAL TRANSFER RESTRICTION. The Cotenants have agreed to co-own together because of their knowledge of and confidence in each other. Accordingly, no Cotenant shall transfer any portion of his/her interest in the Property except as provided in this Agreement. Any other purported transfer is void.

8.2 UNRESTRICTED TRANSFERS OF PARTIAL INTERESTS. A Cotenant may transfer an interest in the Property without restriction if the transferee is (i) a person who is already a Cotenant or one of the individuals comprising a Cotenant, (ii) the current or former spouse of a Cotenant, or (iii) a revocable inter vivos trust of which a Cotenant is a beneficiary.

8.3 RESTRICTED TRANSFERS OF PARTIAL INTERESTS. A Cotenant may transfer an interest in the Property as provided in this Section.

A. *Notice of Intended Partial Sale.* If a sale is intended, the transferring Cotenant shall provide to the other Cotenant a "Notice of Intended Partial Sale" stating (i) the asking price, terms, and conditions (including financing) and (ii) the amount of sales commission, if any, that shall be paid in the event of sale by a real estate agent.

B. *Initial Right to Purchase.* If a sale is intended, the nontransferring Cotenant shall then have the right to purchase the transferring Cotenant's interest on the terms and conditions stated in the Notice of Intended Partial Sale, except that the price and the cash down payment required shall be reduced by the amount of the intended sales commission. The nontransferring Cotenant shall exercise this right by (i) Promptly providing Notice to the transferring Cotenant of his/her tentative intent to purchase (a "Notice of Tentative Intent") and (ii) within ten (10) days of Effective Date of this first Notice, providing a second Notice to the transferring Cotenant reaffirming his/her intent to purchase (a "Notice of Final Intent"). The Notice of Final Intent shall be binding. Failure to complete the purchase on the terms and conditions stated in the Notice of Intended Partial Sale within sixty (60) days of Notice of Final Intent shall be an Actionable Violation. If the nontransferring Cotenant fails to provide either Notice, he/she waives the Initial Right to Purchase and the transferring Cotenant shall be free to solicit purchase offers from other parties.

C. *Additional Right to Purchase.* Prior to accepting any purchase offer, the transferring Cotenant shall provide a copy of the offer to the nontransferring Cotenant. If the offer is one percent (1%) or more lower than the original asking price, the nontransferring Cotenant shall have the right to purchase the transferring Cotenant's interest on the terms and conditions stated in the purchase offer. The nontransferring Cotenant shall exercise this right by Promptly providing Notice to the transferring Cotenant of his/her intent to purchase. This Notice shall be binding, and failure to complete the purchase on the terms and conditions and within the time frames stated in the offer shall be an Actionable Violation. If the nontransferring Cotenant fails to provide the Notice, he/she waives the Additional Right to Purchase. No further purchase rights shall be created as a result of renegotiation of sale price or terms following inspections or other disclosures.

D. *Right to Reject Transferee.* Prior to completing any sale, gift, or other transfer, the transferring Cotenant shall provide to the nontransferring Cotenant a statement of the financial qualifications of the prospective transferee, including a loan application, credit report, and, in the case of a self-employed person, the two most recent years' Federal Tax Returns. The nontransferring Cotenant shall have a period of seven (7) days from delivery of this information to request the transferring Cotenant to arrange an interview of the prospective purchaser. The non-transferring Cotenant shall make himself/herself available to conduct the interview at a reasonable time within forty-eight (48) hours of the request. A Cotenant may reject a prospective transferee, provided the basis for rejection is (i) reasonable and (ii) not prohibited by law. To exercise this right, the nontransferring Cotenant must interview the prospective purchaser and provide Notice of rejection to the transferring Cotenant within forty-eight (48) hours of the interview. This Notice must state the basis for the rejection. A nontransferring Cotenant waives the right to reject a prospective transferee if the Notice is not provided in time.

E. *Transferee Rights.* Following expiration of the rejection period, a prospective transferee shall be entitled to review the financial qualifications of the nontransferring Cotenant, including a loan application, credit report, and, in the case of a self-employed person, the two (2) most recent years' Federal Tax Returns.

F. *Costs of Sale.* All costs associated with any transfer under this Section shall be allocated between transferor and transferee according to local custom.

G. *Property Tax.* A transferee Investor shall be individually and solely responsible for paying any increase in property taxes that results from the transfer, and shall make this payment as an additional Investor Contribution under Section 4.3 A.

ARTICLE 9—DISPUTE RESOLUTION AND DEFAULT

[*Annotation.* See Chapter Six.]

9.1   DECISION MAKING.

A. *Meetings.* Decisions shall be made at meetings which any Cotenant may call at any time provided he/she provides Notice to the other Cotenant at least fourteen (14) days before the meeting. The Notice shall also state the agenda, and no matters not on the agenda may be decided at the meeting unless both Cotenants are represented. Cotenants may vote in person or by proxy. All proxies shall be in writing, dated, and signed by a Cotenant.

B. *Voting Power.* Each Cotenant shall have one (1) vote of equal weight.

C. *Abstention.* If not all individuals comprising a Cotenant attend a meeting, the vote of the individual(s) comprising the

Cotenant who do attend the meeting shall be considered the vote of that Cotenant. If the individuals cannot agree on their collective vote regarding a particular issue, the inability to agree will be considered an abstention. Cotenants absent at the time the vote on an agenda item is taken shall also be considered to have abstained. In the event of an abstention, the vote of the other Cotenant shall control unless it directly conflicts with or invalidates a provision of this Agreement.

D. *Deadlock.* In the event of a deadlock, the matter shall be resolved through mediation or, if mediation is unsuccessful, through Arbitration. Absent law or a provision of this Agreement requiring a particular decision, any Arbitrator shall make his/her decision in accordance with what he/she believes to be the course of action most likely to preserve and enhance the value of the Property without placing an unnecessary financial hardship on either Cotenant.

9.2   MEDIATION.

A. *Agreement to Mediate.* All Cotenants agree to appear for mediation and attempt in good faith to resolve any dispute related to the Property.

B. *Selection of Qualified Mediator.* A "Qualified Mediator" is any person with (i) at least two (2) years' experience mediating real estate disputes and (ii) no prior business or personal relationship with either Cotenant. A Cotenant desiring mediation may select any Qualified Mediator.

C. *Notice of Mediation.* A "Notice of Mediation" shall state (i) the name and address of a Qualified Mediator and (ii) a date and time for mediation. A Cotenant desiring mediation must provide a Notice of Mediation to the other Cotenant at least fourteen (14) days prior to the date set for mediation.

D. *Change of Date.* If a Cotenant is unable to attend mediation on the date stated in the Notice of Mediation, he/she may arrange an alternative date with the mediator provided (i) he/she provides Notice of the alternative date to the Cotenant desiring mediation within forty-eight (48) hours of Effective Date of the Notice of Mediation and (ii) the alternative date is within fourteen (14) days of the date stated in the Notice of Mediation. A Cotenant waives the right to change the date of mediation if the Notice is not provided in time.

E. *Compelling Mediation.* Any Cotenant may petition a court of competent jurisdiction for an order compelling appearance at mediation, and the court shall award all expenses, including attorney's fees, incurred by a Cotenant so petitioning, unless it finds that the Cotenant against whom the petition is filed acted with substantial justification or that other circumstances make the imposition of such expenses unjust. Failure to appear for a duly noticed mediation shall also constitute an Actionable Violation.

F. *Cost of Mediation.* The costs of mediation shall be shared equally by the Cotenants and shall be paid at the time of mediation.

9.3   ARBITRATION.

A. *Agreement to Arbitrate.* Any dispute related to the Property which is not resolved through mediation shall be submitted to binding arbitration in accordance with the provisions of the California Civil Code and Code of Civil Procedure pertaining to contract arbitration. No such dispute shall be resolved through court action except as specifically provided by this Agreement.

B. *Selection of Qualified Arbitrator.* A "Qualified Arbitrator" is any person with (i) at least two (2) years' experience arbitrating real estate disputes and (ii) no prior business or personal relationship with either Cotenant.

C. *Notice of Arbitration.* A "Notice of Arbitration" shall state the name and address of a Qualified Arbitrator. A Cotenant desiring arbitration must provide a Notice of Arbitration to the other Cotenant. Such Cotenant may specify any Qualified Arbitrator in the Notice of Arbitration.

D. *Change of Arbitrator.* A Cotenant may reject the Qualified Arbitrator specified in the Notice of Arbitration if he/she provides a "Notice of Rejection" including the name and address of an alternative Qualified Arbitrator to the Cotenant desiring arbitration within forty-eight (48) hours of Effective Date of the Notice of Arbitration. A Cotenant waives the right to reject a Qualified Arbitrator if the Notice of Rejection is not provided in time. In the absence of a timely Notice of Rejection, the Cotenant desiring arbitration shall select the Qualified Arbitrator specified in the Notice of Arbitration. Otherwise, the Cotenant desiring arbitration may select either the Qualified Arbitrator specified in the Notice of Rejection or the Judicial Arbitration and Mediation Service (JAMS). Once a Qualified Arbitrator has been selected, arbitration shall be initiated pursuant to the rules and procedures of such Qualified Arbitrator for contract arbitration.

E. *Procedure.* Arbitration shall be pursued to conclusion as quickly as reasonably possible and in every case shall be concluded within three (3) months from the date of Notice of Arbitration unless all Cotenants agree to extend that time limit. If the time within which to conclude arbitration is not met, any Cotenant may petition a court of competent jurisdiction for an order compelling the controversy or claim to be arbitrated as soon thereafter as reasonably possible, and the court shall award all expenses, including attorney's fees, incurred by a Cotenant so petitioning unless it finds that the Cotenant against whom the petition is filed acted with substantial justification or that other circumstances make the imposition of such expenses unjust. Failure to appear for arbitration shall also constitute an Actionable Violation. The Cotenants shall have the right to discovery in accordance with California Code of Civil Procedure Section 1283.05. Judgment on an arbitration award may be entered in any court having jurisdiction.

F. *Statutory Notice.*

***NOTICE:* BY INITIALING IN THE SPACE BELOW YOU ARE AGREEING TO HAVE ANY MATTER ARISING OUT OF THE "ARBITRATION" PROVISION DECIDED BY NEUTRAL ARBITRATION AS PROVIDED BY CALIFORNIA LAW AND YOU ARE GIVING UP ANY RIGHTS YOU MIGHT POSSESS TO HAVE THE DISPUTE LITIGATED IN A COURT OR JURY TRIAL. BY INITIALING IN THE SPACE BELOW YOU ARE ALSO GIVING UP YOUR JUDICIAL RIGHTS TO DISCOVERY AND APPEAL, UNLESS SUCH RIGHTS ARE SPECIFICALLY INCLUDED IN THE "ARBITRATION" PROVISION. IF YOU REFUSE TO SUBMIT TO ARBITRATION AFTER AGREEING TO THIS PROVISION, YOU MAY BE COMPELLED TO ARBITRATE UNDER THE AUTHORITY OF THE CALIFORNIA CODE OF CIVIL PROCEDURE. YOUR AGREEMENT TO THIS ARBITRATION PROVISION IS VOLUNTARY.**

WE HAVE READ AND UNDERSTAND THE FOREGOING AND AGREE TO SUBMIT DISPUTES ARISING OUT OF THE MATTERS INCLUDED IN THE "ARBITRATION" PROVISION TO NEUTRAL ARBITRATION.

Occupier _____   Investor _____

9.4   MATTERS EXCLUDED FROM ARBITRATION. The following matters are excluded from mandatory mediation and arbitration:

(i)   An action for injunctive relief or for unlawful detainer;

(ii) An action brought pursuant to the California Small Claims Act;

(iii) An action or proceeding which is within the jurisdiction of a probate or domestic relations court;

(iv) An action or proceeding to compel arbitration and/or mediation, including an action to impose sanctions for frivolous or bad faith activity designed to delay or frustrate arbitration and/or mediation; and

(v) An action to record a notice of pending action, or for an order of attachment, receivership, injunction, or other provisional remedy, which action shall not constitute a waiver of the right to compel arbitration and/or mediation.

[*Annotation.* Items (i) and (ii) are exempt from mandatory mediation and arbitration because they can generally be handled more quickly and easily in court. Items (iii), (iv), and (v) are exempt because they cannot be resolved except through the courts.]

9.5   OCCUPIER RESERVE FUND. No later than the Effective Date of this Agreement, Occupier shall provide a check to Investor for ONE THOUSAND FIVE HUNDRED AND 00/100 DOLLARS ($1,500.00). In the event of an Actionable Violation by Occupier, Investor may use this sum (the "Reserve Fund") for any expense incurred in connection with (i) the Property or (ii) the enforcement of Occupier's obligations. Use of the Reserve Fund shall not cure any Actionable Violation or waive any right to pursue other remedies. Investor shall Promptly provide Notice to Occupier following use of any portion of the Reserve Fund and Occupier shall provide a check to Investor for reimbursement of such portion within fourteen (14) days of the Effective Date of the Notice. Investor shall return any balance remaining in the Reserve Fund to Occupier upon closing of the Disposition Escrow.

9.6   EQUITY SHARING NOTE AND TRUST DEED. Concurrent with the signing of this Agreement, Occupier shall execute a note payable to Investor (the "Equity Sharing Note") secured by a deed of trust on his/her interest in the Property (the "Equity Sharing Deed of Trust").

A. *Purpose.* The purpose of the Equity Sharing Note and Equity Sharing Deed of Trust is to provide a remedy to Investor in the event Occupier does not fulfill his/her obligations to Investor regarding the Property.

B. *Amount.* The amount stated in the Equity Sharing Note and Equity Sharing Deed of Trust is the total of the original principal amount of the Acquisition Loan plus FIFTEEN THOUSAND

FIVE HUNDRED AND 00/100 DOLLARS ($15,500.00). Occupier agrees that this amount is an accurate valuation of his/her minimum obligation to Investor in the event of a Default.

C. *Liquidated Damages.* Occupier and Investor agree that, in the event of a Default, the loss and extra expense incurred by Investor would be difficult to ascertain. The amount stated in the Equity Sharing Note and Equity Sharing Deed of Trust is a reasonable estimate of such loss and extra expense and shall and is therefore appropriate as the amount of liquidated damages.

D. *Power of Sale.* The Equity Sharing Deed of Trust shall contain a power of sale, which allows Investor to cause Occupier's interest in the Property to be sold upon Default. Any demand preceding sale shall be reduced by the unpaid balance of the Acquisition Loan.

E. *Reconveyance.* Investor shall cause full reconveyance of the Equity Sharing Deed of Trust at the close of the Disposition Escrow.

9.7   ACTIONABLE VIOLATION.

A. *Definition.* An "Actionable Violation" shall be any of the following:

(i)   *Breach of Promise.* Failure to timely fulfill any obligation stated in this Agreement, any amendment or supplement to this Agreement, the Equity Sharing Note, or the Equity Sharing Deed of Trust;

(ii) *Nuisance.* Use of the Property which (a) unreasonably interferes with the quiet enjoyment of the Property, (b) is noxious, illegal, seriously annoying, or offensive to a person of reasonable sensibility, (c) increases the rate of insurance for the Property or causes any insurance policy to be canceled or not renewed, (d) impairs the structural integrity of the Property, (e) is in violation of a Governmental Regulation, or (f) will or may decrease the attractiveness or desirability of the Property;

(iii) *Creation of Lien.* Any act or omission (not authorized by this Agreement) that results in the creation of a lien or encumbrance of any kind on the Property; and

(iv) *Frustration of Purpose.* Any act that is in contravention of this Agreement or makes the performance of the obligations described in this Agreement impossible.

B. *Consequences of Actionable Violation.*

(i)   *Right of Nonviolating Cotenant to Perform.* If a Cotenant commits an Actionable Violation, the other Cotenant shall have the right (but not the obligation) to perform any act required to negate the Actionable Violation and to assess all related costs and expenses against the violating Cotenant.

(ii) *Consequential Losses.* A Cotenant who commits an Actionable Violation shall be individually and solely responsible for payment of any damages or losses that result, including late charges, penalties, fines, attorney's fees, and court costs.

(iii) *Liquidated Damages.* The Cotenants agree that a portion of the loss and extra expense incurred by a Cotenant as a consequence of an Actionable Violation by the other Cotenant would be difficult to ascertain and that THREE HUNDRED AND 00/100 DOLLARS ($300.00) is a reasonable estimate of such loss and extra expense. A Cotenant who commits an Actionable Violation shall pay this amount to the other Cotenant as liquidated damages in addition to all other compensation due under this Section.

C. *Notice of Actionable Violation.* A "Notice of Actionable Violation" shall include (i) a description of an Actionable Violation and (ii) a statement of all acts and/or omissions required to negate the Actionable Violation and satisfy the other obligations described in the preceding Subsection. Any Cotenant may provide a Notice of Actionable Violation.

D. *Cure of Actionable Violation.* A Cotenant shall have fourteen (14) days from the Effective Date of a Notice of Actionable Violation to "Cure" the Actionable Violation by (i) performing all acts and/or omissions described in the Notice of Actionable Violation and (ii) providing Notice of such performance with supporting documentation to the other Cotenant. A Cotenant waives his/her right to Cure an Actionable Violation if he/she (a) fails to fulfill either of these requirements in time or (b) has previously received more than four (4) Notices of Actionable Violation. A Cotenant who waives his/her right to cure an Actionable Violation has committed a Default.

9.8   DEFAULT.

A. *Definition.* "Default" means (i) failure or inability to timely cure an Actionable Violation or (ii) Bankruptcy of a Cotenant.

B. *Bankruptcy of a Cotenant.* "Bankruptcy of a Cotenant" occurs if (i) any individual comprising a Cotenant files a voluntary petition in bankruptcy, is adjudicated a bankrupt, becomes insolvent, makes an assignment for the benefit of creditors, or applies for or consents to the appointment of a receiver or trustee with respect to any substantial part of his or her assets, or if (ii) a receiver or trustee is appointed or an attachment or execution levied with respect to any substantial part of the assets of any individual comprising a Cotenant and the appointment is not vacated or the attachment or execution is not released within thirty (30) days, or if (iii) a charging order is issued against any interest in the Property and is not released or satisfied within thirty (30) days.

C. *Remedies for Default.* If a Cotenant Defaults, the other Cotenant shall be immediately entitled to one or more of the following remedies, serially or concurrently: Forced Disposition, Foreclosure, Eviction and/or any other remedy available under California Law. The pursuit of any of these remedies is not a waiver of the right to subsequently elect any other remedy.

D. *Liquidated Damages.* A Cotenant who Defaults under Subsection 9.8 A (i) shall pay to the other Cotenant the sum of FIVE THOUSAND AND 00/100 DOLLARS ($5,000.00) as liquidated damages in addition to all other compensation due under this Section. The Cotenants agree that a portion of the loss and extra expense incurred by a Cotenant as a consequence of a Default by the other Cotenant would be difficult to ascertain and that this amount is a reasonable estimate of such loss and extra expense.

9.9   FORCED DISPOSITION.

A. *Notice of Forced Disposition.* A Cotenant intending to cause Forced Disposition shall provide Notice to the other Cotenant (the "Notice of Forced Disposition") including (i) a description of the Default underlying the Forced Disposition, (ii) the name and address of the escrow officer for the Disposition Escrow, and (iii) a statement of whether the non-Defaulting Cotenant intends to purchase the remainder of the Property or cause the Property to be sold.

B. *Valuation.* Not later than five (5) calendar days from the Effective Date of the Notice of Forced Disposition, the Cotenants shall initiate determination of the Appraised Value of the Property pursuant to Section 10.1.

C. *Defaulting Cotenant Equity.* "Defaulting Cotenant Equity" is the amount a Defaulting Cotenant shall receive following a Forced Disposition. Defaulting Cotenant Equity is Cotenant Equity less the following amounts:

(i)   *Outstanding Monetary Obligations.* All sums owed by the Defaulting Cotenant under this Agreement which are due on or before the close of the Disposition Escrow.

(ii) *Outstanding Service Obligations.* The reasonable cost of fulfilling all service obligations of the Defaulting Cotenant under this Agreement which are required on or before the close of the Disposition Escrow.

(iii) *Actionable Violation Damages.* Any outstanding damages or losses which resulted from an Actionable Violation, including late charges, penalties, fines, attorney's fees, and court costs.

(iv) *Advanced Amounts.* Any sums advanced by the non-Defaulting Cotenant on behalf of the Defaulting Cotenant, together with simple interest on such sums at the maximum rate allowed by law.

(v) *Enforcement Expenses.* All costs and expenses incurred by the non-Defaulting Cotenant in enforcing this Agreement, including reasonable attorney's fees.

(vi) *Liquidated Damages.* The sum of FIVE THOUSAND AND 00/100 DOLLARS ($5,000.00) for liquidated damages pursuant to Section 9.8 D.

D. *Cotenant Purchase.* If the Notice of Forced Disposition states intent to purchase the remainder of the Property, the Cotenants shall proceed as follows:

(i) *Cotenant Purchase Date.* For the purposes of this Section only, the "Cotenant Purchase Date" shall be the first business day that occurs after the lapse of thirty (30) days from the Effective Date of the Notice of Forced Disposition.

(ii) *Cash Payment and Transfer.* On or prior to the Cotenant Purchase Date, the following shall be deposited into the Disposition Escrow:

(a) *Non-Defaulting Cotenant.* The non-Defaulting Cotenant shall deposit (1) twenty five percent (25%) of the Defaulting Cotenant Equity in cash, (2) a note payable to the Defaulting Cotenant for the remaining balance of the Defaulting Cotenant Equity payable in thirty-six (36) equal monthly installments, and (3) a Recision of Notice of Default on the Equity Sharing Deed of Trust (if applicable). If the Defaulting Cotenant Equity is zero or less, the non-Defaulting Cotenant shall not be required to deposit any funds.

(b) *Defaulting Cotenant.* The Defaulting Cotenant shall sign and deposit (1) a fully executed grant deed conveying his/her interest in the Property to the non-Defaulting Cotenant, (2) escrow instruction in accordance with the terms of this Agreement, and (3) all documents necessary to fulfill the requirements of this Agreement. If the Defaulting Cotenant Equity is less than zero, the Defaulting Cotenant shall also deposit a note payable to the non-Defaulting Cotenant in the amount of the shortfall at an interest rate of eight percent (8%) fully amortized over three (3) years and payable in monthly installments.

Release of funds and title recordation shall occur on the Cotenant Purchase Date.

(iii) *Transaction Costs*. The non-Defaulting Cotenant shall be individually and solely responsible for any costs associated with a Cotenant purchase under this Subsection.

E. *Sale*. If the Notice of Forced Disposition states intent to cause the Property to be sold, the Cotenants shall follow the procedures described in Subsections 6.4 A–E except that (i) the "Offering Date" shall be the first (1st) business day after the Effective Date of the Notice of Forced Disposition, (ii) the non-Defaulting Cotenant shall be permitted to list the Property with any licensed real estate agent, and (iii) the non-Defaulting Cotenant shall deposit into the Disposition Escrow a Recision of Notice of Default on the Equity Sharing Deed of Trust (if applicable). An Occupier in possession of the Property during a Forced Disposition shall allow the Property to be shown to prospective purchasers following twenty-four (24) hours' Notice. Sale proceeds shall be used to retire all outstanding obligations secured by the Property and pay all Disposition Expense. From any remaining balance, the Defaulting Cotenant shall receive the Defaulting Cotenant Equity and the non-Defaulting Cotenant shall receive the balance. If the Defaulting Cotenant Equity is less than zero, the Defaulting Cotenant shall execute a note payable to the non-Defaulting Cotenant in the amount of the shortfall at an interest rate of eight percent (8%) fully amortized over three (3) years and payable in monthly installments.

F. *Homestead Waiver*. In the context of a Forced Disposition, a defaulting Cotenant hereby waives the benefit of any homestead or exemption or redemption rights to the fullest extent permitted by law, and shall be deemed estopped to assert such rights.

9.10 FORECLOSURE. "Foreclosure" means a foreclosure under the Equity Sharing Deed of Trust or any common law lien. Each Cotenant pledges his/her interest to the other as security for the obligations described in this Agreement and acknowledges that such interest is subject to common law liens and associated foreclosure rights. A Cotenant may proceed with required notices related to Foreclosure immediately upon Default by the other Cotenant.

9.11   EVICTION. "Eviction" means any action to recover possession of the Property from a Cotenant or that Cotenant's relatives, guests, tenants, or subtenants. A Cotenant's right to occupy any portion of the Property under the lease provisions of this Agreement shall terminate immediately upon Default, and the Defaulting Cotenant and such Cotenant's relatives, guests, tenants, or subtenants shall be subject to Eviction from the premises following service of any legally required notices. By executing this Agreement, each Cotenant expressly agrees to waive any legal right to occupy the premises following Default. A Cotenant may proceed with legally required notices related to Eviction immediately upon Default by the other Cotenant. Following vacation of the premises, the non-Defaulting Cotenant may rent the Property to outside parties and retain all proceeds from such rental.

ARTICLE 10—GENERAL PROVISIONS

10.1   VALUATION. The "Appraised Value" of the Property shall be its fair market value determined as provided in this Section.

A. *Qualified Appraiser.* A "Qualified Appraiser" is any person who (i) has at least two (2) years' experience appraising real estate similar to the Property in the area where the Property is located, (ii) holds a valid real estate sales, brokerage, or appraisal license, (iii) had no prior business or personal relationship with either Cotenant, and (iv) agrees in writing to complete his/her appraisal within fourteen (14) calendar days of retention.

B. *Initiation of Determination.* Not later than the date on which this Agreement requires the Cotenants to initiate determination of Appraised Value (the "Appraisal Initiation Date"), the Cotenants shall either (i) jointly retain a Qualified Appraiser, or (ii) each separately retain a Qualified Appraiser. Within fourteen (14) calendar days of the Appraisal Initiation Date, any Cotenant who retains a Qualified Appraiser shall provide a complete and unaltered copy of his/her appraisal of the value of the Property as of the Appraisal Initiation Date to the other Cotenant. A Cotenant waives the right to retain a Qualified Appraiser if he/she fails to fulfill all of the requirements of the preceding sentence in time.

C. *Determination of Value.* If only one Qualified Appraiser is retained, either by joint agreement or through wavier by one Cotenant, the Appraised Value shall be the value stated in his/

her appraisal. If two qualified Appraisers are retained, the Appraised Value shall be the average of the values stated in their appraisals.

D. *Appraisal Fees.* If the Cotenants jointly retain a Qualified Appraiser, they shall each pay one half (½) of his/her fees. Otherwise, each Cotenant shall pay the fees of the Qualified Appraiser that he/she retains.

[*Annotation.* See Chapter Three.]

10.2   NOTICES. Any notice required by this Agreement must be in writing and delivered to the intended recipient either personally or by first class mail, postage prepaid. Notices shall be considered personally delivered to Cotenants when they are handed to any one of the individuals comprising the Cotenant. Notices mailed to Cotenants shall be addressed as follows:

OCCUPIER: George C. and Mary A. Smith
3321 Elm Street
San Francisco, CA 94133

INVESTOR: Laura M. Davidson
12 Windy Alley
Chicago, IL 60619

The "Effective Date" of a notice shall be the date of personal delivery or three (3) business days after mailing.

[*Annotation.* Note that this section does not require registered or certified mail. People are often not at home when registered or certified mail is delivered, and they fail to pick up the material at the post office in response to notice of an attempted delivery. We presume that regular mail is received three business days after it is sent.]

10.3   EFFECTIVE DATE OF AGREEMENT. The "Effective Date" of this Agreement shall be the earlier of (i) the date the Agreement is signed by both Cotenants or (ii) the first date on which both Cotenants hold title to the Property as tenants-in-common.

10.4   TERM OF AGREEMENT. This Agreement shall bind the Cotenants for ninety (90) years or until such time as one of the following events occurs:

A. *Sale of Entire Property.* One hundred percent (100%) of the Property is resold in a single transaction;

B. *Buy out.* One Cotenant transfers his/her entire interest in the Property to the other Cotenant;

C. *Replacement.* The Cotenants explicitly agree in writing to no longer be bound by this Agreement; or

D. *Operation of Law.* This Agreement is superseded or lapses by operation of law.

10.5   OCCUPIER VACANCY. Notwithstanding anything to the contrary in this Agreement, Occupier's Cotenant Equity shall not be distributed until (i) Occupier and all of Occupier's relatives, guests, pets, tenants, or subtenants have vacated the Property and removed all personal property and debris, and (ii) Occupier has broom-cleaned the Property.

[*Annotation.* This section provides a simple additional tool to ensure that a reluctant occupier will vacate the property promptly at the end of the equity share, and will leave it in relatively good condition.]

10.6   NONALLOCATED EXPENSES. Any cost or expense involuntarily imposed on the Cotenants as a result of their co-ownership of the Property and not otherwise allocated or mentioned by this Agreement shall be a Required Additional Capital Contribution.

10.7   NONAUTHORIZED COMPENSATION. Under no circumstances shall a Cotenant be entitled to any reimbursement for any expenditure of time or money related to the Property unless such expenditure has been specifically authorized by this Agreement or explicitly approved by the other Cotenant as provided in this Agreement.

[*Annotation.* This section reaffirms yet again that neither owner gets paid for any financial contributions, service contributions, or improvements unless both owners had agreed to the reimbursement in advance.]

10.8   INDEMNITY. If a Cotenant or an individual comprising a Cotenant becomes subject to any claim, liability, obligation, or loss arising from or related to the willful or negligent act or omission of the other Cotenant, such other Cotenant shall fully indemnify him/her from all associated costs and expenses including attorney's fees.

[*Annotation.* This section provides that an owner is responsible when he/she causes the other to suffer a loss.]

10.9   RECORD KEEPING. Occupier shall keep complete books and records accurately reflecting the accounts, business, and transactions of the Cotenants in connection with the Property. The books shall be kept on a cash basis and maintained at the Property or at such other location designated for such purpose by agreement of both Cotenants. Investor shall have the right to inspect and examine such books and records at any reasonable time.

[*Annotation.* This section requires that the occupier maintain records of the property expenses. Records will be essential if a dispute arises between the owners.]

10.10 MEMORANDUM OF AGREEMENT. Each of the Cotenants shall deposit into the Acquisition Escrow an executed and recordable short form "Memorandum of Agreement" which shall be recorded in the Official Records of the County of San Francisco, California.

[*Annotation.* See Chapter Six.]

10.11 CONDEMNATION. In the event a condemnation or eminent domain proceeding results in the transfer of the Property, the proceeds shall (i) be considered the Termination Value for the purpose of determining Cotenant Equity and (ii) be distributed as provided in Subsection 6.4 F.

[*Annotation.* This section concerns sales of the property that are forced by the government. This might arise, for example, if the government plans to construct a highway across the property. In such a case, the equity share ends and the parties distribute the proceeds the same way as they would at the planned end of the equity share term.]

10.12 INTERPRETATION. The provisions of this Agreement shall be liberally construed to effect its purpose of creating a general plan for the operation of the Property. The various headings used are for convenience only and shall not affect meaning or interpretation. Any exhibit mentioned in this Agreement is attached and deemed incorporated by this reference.

10.13 GOVERNING LAW. This Agreement is executed in and shall be governed by the laws of the State of California.

10.14 AMENDMENTS. This Agreement may be amended at any time and from time to time, but any amendment must be in writing and signed by both Cotenants.

[*Annotation.* The importance of this section is often overlooked. If there is a conflict between the written Agreement and later informal discussions or meetings of the owners, the Agreement will control.

For example, suppose the Smiths call Laura on the telephone early in the equity share and they all discuss the many improvements that the Smiths plan to make on the property. The improvements all sound great and everyone agrees they will enhance the value of the property. But the discussion is general and no specific work, prices, or time frames are mentioned. At the end of the conversation, the Smiths have the understanding that they can go ahead with the work at their own pace, and Laura will reimburse them 45 percent of the cost at the end of the equity share. Laura has the understanding that when the Smiths are actually ready to make a specific improvement, they will discuss it with her in depth and make a decision.

The end of the equity share term arrives, and the Smiths seek reimbursement for $15,000 in improvement costs. Unfortunately, the property value has not increased, and Laura feels the improvements (including purple kitchen cabinets and consolidation of two bedrooms into one) are to blame. She feels that if she had been consulted about the specific improvements, she would never have agreed. Under these circumstances, if the owners cannot agree on a compromise, the Smiths will not get reimbursement. This is because the Agreement, which requires written consent to each specific improvement, takes precedence over an oral conversation. The story illustrates a basic rule: Avoid disputes over the meaning of vague conversations where either or both parties may "hear what they want to hear" and "remember what they want to remember."]

10.15 SEVERABILITY. Each provision of this Agreement shall be deemed independent. The invalidity or unenforceability of any provision shall not affect the validity or enforceability of any other provision.

10.16 TIME. Time is expressly declared to be of the essence in this Agreement.

10.17 WAIVER. Except as specifically provided in this Agreement, a Cotenant may waive a term or provision of this Agreement only by preparing and signing a written document explicitly describing the waiver. No waiver by any Cotenant of any breach of this Agreement shall constitute a waiver of any subsequent breach of the same or different provision of this Agreement.

10.18 ENTIRE AGREEMENT. This document together with the associated Equity Sharing Note and Equity Sharing Deed of Trust contain the entire agreement of the Cotenants relating to any matter regarding the Property. Any written or oral representations, modifications, or agreements regarding these matters, including but not limited to those contained in any purchase agreement or preliminary commitment, shall be of no force and effect unless contained in a subsequently dated, written document expressly stating such representation, modification, or agreement, signed by both Cotenants.

10.19 COSTS AND ATTORNEY'S FEES. In the event of any arbitration or litigation arising out of this Agreement, the prevailing party shall be entitled to reasonable costs and reasonable attorney's fees from the party not prevailing.

10.20 ATTORNEY DISCLOSURES. This Agreement was prepared by an attorney representing both Cotenants. Each Cotenant understands and acknowledges that his/her interests conflict with the interests of the other Cotenant and that the attorney preparing this Agreement is unable to adequately represent the interests of any Cotenant individually. The parties acknowledge that the legal and tax aspects of equity sharing have not yet been fully tested through litigation in the court or tax system. The Cotenants acknowledge that they have been advised to independently hire economic, tax, and legal counsel to evaluate and review the financial, tax, and legal consequences of this transaction and this Agreement. The Cotenants acknowledge that they have either conducted their own independent tax and legal analysis of each of the terms of this Agreement or hereby knowingly waive their right to do so.

_____   DATE
George C. Smith

_____   DATE
Mary A. Smith

_____   DATE
Laura M. Davidson

INTRODUCTION TO THE MEMORANDUM
OF AGREEMENT

The purpose of the Memorandum of Agreement is discussed in Chapter Six. The "Exhibit A" mentioned in the Memorandum is the legal description of the property, which must be attached so that the Memorandum can be recorded in the government records. Exhibit A is not shown here.

MEMORANDUM OF AGREEMENT
FOR 3321 ELM STREET

When Recorded Mail To:

D. Andrew Sirkin
500 Main Street
San Francisco, CA 94111

This Memorandum of Agreement is entered into by and among George C. Smith, Mary A. Smith, and Laura M. Davidson. The parties are owners as Tenants-in-Common of a parcel of real property commonly known as 3321 Elm Street, San Francisco, California, and more particularly described as set forth in "Exhibit A" attached hereto and incorporated herein by reference.

The parties have entered into a co-ownership agreement. The rights and duties of the parties with regard to the real property described above are governed by this agreement. The agreement provides, among other things:

(1) Restrictions on the rights of all owners to transfer or encumber any portion of or interest in the property without the consent of the other owners; and

(2) Options and rights of first refusal granted by each owner to the other owners in the event of any proposed transfer of any portion of or interest in the property.

This Memorandum is intended to give record notice of the existence of the above agreement, but shall in no way affect or modify the provisions of that agreement.

_____
George C. Smith   DATE

_____
Mary A. Smith   DATE

_____
Laura M. Davidson   DATE

[*Annotation.* Because the Memorandum must be recorded in government records, the signatures must be witnessed and acknowledged by a Notary Public.]

INTRODUCTION TO THE EQUITY SHARING PROMISSORY NOTE

The purpose and use of the Promissory Note are discussed in Chapter Six.

EQUITY SHARING PROMISSORY NOTE
FOR 3321 ELM STREET

$195,500.00   June 15, 1994

San Francisco, California

1. OTHER RELATED DOCUMENTS. George C. Smith and Mary A. Smith (collectively hereinafter "Borrower") and Laura M. Davidson (hereinafter "Lender") co-own real property commonly known as 3321 Elm Street, San Francisco, California (the "Property"), as tenants-in-common. In connection with their co-ownership of the Property, Borrower and Lender have executed the following documents in addition to this Note:

A. *Senior Loan.* A note and deed of trust in the amount of ONE HUNDRED EIGHTY THOUSAND AND 00/100 DOLLARS ($180,000.00) in favor of National Bank, 555 Main Street, San Francisco, California 94111, executed on June 15, 1994 (the "Senior Note" and "Senior Deed of Trust");

B. *Equity Sharing Agreement.* A document entitled "Equity Sharing and Lease Agreement for 3321 Elm Street" executed June 15, 1994 (the "Equity Sharing Agreement"), which describes the rights and obligations of Borrower and Lender with regard to their co-ownership of the Property. The Equity Sharing Agreement provides, among other things:

(i) *Contribution of Lender.* Lender has contributed the amount of TEN THOUSAND FIVE HUNDRED AND 00/100 DOLLARS ($10,500.00) toward the cost of acquiring the Property;

(ii) *Payment of Senior Note.* Borrower shall make all payments of principal and interest required by the Senior Note; and

(iii) *Liquidated Damages.* In the event of "Default" under the terms of the Equity Sharing Agreement, Borrower shall pay to Lender the sum of FIVE THOUSAND AND 00/100 DOLLARS ($5,000.00) as liquidated damages.

C. *Equity Sharing Deed of Trust.* A document entitled "Equity Sharing Deed of Trust" executed by Borrower and Lender June 15, 1994 (the "Equity Sharing Deed of Trust"). The Equity Sharing Deed of Trust secures this Note and contains provisions that permit the acceleration of the maturity of this Note as described below.

2. BORROWER'S PROMISE TO PAY. For value received, George C. Smith and Mary A. Smith, jointly and severally, promise to pay to or for Laura M. Davidson the following sums:

A. ONE HUNDRED EIGHTY THOUSAND AND 00/100 DOLLARS ($180,000.00) payable to and at National Bank, 555 Main Street, San Francisco, CA 94111, according to terms and provisions of the Senior Note and Senior Deed of Trust; and

B. FIFTEEN THOUSAND FIVE HUNDRED AND 00/100 DOLLARS ($15,500.00) payable to Lender at 12 Windy Alley, Chicago, IL 60619, in full within five (5) calendar days of written demand which may be made any time following "Default" as defined in the Equity Sharing Agreement.

3. CALCULATION OF NOTE AMOUNT. The total principal amount of this Note reflects and affirms (i) Borrower's obligation to make all payments required on the Senior Note, and (ii) Borrower's other responsibilities and obligations under the Equity Sharing Agreement. The Note amount is a true and accurate valuation of the amounts Borrower owes Lender in the event of a "Default" under the Equity Sharing Agreement. Borrower expressly agrees that it would be extremely difficult to fix Lender's actual loss, damage, and extra expense upon such "Default" and that the amount set forth herein and in the Equity Sharing Deed of Trust is a reasonable estimate of such loss, damage, and expense.

4. BORROWER'S FAILURE TO PAY OR OTHER DEFAULT.

A. *Late Payments.* If Lender is required to pay, or becomes obligated to pay any penalties, late charges, or interest under the terms of the Senior Note by reason of Borrower's failure to make timely payments under this Note, Borrower promises to pay the amount of the penalties, late charges, or interest to Lender upon demand.

B. *Nonperformance.* Should Borrower default in the payment of any installment when due or in the performance of any other obligation described in this Note, the Equity Sharing Agreement, or the Equity Sharing Deed of Trust, the whole sum of principal under this Note shall, at the option of Lender, become immediately due and payable. Lender may then proceed to exercise any rights or remedies that he/she may have under the Equity Sharing Deed of Trust or under this Note or such other rights and remedies which Lender may have at law, equity, or otherwise.

C. *Collection Costs.* After default, in addition to principal, interest, and late charges, Lender shall be entitled to collect all costs of collection, including but not limited to reasonable attorney's fees, incurred in connection with the protection or realization of collateral or in connection with any of Lender's collection efforts, whether or not suit on this Note or any foreclosure proceeding is filed, and all such costs and expenses shall be payable on demand and until paid shall also be secured by the Equity Sharing Deed of Trust and by all other collateral held by Lender as security for Borrower's obligations to Lender.

D. *Waiver of Borrower Protections.* Borrower hereby waives "notice or dishonor" (the right to require Lender to give notice that amounts due have not been paid before commencing collection efforts), presentment (the right to require Lender to demand payment of amounts due before commencing collection efforts), and protest (the right to demand an official certification of nonpayment before Lender commences collection efforts). Borrower also hereby waives and renounces all rights to the benefits of any statute of limitations and any moratorium, appraisement, exemption, and homestead now provided or which may later be provided by any federal or state statute, including but not limited to exemptions provided by or allowed under Title 11 of the United States Code, as at any time amended, both as to himself/herself personally and as to all of his/her property, whether real or personal, against the enforcement and collection of the obligations evidenced by this Note and any and all extensions, renewals, and modifications hereof.

[*Annotation.* Section 4 D provides that the occupier waives many of the formal procedures normally required of a lender. This waiver is justified because the equity sharing agreement has its own Actionable Violation and Default procedures, which provide adequate protection to the occupier.]

5. WAIVER. No failure on the part of Lender to exercise any right or remedy hereunder, whether before or after the occurrence of a default, shall constitute a waiver thereof, and no waiver of any past default shall constitute waiver of any future default or of any other default. No failure to accelerate the debt evidenced hereby by reason

of default hereunder, or acceptance of a past due installment of principal or interest, or indulgence granted from time to time, shall be construed to be a waiver of the right to insist on prompt payment thereafter or the right to impose late charges retroactively or prospectively, or shall be deemed to be a novation of this Note or as a reinstatement of the debt evidenced hereby or as a waiver of such right of acceleration or any other right, or be construed so as to preclude the exercise of any right which Lender may have, whether by the laws of California, by agreement or otherwise, and Borrower hereby expressly waives the benefit of any statute or rule of law or equity which would produce a result contrary to or in conflict with the foregoing. This Note may not be changed orally, but only by an agreement in writing signed by the party against whom such agreement is sought to be enforced.

[*Annotation.* This section means that the terms of the Promissory Note cannot be changed accidentally through the investor's behavior; instead, any changes must be formal and written.]

6.   TRANSFER OR ENCUMBRANCE OF THE PROPERTY. If Borrower sells, contracts to sell, gives an option to purchase, conveys, leases, encumbers, or alienates the Property, or any interest in the Property, or suffers his title, or any interest in the Property, to be divested, whether voluntarily or involuntarily; or if title to such property be subject to any lien or charge, voluntarily or involuntarily, contractual or statutory, without the written consent of Lender being first had and obtained, Lender, at Lender's option, may, without prior notice, declare all sums due under this Note, irrespective of their stated due date(s), immediately due and payable, and may exercise all rights and remedies provided in the Equity Sharing Deed of Trust.

[*Annotation.* This section reaffirms the portions of the equity sharing agreement that prohibit the occupier from selling or giving away his/her interest, or borrowing against the property, without the investor's consent.]

7.   NOTICES. Any notice that must be given to Borrower under this Note will be delivered either personally or by first class mail, postage prepaid, to George C. and Mary A. Smith, 3321 Elm Street, San Francisco, CA 94133.

8.   RESPONSIBILITY. If more than one person signs this Note, each is fully and personally obligated to pay the full amount owed

and to keep all of the promises made in this Note. Lender may enforce all of his/her rights under this Note against any signer individually. This means that any signer may be required to pay all of the amounts owed under this Note. Any person who assumes any of the obligations of Borrower under the Equity Sharing Agreement also becomes fully and personally obligated to pay the full amount owed and to keep all of the promises made in this Note.

George C. Smith	DATE
Mary A. Smith	DATE

INTRODUCTION TO THE EQUITY SHARING DEED OF TRUST

The purpose and use of the Deed of Trust are discussed in Chapter 6. Because state law requirements dictate much of the content of a deed of trust or other real estate lien document, this sample is intended only as a demonstration of how a lien can be adapted to equity sharing use. A deed of trust is one of several types of documents used for real estate liens. Equity sharing owners who intend to use a secured promissory note need to determine what type of document is most appropriate under their state's law, and then adapt that document to equity sharing usage.

EQUITY SHARING DEED OF TRUST FOR 3321 ELM STREET
(All-Inclusive with Assignment of Rents)

When Recorded Return To:

D. Andrew Sirkin
500 Main Street
San Francisco, CA 94111

This Equity Sharing Deed of Trust (the "Deed of Trust") is made this 15th day of June, 1994, among George C. Smith and Mary A. Smith (the "Trustor"), Friendly Title Company, a California Corporation (the "Trustee"), and Laura M. Davidson (the "Beneficiary").

TRUSTOR IRREVOCABLY GRANTS, TRANSFERS, AND ASSIGNS TO TRUSTEE IN TRUST, WITH POWER OF SALE:

I. TRUSTOR'S FIFTY FIVE PERCENT (55.00%) tenancy-in-common interest in that certain lot, piece, or parcel of land, together with all water rights and any and all buildings and improvements now or hereafter erected thereon situated in the County of San Francisco, State of California, and more particularly described in "Exhibit A." The entirety of this lot, piece, or parcel of land, together with all said buildings and improvements, shall be herein referred to as the "Property."

II. TOGETHER with all right, title, and interest of Trustor, if any, in and to the land lying in the bed of any street, road, or avenue, opened or proposed, in front of or adjoining the Property to the center line thereof, and in and to the appurtenances to all right, title, and interest of Trustor in and to said real estate.

III. TOGETHER with any and all awards or payments, including interest thereon, and the right to receive the same, which may be made to Trustor with respect to the Property as a result of (a) the exercise of the right of eminent domain, (b) the alteration of the grade of any street, or (c) any other injury to or decrease in the value of the Property, to the extent of all amounts which may be secured by this Deed of Trust at the date of receipt of any such award or payment by Beneficiary and of the reasonable counsel fees, costs, and disbursements incurred by Beneficiary in connection with the collection of such award or payment. Trustor agrees to execute and deliver, from time to time, such further instruments as may be requested by Beneficiary to confirm such assignment to Beneficiary of any such award or payment.

IV. TOGETHER with Trustor's interest in the rents issues and profits thereof, subject, however, to the right, power, and authority hereinafter given to and conferred on Beneficiary to collect and apply such rents, issues, and profits.

[*Annotation.* This section identifies how the property that may be sold at public sale if the occupier defaults. This description attempts to include any interest in the property which the occupier may have. The "Exhibit A" mentioned here, which is not shown, is the legal description of the property.]

FOR THE PURPOSE OF SECURING:

I.   Payment of an indebtedness in the principal sum of ONE HUNDRED NINETY FIVE THOUSAND FIVE HUNDRED AND 00/100 DOLLARS ($195,500.00) with interest thereon according to the terms of a document entitled "Equity Sharing Promissory Note" of even date herewith executed by Trustor, delivered to Beneficiary and payable to him/her order (the "Note," which is incorporated by reference), and any and all extensions or renewals thereof, and the performance and discharge of each and every obligation, covenant, and agreement of Trustor contained in the Note. The principal amount of the Note and this Deed of Trust represents the sum of:

(i)   ONE HUNDRED EIGHTY THOUSAND AND 00/100 DOLLARS ($180,000.00) as the "all-included" note and deed of trust recorded concurrent herewith but prior hereto and executed by George C. Smith, Mary A. Smith, and Laura M. Davidson as Trustors, in favor of National Bank, as Beneficiary, and National Bank Title Company, a California corporation, as Trustee (the "Senior Note" and "Senior Deed of Trust"), and

(ii) The sum of FIFTEEN THOUSAND FIVE HUNDRED AND 00/100 DOLLARS ($15,500.00) as the "unincluded" amount of the Equity Sharing Promissory Note.

Beneficiary's demand at Trustee sale shall specifically exclude the principal and interest due under the Senior Note (the "Included Amount"), thereby reducing the demand to reflect only the amount described in subsection (ii) above (the "Unincluded Amount") and all other amounts authorized under this Deed of Trust, the Note, and the document entitled "Equity Sharing and Lease Agreement for 3321 Elm Street" and executed June 15, 1994 by Trustor and Beneficiary (the "Equity Sharing Agreement," which is incorporated by reference);

II. And additional sums and interest that may hereafter be loaned to then record owner of the Property by Beneficiary, when evidenced by another note reciting that it is secured by this Deed of Trust;

III. The performance and discharge of each and every obligation, covenant, and agreement of Trustor contained in this Deed of Trust, the Note, and the Equity Sharing Agreement; and

IV. Payment of all other sums with interest thereon becoming due and payable under the provisions hereof to either Trustee or Beneficiary.

[*Annotation.* This section describes the occupier's basic promises, which are secured by the deed of trust. They include all of the occupier's obligations under the equity sharing agreement. The remaining section lists the acts by occupier that can trigger sale of the property under the deed of trust.]

TO PROTECT THE SECURITY OF THIS DEED OF TRUST, TRUSTOR AGREES THAT:

1. WARRANTIES. Trustor warrants that Trustor has good title to his/her FIFTY FIVE PERCENT (55.00%) tenancy-in-common interest in the Property and has a right to encumber the same by this Deed of Trust. Trustor shall and will make, execute, acknowledge, and deliver, in due form of law, all such further or other deeds or assurances as may at any time hereafter be reasonably desired or required for more fully and effectually conveying the Trustor's interest in the Property by this Deed of Trust.

2. TRANSFER OR ENCUMBRANCE OF THE PROPERTY. If Trustor sells, contracts to sell, gives an option to purchase, conveys, leases, encumbers, or alienates the Property, or any interest in the

Property, or suffers his title, or any interest in the Property, to be divested, whether voluntarily or involuntarily; or if title to such Property be subject to any lien or charge, voluntarily or involuntarily, contractual or statutory, without the written consent of Beneficiary being first obtained, Beneficiary, at Beneficiary's option, may, without prior notice, declare all sums secured by this Deed of Trust, irrespective of their stated due date(s), immediately due and payable, and may exercise all rights and remedies provided in this Deed of Trust.

3.   INSURANCE. Trustor will keep the building on the Property and all equipment thereon insured for the benefit of Beneficiary in accordance with the terms of the Equity Sharing Agreement. If Trustor defaults in so insuring the Property, Beneficiary may, at the option of the Beneficiary, effect such insurance from year to year and pay the premiums therefor. Trustor will reimburse Beneficiary for any Premiums so paid, with interest from the time of payment, on demand; this obligation to reimburse shall also be secured by this Deed of Trust. If Beneficiary, by reason of such insurance, receives any money for loss or damage, such amount may, according to the terms of the Equity Sharing Agreement, be retained and applied by Beneficiary toward payment of the moneys secured by this Deed of Trust, or be paid over wholly or in part to Trustor for the repair of said buildings or for the erection of new buildings in their place. In the event of a foreclosure sale hereunder, the purchaser or purchasers of the Property shall succeed to all the rights of Trustor, including any right to unearned premiums in and to all policies of insurance assigned and delivered to Beneficiary pursuant to the provisions of this Article. The provisions of this Article shall apply to all policies of insurance related to the Property which Trustor may take out in addition to the policies required under this Article.

4.   REPAIR AND MAINTENANCE. Trustor shall repair and maintain the Property in accordance with the terms of the Equity Sharing Agreement. Trustor will not substantially alter, remove, or demolish the Property or any portion of the Property, except when incident to required repair or maintenance. Trustor will pay when due all claims for labor performed and materials furnished in connection with the Property and not permit mechanic's or materialman's lien to arise against the Property. Trustor will comply with all laws affecting the Property or requiring that any alterations or improvements be made to the Property. Trustor will not initiate, join in, or consent to any change in, any private restrictive covenant, any zoning ordinance, or other public or private restriction, limiting or defining the uses that may be made of the Property or any part thereof without written consent of Beneficiary.

5.   TAXES AND ASSESSMENTS. Trustor will pay all taxes, assessments, water and sewer fees and other charges, and any prior liens now or hereafter assessed or liens on or levied against the Property or any part thereof. Trustor shall pay all such taxes and assessments at least thirty (30) days before they become delinquent. If Trustor defaults on the obligation, Beneficiary may, at the option of Beneficiary, pay the same, and Trustor will repay the same with interest at the rate set forth in the note from and after maturity, and the same shall be liens on the Property and secured by this Deed of Trust.

6.   ASSIGNMENT OF RENTS. As additional security, Trustor hereby gives to and confers on Beneficiary the right, power, and authority to collect the rents, issues, and profits of the Property, reserving unto Trustor the right, prior to any default by Trustor in payment of any indebtedness secured hereby or in performance of any agreement hereunder, to collect and retain such rents, issues, and profits as they become due and payable. Upon any such default, Beneficiary may at any time without notice, either in person, by agent, or by a receiver to be appointed by a court, and without regard to the adequacy of any security for the indebtedness hereby secured, enter upon and take possession of said property or any part hereof, and/or sue for or otherwise collect such rents, issues, and profits, including those past due and unpaid, and apply the same, less costs and expenses of operation and collection, including reasonable attorney's fees, upon any indebtedness secured hereby, in such order as Beneficiary may determine. The entering upon and taking possession of said property, the collection of such rents, issues, and profits, and the application thereof as aforesaid, shall not cure or waive any default or notice of default hereunder or invalidate any act done pursuant to such notice. At any time or from time to time upon the request of Beneficiary, Trustor shall, upon notice and demand, transfer and assign to Beneficiary, in form satisfactory to Beneficiary, Trustor's interest in any lease now or hereafter affecting the whole or any part of the Property, upon the condition, however, that until Trustor shall default in the payment of any indebtedness secured by this Deed of Trust or by said assignment, or shall default in the performance of any agreement herein or in said assignment contained, Trustor shall have the right to collect all such rents, issues, and profits upon accrual, but not prior thereto, and to retain, use, and enjoy the same.

7.   STATEMENT OF AMOUNTS DUE. Upon request of Beneficiary, made either personally or by mail, Trustor shall certify in a duly acknowledged writing to Beneficiary or to any proposed assignee or transferee of this Deed of Trust and the Note, the amount of principal and interest then owing on the Note and whether any offsets or

defenses exist against the indebtedness secured hereby. Trustor shall provide such certification within six (6) days if the request is made personally or within ten (10) if the request is made by mail.

8.   JOINT AND SEVERAL LIABILITY. If Trustor consists of more than one party, such Trustors shall be jointly and severally liable under any and all obligations, covenants, and agreements of Trustor contained herein.

9.   CONTINUITY OF OBLIGATIONS. Notwithstanding any taking by eminent domain, alteration of the grade of any street or to the injury to or decrease in value of the Property by any public or quasi-public authority or corporation, Trustor shall continue to fulfill all obligations under this Deed of Trust, the Note, and the Equity Sharing Agreement until such time as the disposition of the Property is completed in accordance with the Equity Sharing Agreement.

10. SUBSTITUTE PERFORMANCE. In the event of default in the performance of any of Trustor's covenants or agreements hereunder, Beneficiary may, at the option of Beneficiary, perform the same; and the cost thereof, with interest at the rate set forth in the Note from and after maturity, shall immediately be due from Trustor to Beneficiary to be secured by this Deed of Trust.

11. ACCELERATION. The whole of the principal sum and the interest shall become due at the option of Beneficiary:

(i)   After default in the fulfillment of any obligation described in the Equity Sharing Agreement and the continuance of any such default for fourteen (14) days; or

(ii)   After default in the payment of any installment of principal and/or of interest on the note secured hereby and the continuance of any such default for fourteen (14) days; or

(iii) After failure to provide the certification required by Article 7; or

(iv)   Upon the actual or threatened waste, removal, or demolition of, or material alteration to, any part of the Property, except as permitted by this Deed of Trust; or

(v)   Upon default in keeping in force the insurance required by this Deed of Trust or in delivering renewal policies as required by this Deed of Trust or in reimbursing Beneficiary for premiums paid under this Deed of Trust; or

(vi)   After default for fourteen (14) days after notice and demand in the removal of any lien on the Property; or

(vii)   Upon default in the observance or performance of any other covenants or agreements of Trustor hereunder; or

(viii) If Trustor shall generally not pay his/her debts as they become due or shall admit in writing his/her inability to pay his/her debts, or shall make a general assignment for the benefit of creditors; or

(ix)   If Trustor shall commence any case, proceeding, or other action seeking reorganization, liquidation, dissolution, or relief of debts under any law relating to bankruptcy, insolvency, reorganization, or relief of debtors, or seek an appointment of receiver, trustee, custodian, or other similar official for himself/herself or for all or any substantial part of his/her properties; or

(x)   If any case, proceeding, or other action against the Trustor shall be commenced seeking to have an order for relief entered against him/her as debtor or seek an appointment of receiver, trustee, custodian, or other similar official for him/her or for all or any substantial part of his/her property, and such case, proceeding, or other action either results in the entry for an order for relief against it which is not fully stayed within seven (7) business days of its entry, or remains undismissed for a period of forty-five (45) days.

[*Annotation.* Ordinarily, an "Acceleration" provision of a deed of trust makes the entire amount of the underlying loan due all at once following a default. In an equity sharing deed of trust, the purpose is to reaffirm the investor's right to foreclose following a default.]

12. NOTICE AND DEMAND. The election of Beneficiary to accelerate the maturity of the principal sum of the Note pursuant to this Deed of Trust shall be evidenced by delivery to Trustee of a written declaration by Beneficiary of default and demand for sale, and Trustee or Beneficiary shall thereafter file or cause to be filed for record a notice of such default and of election to cause the Property to be sold. Beneficiary also shall deposit with Trustee this Deed of Trust, the Note, and all documents evidencing expenditures secured hereby. Notwithstanding any other provision of this Deed of Trust or Note, any demand for sale delivered to the Trustee for the foreclosure of this Deed of Trust shall be reduced by the unpaid balance, if any, at the time of the Trustee sale, of the principal and interest due on the Senior Note and of any other sums payable under the terms of the Senior Note or Senior Deed of Trust. Satisfactory evidence of the unpaid balance (which may consist of the written statement of the holder of the Senior Note) must be submitted to the Trustee prior to sale.

13. SALE. Notice of sale having been given as then required by law and three (3) months having elapsed after recordation of such notice of default, Trustee, without demand on Trustor, shall sell Trustor's interest in the Property at the time and place of sale fixed by it on said notice of sale, either as a whole or in separate parcels in such order as it may determine, at public auction to the highest bidder for cash in lawful money of the United States, payable at time of sale. Trustee may postpone sale of all or any portion of Trustor's interest in the Property by public announcement at such time and place of sale, and from time to time thereafter may postpone such sale by public announcement at the time fixed by the preceding postponement. Any person, including Trustor, Trustee, or Beneficiary, may purchase at such sale. Beneficiary agrees to bid an amount not in excess of the amount then due upon the obligation secured by this Deed of Trust, including late charges, penalties, and/or advances, minus the balance then due on the Senior Note, including late charges, interest penalties, advances, and/or impounds. Trustee shall deliver to any purchaser its deed conveying the property so sold, but without any covenant or warranty, express or implied. The recitals in such deed of any matters or facts shall be conclusive proof of the truthfulness thereof.

14. PROCEEDS. After deducting all costs, fees, and expenses of Trustee and of this Trust, including cost of evidence of title in connection with sale, Trustee shall apply the proceeds of sale to payment of: all sums expended under the terms hereof, not then repaid, with accrued interest at the maximum rate allowed by law; all other sums then secured hereby; and the remainder, if any, to the person or persons legally entitled thereto.

15. OTHER REMEDIES. The provisions contained in this Deed of Trust shall not be construed to preclude Trustee or Beneficiary, in the event of any default thereunder, from enforcing any appropriate remedy against Trustor or from proceeding by suit to foreclose or by suits at law or in equity, as Beneficiary may elect or as Trustee may be advised, to enforce payment of all sums secured hereby.

16. RIGHT TO RECONVEY. Upon written request of Beneficiary and the surrender of this Deed of Trust and the Note to Trustee for cancellation and retention and upon payment of its fees, Trustee shall reconvey, without warranty, the property then held hereunder. The recitals in such reconveyance of any matters or facts shall be conclusive proof of the truthfulness thereof. The grantee in such reconveyance may be described as the person or persons legally entitled

thereto. As to Trustee, any such request for reconveyance shall be conclusive evidence of the fulfillment of the trusts hereby created.

17. SUBSTITUTE TRUSTEES. Beneficiary may from time to time substitute in such manner as may be provided by law a successor or successors to any Trustee named herein or acting hereunder, which successor Trustee shall thereupon succeed, without conveyance from the Trustee's predecessor, to all of its powers, duties, authority, and title; or, in the event of the absence of any such law providing for the substitution of trustees in deeds of trust, Beneficiary may, with like effect, make such substitution from time to time by instruments of writing executed and acknowledged by Beneficiary and recorded in the office of the recorder of the county or counties in which the Property is situated. Such instrument shall contain the date of the execution of this Deed of Trust, the name of the original Trustor, Trustee, and Beneficiary, the book and page where this Deed of Trust is recorded, and the name of the new Trustee.

18. SERVICE OF NOTICES. Every provision for notice and demand or request shall be deemed fulfilled by written notice and demand or request personally served on one or more of the persons who shall at the time hold record title to the Property, or on their heirs or successors, or mailed by depositing it in any post office station or letter box, enclosed in a postpaid envelope addressed to such person or persons, or to their heirs or successors, at his/her, their, or its address last known to Beneficiary.

19. COLLECTION COSTS. If Beneficiary shall incur or expend any sums, including reasonable attorney's fees, to sustain the lien of this Deed of Trust or its priority, or to protect or enforce any of his/her rights hereunder, or to recover any indebtedness hereby secured, or for any title examination or title insurance policy relating to the title to the Property, all such sums shall on notice and demand be paid by Trustor, together with the interest thereon at the maximum rate allowed by law. Such sums shall be a lien on the Property, prior to any right or title to, interest in, or any claim upon the Property subordinate to the lien of this Deed of Trust and evidenced by the Note. In any action or proceeding to foreclose this Deed of Trust, or to recover or collect the debt secured thereby, the provisions of law respecting the recovery of costs, disbursements, and allowances shall prevail unaffected by this covenant.

20. WAIVER. Any failure by Beneficiary to insist on the strict performance by Trustor of any of these terms and provisions shall not be deemed to be a waiver of any of the terms and provisions. Beneficiary,

notwithstanding any such failure, shall have the right thereafter to insist on the strict performance by Trustor of any and all of the terms and provisions of this Deed of Trust to be performed by Trustor. Neither Trustor, nor any other person now or hereafter obligated for the payment of the whole or any part of the sums now or hereafter secured by this Deed of Trust, shall be relieved of such obligation by reason of (i) the failure of Beneficiary to comply with any request of Trustor, or of any other person so obligated, to take action to foreclose this Deed of Trust; (ii) the failure of Beneficiary to enforce any of the provisions of this Deed of Trust or of any obligations secured hereby; (iii) the release, regardless of consideration, of the whole or any part of the security held for the indebtedness secured by this Deed of Trust; (iv) any agreement or stipulation between any subsequent owner or owners of the Property and Beneficiary extending the time of payment or modifying the terms of the Note or this Deed of Trust without first having obtained the consent of Trustor or such other person. In the latter event, Trustor and all such other persons shall continue to be liable to make such payments according to the terms of any such agreement or extension or modification unless expressly released and discharged in writing by Beneficiary.

21. TERMINOLOGY. Whenever used in this Deed of Trust, unless the context clearly indicates a contrary intent or unless otherwise specifically provided here, the word "Trustor" shall mean "Trustor and/or any subsequent owner or owners of the Property," the word "Beneficiary" shall mean "Beneficiary and/or any subsequent holder or holders of the Note," the word "Note" shall mean "the Equity Sharing Promissory Note of the same date as the Equity Sharing Deed of Trust and any additional promissory note or notes at any time secured by this Equity Sharing Deed of Trust" and the word "person" shall mean "an individual, corporation, partnership, or unincorporated association." In this Deed of Trust, whenever the context so requires, the masculine gender includes the feminine and/or neuter, and the singular number includes the plural and conversely.

22. MODIFICATION. This Deed of Trust cannot be changed except by agreement in writing, signed by the party against whom the enforcement of the change is sought.

23. STATUTE OF LIMITATIONS. Except insofar as now or hereafter prohibited by law, the right to plead, use, or assert any statute of limitations is hereby waived as a plea or defense or a bar of any kind, or for any purpose, to any debt, demand, or obligation secured or to be secured hereby, or to any complaint or other pleading

or proceeding filed, instituted, or maintained for the purpose of enforcing this trust or any rights hereunder.

24. ACCEPTANCE. Trustee accepts this trust when this Deed of Trust, duly executed and acknowledged, is made a public record as provided by law. Trustee is not obligated to notify any party hereto of pending sale under any other deed of trust or of any action or proceeding in which Trustor, Beneficiary, or Trustee shall be a party unless brought by Trustee.

25. INTERPRETATION. This Deed of Trust shall be construed according to the laws of the State of California.

_____   _____
George C. Smith   DATE

_____   _____
Mary A. Smith   DATE

[*Annotation.* Because the Deed of Trust must be recorded in government records, the signatures must be witnessed and acknowledged by a Notary Public.]

Appendix A

Why Equity Share?

Equity sharing has advantages and disadvantages for any given person in any given situation. This appendix examines these advantages and disadvantages from the perspective of home buyer, investor, seller, parent/relative, employer, and real estate agent. This analysis will provide the tools for two important tasks: (1) to decide whether you should equity share, and (2) to convince others to equity share with you.

HOME BUYER ANALYSIS—ADVANTAGES AND DISADVANTAGES

Equity Sharing versus Renting

Advantage 1: Tax deductible monthly payments. Mortgage interest and property taxes are tax-deductible; rent is not. Determine what percentage of income you pay as tax, and compare the *after-tax* monthly payments in an equity share with rent for a comparable residence. Your tax preparer can help.

Advantage 2: Better return on savings. In the short term, home values go up and down in cycles. But over terms of five-years or longer, home values have consistently risen, and home owners' investment return is consistently higher than returns on almost any other type of investment. These were the return percentages over three recent decades:

Period	Nationwide Average Home Appreciation	Return on 10 Percent Down Payment after Deduction of Buyer Closing Costs and Costs of Sale
1960–1970	42.9%	313% or 31.3% per year
1970–1980	177.6%	1,566% or 156.6% per year
1980–1990	67.6%	537% or 53.7% per year

Moreover, you can defer tax on your investment return by reinvesting in a new home when you sell.

Advantage 3: Security and pride. Owning offers the security of never being subject to eviction, the satisfaction of being able to customize your living space, and the pride of ownership.

Disadvantage 1: Investment risk. An owner's investment could be partially or totally lost if the property has hidden problems, an uninsured loss occurs, or market value declines. Risk of investment loss is much lower with some other investments, such as federally insured bank deposits.

Disadvantage 2: More responsibility. Owners are responsible for unforeseen maintenance costs, and cannot move without worrying about selling or renting out their home.

Equity Sharing versus Buying Alone

Advantage 1: More down payment. Equity sharing funds are considered down payment by mortgage lenders; if a lender requires a

---

Example A.1   Financial Comparison of Equity Sharing versus Renting

This example assumes you have $10,000 in savings and are comparing renting a two-bedroom home for $800 per month with buying a similar home for $150,000. If you rent, you will invest your $10,000 savings in a long-term certificate of deposit paying 6.5% interest. If you equity share on the $150,000 home, your investor will contribute $8,000 and you will contribute $10,000; he will get 30 percent of the appreciation and you will get 70 percent. Assume the equity share property appreciates 20 percent over five years and you pay 33 percent of your income in taxes.

The monthly cost comparison shows that your after-tax cost of living in the $150,000 equity share home is $787, $13 less than rent on a comparable home. The investment return comparison shows that, if you equity share, you will have $20,710 in equity after five years; if you rent, you will have only $12,523.

(Continued)

(Example Continued)

Monthly Costs—Equity Sharing vs. Renting

Equity Sharing (Calculation A)

Monthly mortgage payment (30-yr. mortgage at 7.25%)	$ 921
Property tax	151
Insurance	30
Total PITI	$ 1,102
Less: Tax savings (33% of $802 mortgage *interest**)	(265)
Tax savings (33% of $151 property taxes)	(50)
After-tax monthly payment	$ 787
Rent	$ 800
Extra cost of renting	$ 13

*The portion of your monthly interest payment that is interest (as opposed to repayment of the loan) will decrease slightly over time.

Investment Return—Equity Sharing vs. Renting

CD

Principal	$10,000
Interest over 5 years (compound)	3,765
Less: Tax on interest (33% of $3,765)	(1,242)
Funds available for down payment in 5 years	$12,523

Equity Sharing (Calculation B)

Appreciation (20% of $150,000)	$30,000
Less: Closing costs on purchase (2% of $150,000)	(3,000)
Costs of sale (6.5% of $180,000 sale price)	(11,700)
Net appreciation	$15,300
Less: Investor split (30% of $15,300)	(4,590)
Your return	$10,710
Less: Tax on return	(0)
Principal	10,000
Funds available for down payment in 5 years	$20,710
Extra funds available from equity sharing	$ 8,187

minimum down payment of 5 percent, 10 percent, or 20 percent, equity sharing funds will count toward that minimum. Equity sharing will increase your buying power.

Advantage 2: No interest payment. You pay no monthly interest on equity sharing funds. If buying alone would require borrowing, the extra monthly interest cost could be substantial.

Advantage 3: Mortgage qualification strength. Mortgage lenders combine the earnings, savings, and creditworthiness of both equity sharing owners to determine whether they qualify for a mortgage. Your investor's financial strength will help you qualify for a bigger and better mortgage.

Advantage 4: Help with major repairs. The investor helps pay the cost of major repairs, and may agree to share the cost of some improvements.

Disadvantage 1: Lost appreciation. If your home appreciates well, paying your investor his share may cost you more than interest payments would have.

Disadvantage 2: Lost freedom. You are not free to make your own decisions about the equity sharing property. You must maintain the property well and consult with the investor before making major improvements. You can't sell the property at will. You must repay the investor at the end of the term by refinancing the property, obtaining a home equity loan, or using savings. If you can't afford repayment, you may have to sell.

Example A.2   Financial Comparison of Equity Sharing versus Buying Alone

Assume you have $12,000 in savings and are comparing the equity sharing purchase described above with buying the same $150,000 home using a 5 percent down payment and a 95 percent mortgage. If you equity share, you need only $10,000 for down payment and closing costs, so you invest your extra $2,000 in a 6.5 percent certificate of deposit. If you buy alone, you need that extra $2,000 for closing costs. At the time of writing, a 95 percent mortgage costs an extra loan point, has a ¼ percent higher interest rate, and requires private mortgage insurance (PMI), which costs another 1 percent of the mortgage amount per year.

The monthly cost comparison shows that your after-tax cost of buying alone is $951, or $164 more than the cost of equity sharing. The first investment return comparison presumes the property appreciates 20 percent over five years. In that case, if you deposit your $164 monthly savings in a money market account at 5.5 percent, you will have $34,031 in equity after five years, $8,231 more than if you purchased alone. Note that your $164 in monthly savings makes this result possible. If you spend this money, you will have only $23,463 in equity after five years, $2,337 less than if you purchased alone.

The second investment return comparison presumes the property appreciates only 5 percent over five years. If you deposit your $164 monthly

(Continued)

(Example Continued)
savings in a money market account, you will have $20,188 in equity after five years, $10,816 more than if you purchased alone. If you spend the $164, you will have $9,372 in equity, $4,610 more than if you purchased alone.

Equity sharing lessens the investment risk of buying a home by allowing you to share that risk with the investor. If you were forced to sell after only 5 percent appreciation, you would lose $7,238 if you purchased alone, but only $2,628 if you equity shared.

Monthly Costs—Equity Sharing vs. Buying Alone

Equity Sharing
After-tax monthly payment (Calculation A in Example A.1) $ 787

Buying Alone

Monthly mortgage payment (30-yr. mortgage at 7.5%)	$ 996
PMI	118
Property tax	151
Insurance	30
Total PITI + PMI	$1,295
Less: Tax savings (33% of $891 mortgage *interest**)	(294)
Tax savings (33% of $151 property taxes)	(50)
After-tax monthly payment	$ 951
Extra cost of buying alone	$ 164

*The portion of your monthly interest payment that is interest (as opposed to repayment of the loan) will decrease slightly over time.

To qualify for the 95 percent LTV loan with its much tougher underwriting guidelines, you would need annual gross income of $52,000. In the equity sharing transaction, you would need gross income of only $38,000, and probably less when the investor's added financial strength was considered.

Investment Return (20% Appreciation)—Equity Sharing vs. Buying Alone

Equity Sharing with 20% Appreciation

Your return (Calculation B in Example A.1)	$10,710
Less: Tax on return	(0)
Principal	12,000
CD interest on extra $2,000 at 6.5%	753
Less: Taxes on CD interest (33% of $753)	(248)
Value of $164/month invested at 5.5%	11,296
Less: Tax on interest ($11,296 − (60 × 164) = $1,456 in interest; 33% of $1,456 = $480)	(480)
Funds available for down payment in 5 years	$34,031

(Example Continued)
Buying Alone with 20% Appreciation

Appreciation (20% of $150,000)	$30,000
Less: Closing costs on purchase (3% of $150,000)	(4,500)
Costs of sale (6.5% of $180,000 sale price)	(11,700)
Net appreciation	$13,800
Less: Tax on return	(0)
Principal	12,000
Funds available for down payment in 5 years	$25,800
Extra funds from equity sharing	$ 8,231

Investment Return (5% Appreciation)—Equity
Sharing vs. Buying Alone

Equity Share with 5% Appreciation

Appreciation (5% of $150,000)	$ 7,500
Less: Closing costs on purchase (2% of $150,000)	(3,000)
Costs of sale (6.5% of $157,500 sale price)	(10,238)
Total loss	$ (5,738)
Less: Investor share of loss	2,605
Your loss	$ (3,133)
Principal	12,000
CD interest on extra $2,000 at 6.5%	753
Less: Taxes on CD interest (33% of $753)	(248)
Value of $164/month invested at 5.5%	11,296
Less: Tax on interest ($11,926 − (60 × 164) = $1,456 in interest; 33% of $1,456 = $480)	(480)
Funds available for down payment in 5 years	$20,188

Buying Alone with 5% Appreciation

Appreciation (5% of $150,000)	$ 7,500
Less: Closing costs on purchase (3% of $150,000)	(4,500)
Costs of sale (6.5% of $157,500 sale price)	(10,238)
Net appreciation	$ (7,238)
Principal	12,000
Funds available for down payment in 5 years	$ 4,762
Extra funds from equity sharing	$15,426

INVESTOR ANALYSIS—ADVANTAGES AND DISADVANTAGES

Equity Sharing versus Certificate of Deposit

Advantage 1: Higher returns. Investment returns on a 10 percent home down payment have averaged from 31 to 156 percent per year over the past 30 years. You can defer income tax on this return indefinitely by reinvesting in other real estate.

Advantage 2: Tax shelter. For most investors, the equity share will generate tax deductions that shelter income from other earnings or investments.

Disadvantage 1: Investment risk. See comparison of equity sharing to renting.

Disadvantage 2: Not liquid. It could be difficult to sell an equity sharing interest. A CD can always be liquidated, although you may pay a penalty.

Disadvantage 3: Risk of credit damage. A default by the occupier could damage your credit.

Disadvantage 4: Additional cash needs. In the case of uninsured damage to the property or default by the occupier, you may be required to invest additional funds in the equity share.

Disadvantage 5: Loss of control. You can't make decisions regarding the equity share without consulting the occupier.

Example A.3   Financial Comparison of Equity Sharing versus Certificate of Deposit

Assume you have $8,000 in savings and are comparing the equity sharing investment described in Example A.2 with a 6.5 percent certificate of deposit. Interest in the CD is compounded, and no return is payable until the end of the five-year term. You pay 33 percent of your income in taxes.

The monthly cost comparison shows a return of $35 per month in tax savings from the equity share. There is no monthly return from the CD because the interest is compounded and added to principal. At the conclusion of the five-year term, your equity share is worth $14,898, giving you an annual return of 17.25 percent. After taxes, your CD is worth $10,039, an annual return of 5.09 percent.

(Continued)

(Example Continued)

Monthly After-Tax Return—Equity Sharing vs. CD

Equity Share (Calculation C)
Rental income calculation

Fair market rental (30% of $800)	$ 240	
Less: 10% Good tenant discount	(24)	
Management discount	(100)	
Fair rental		116
Less: Investor expenses		(116)
Monthly negative cash flow		$ 0

Depreciation (see Chapter 4)

Cost of building (75% of $150,000)	$112,500	
Closing costs	3,000	
Total cost basis	115,500	
Investor share (30% of $115,500)	34,650	
Monthly depreciation ($34,650/27.5%/12)	(105)	
Net tax loss	$ (105)	
Monthly tax savings (33% of $105)		$ 35
After-tax return (negative cash flow + tax savings)		$ 35

Certificate of Deposit

Monthly return	0
Extra funds from equity sharing	$ 35

Return at Conclusion—Equity Sharing vs. CD

CD Investment

Principal	$ 8,000
Interest over 5 years (compound)	3,043
Less: Tax on interest (30% of $3,765)	(1,004)
Funds for reinvestment	$10,039
Annual return	5.09%

Equity Share (Calculation D)

Appreciation (20% of $150,000)	$30,000
Less: Closing costs on purchase (2% of $150,000)	(3,000)
Costs of sale (6.5% of $180,000 sale price)	(11,700)
Net appreciation	$15,300
Less: Occupier split (70% of $15,300)	(10,710)
Your return	$ 4,590
Less: Tax on return	(0)
Principal	8,000
Value of $35/month invested at 5.5%	2,411
Less: Tax on interest ($2,411 − (60 × 35) = $311	
in interest; 33% of $311 = $103)	(103)
Funds for reinvestment	$14,898
Annual return (not including tax savings)	17.25%

Equity Sharing versus Rental Property

This comparison is difficult to make because there are so many different types of possible rental property investments to consider, with widely varying levels of risk and return. Moreover, an investor with $8,000 in savings cannot afford the minimum down payment and closing costs of rental property in most of the country. Mortgage lenders currently require at least a 25 percent down payment on small residential rental properties, and 30 to 40 percent on larger residential properties, commercial properties, and mixed-use properties.

Advantage 1: Smaller investment needed. If you have limited resources, equity sharing provides one of the few real estate investment opportunities available to you. If you have more substantial resources, it offers the opportunity to spread your investment over several properties instead of investing in just one. Spreading the investment lowers the risk that one event or series of events affecting a particular property will prove financially disastrous.

Advantage 2: No negative cash flow. Equity sharing investors have no monthly expenses; additional investment would be required only in the case of uninsured damage to the property or default by the occupier. In many areas of the country, it is impossible to match this feature in a rental property unless you make a 50 percent or greater down payment.

Advantage 3: Less management and no management fees. Rental property owners have significant management duties, including cleaning and maintaining the property, collecting rent, and rerenting units when they become vacant. Owners with no time for these burdens must retain a management company at significant cost. By contrast, an equity sharing investor has no management burdens or costs.

Advantage 4: Less risk of vacancy. Each time a tenant vacates, a rental property owner incurs the cost of lost rent, cleaning and "sprucing up" the vacant unit, advertising, and showing the property to prospective tenants or paying a rental commission to have a management company show it.

Advantage 5: Lower maintenance costs. Equity sharing occupiers bear the cost of all routine maintenance and minor repairs.

Disadvantage 1: Risk of default. If you are comparing equity sharing to owning alone, the possibility of occupier default adds substantial risk. If you are comparing equity sharing to participating in a rental property partnership, the risk of default is probably lower in equity sharing. An occupier has much more to lose from default than an investment partner and is therefore less likely to default.

Example A.4   Financial Comparison of Equity Sharing versus Rental Property

Assume you have $8,000 in savings and are comparing the equity sharing investment described in Example A.3 with buying the same property in partnership with other investors. The investor group will make a 25 percent down payment, have closing costs of 3 percent, and get a fixed-rate loan at 7.5 percent. Your $8,000 will be enough to get you a 19 percent ownership in the partnership.

The monthly cost comparison shows that, even after depreciation and other tax benefits, the rental property will cost you $42 per month. This type of negative cash flow is typical for small rental property investments in much of the country. By contrast, the equity share has no monthly expenses and yields $35 in tax savings, making you $77 better off. At the end of a five-year period, your equity share investment is worth $17,668; your investment partnership interest, $4,660.

Monthly After-Tax Return—Equity Sharing vs. Rental Property

Equity Share

After-tax return (Calculation C in Example A.3)		$ 35
Rental Property (Calculation E)		
Rental income	$ 800	
Less: Vacancy factor (20% of $800)	(160)	
Property tax	(151)	
Insurance	(25)	
Maintenance and repair	(100)	
Management	(100)	
Mortgage	(787)	
Total monthly negative cash flow	$ (523)	
Your monthly negative cash flow (20% of $523)		(99)
Tax savings from negative cash flow (33% of $105)		35
Depreciation (see Chapter Four)		
Cost of building (75% of $150,000)	$112,500	
Closing costs (3% of $150,000)	4,500	
Total cost basis	117,000	
Investor share (19% of $117,000)	22,230	
Monthly depreciation (22,230/27.5/12)	(67)	
Tax savings from depreciation (33% of $67)		22
After-tax cost (negative cash flow + tax savings)		$ (42)
Extra funds from equity sharing		$ 77

(Continued)

(Example Continued)
       Return at Conclusion—Equity Sharing vs. Rental Property

Equity Share

Appreciation (20% of $150,000)	$30,000
Less: Closing costs on purchase (2% of $150,000)	(3,000)
Costs of sale (6.5% of $180,000 sale price)	(11,700)
Net appreciation	$15,300
Less: Occupier split (70% of $15,300)	(10,710)
Your return	$ 4,590
Less: Tax on return	(0)
Principal	8,000
Value of $77/month invested at 5.5%	5,304
Less: Tax on interest ($5,304 − (60 × 77) = $684	
in interest; 33% of $684 = $226)	(226)
Total funds for reinvestment	$17,668

Rental Property

Appreciation (20% of $150,000)	$30,000
Less: Closing costs on purchase (2% of $150,000)	(4,500)
Costs of sale (6.5% of $180,000 sale price)	(11,700)
Negative cash flow ($523 × 60)	(31,380)
Net Loss	(17,580)
Investor share (19% of $17,580)	(3,340)
Principal	8,000
Total funds for reinvestment	$ 4,660

SELLER ANALYSIS—ADVANTAGES AND DISADVANTAGES

As a seller, you should consider equity sharing if even one of the following statements is untrue:

- You plan to reinvest all of your sale proceeds in your new residence.
- You have received an all-cash offer for your property at or above your asking price.
- You will be able to defer all income tax on your resale profit by purchasing a replacement residence of equal or greater value.

If the first statement is untrue, consider investing the extra portion of your sale proceeds in an equity share in your former home. Use the investor analysis previously discussed. If either of the remaining statements is untrue, use this section to analyze whether equity sharing might enhance the salability of your home or allow you to defer taxes even though you are trading down.

Equity Sharing versus Cashing Out

Advantage 1: Higher sale price. In many parts of the country, 95 percent LTV mortgages are difficult or impossible to get, and the very tough underwriting guidelines for 90 percent LTV mortgages disqualify many borrowers. Through equity sharing, you enable buyers with otherwise inadequate down payment and/or loan qualification strength to purchase your home. More buyers means a quicker sale and a higher price.

Advantage 2: Hedge against market rebound. Home prices move up and down in cycles. If you find yourself selling at a low point in the cycle, equity sharing will allow you to participate in the market rebound.

Advantage 3: Defer gains tax. If you are trading down, you will pay income tax on your resale profit. Equity sharing may allow you to defer this tax indefinitely.

Advantage 4: Investment return. If your alternatives to equity sharing are either taking a lower price or paying income tax, you are equity sharing with money you would otherwise have left in the home or paid the government. Any profit you make is money you would not otherwise have.

Disadvantage 1: Additional cash needs. See comparison of equity sharing to certificate of deposit.

Example A.5   Financial Comparison of Equity Sharing versus Cashing Out

Assume you paid $100,000 for your house, plus closing costs of $2,000, and have a mortgage balance of $75,000. In the first comparison, assume that you plan to trade up but have been unable to sell your home for $150,000. You are considering whether to accept the equity sharing offer from Example A.4 or sell "all cash" for $135,000. At the time of sale, the equity share will leave you with $57,250 compared with $51,225 from the all-cash sale at $135,000. In addition to this extra $6,025 at sale, you make $14,898 from the equity share over five years. In the second comparison, assume you plan to trade down and purchase a replacement residence for $105,000. You are considering whether to accept an equity sharing offer or an all-cash offer, both at $150,000. The equity share gives you an extra $4,646 at the time of sale, plus $14,898 over five years.

(Continued)

(Example Continued)
Cash at Sale—Equity Sharing vs. Cashing Out

Equity Share (Calculation F)

Buyer down payment	$ 10,000	
New mortgage (90% of $150,000)	135,000	
Less: Seller closing costs (6.5% of $150,000)	(9,750)	
Equity sharing closing costs (including fees on new mortgage)	(3,000)	
Repayment of original mortgage	(75,000)	
Cash proceeds		$57,250
Less: Income tax on gain (assuming you sold 70% of the home and reinvested in a home worth $105,000 or more)		(0)
Cash available for new home		$57,250

All-Cash Sale at $135,000 (Alternative 1)

Sale price	$135,000	
Less: Seller closing costs (6.5% of $135,000)	(8,775)	
Repayment of original mortgage	(75,000)	
Cash proceeds		$51,225
Less: Income tax on gain (assuming you reinvested in a home worth $135,000 or more)		(0)
Cash available for new home		$51,225

All-Cash Sale at $150,000—Trading Down (Alternative 2)

Sale price	$150,000	
Less: Seller closing costs (6.5% of $150,000)	(9,750)	
Repayment of original mortgage	(75,000)	
Cash proceeds		$65,250
Sale price	$150,000	
Less: Seller closing costs (6.5% of $150,000)	(9,750)	
Original purchase price	(100,000)	
Original closing cost	(2,000)	
Taxable gain	$ 38,320	
Income tax on gain (33% of $38,320)		(12,646)
Cash available for new home		$52,604
Extra cash out from equity sharing (compared with Alternative 1)	$ 6,025	
Extra cash out from equity sharing (compared with Alternative 2)	$ 4,646	

(Continued)

(Example Continued)
Return after 5 years—Equity Sharing vs. Cashing Out

Equity Share	Alternative 1	Alternative 2
Funds for reinvestment from equity share		
(Calculation D in Example A.3)	$14,898	$14,898
Extra cash out invested in 6.5% CD	8,294	6,395
Less: Income tax on interest	(749)	(577)
Funds available for reinvestment	$22,443	$20,716
All-Cash Sale at $135,000		
No investment—too little sale proceeds		0
All-Cash Sale at $150,000—Trading Down		
No investment—paid it in taxes		0

Equity Sharing versus Seller Financing

Advantage 1: Indefinite tax deferral. If you are trading down and therefore paying tax on your profit from resale, seller financing will allow you to defer *some* of the tax *temporarily* until the seller financing is repaid. By contrast, equity sharing will generally allow you to defer *all* of the tax *indefinitely*.

Advantage 2: Tax shelter. See comparison of equity sharing to certificate of deposit.

Advantage 3: Higher returns. See comparison of equity sharing to certificate of deposit.

Disadvantage 1: No guaranteed return. The interest on seller financing is not dependent on property appreciation.

Disadvantage 2: Credit damage. As an equity sharing investor, you will be a coborrower with the occupier on the mortgage, and a default by the occupier could damage your credit. You will not be a coborrower if you provide seller financing.

Disadvantage 3: Additional cash needs. See comparison of equity sharing to certificate of deposit.

Example A.6   Financial Comparison of Equity Sharing versus Seller Financing

You are comparing the equity share of the previous examples with carrying a note in the amount of $8,000 at 8 percent interest for five years. In the first comparison, assume you are trading up. Your cash proceeds at sale will be $57,250 whether you equity share or carry a note. Over the next five years, the note will provide you with after-tax income of $36. The equity share provides no direct income, but gives you a tax savings of $24. At the end of the five-year term, the equity share will be worth $12,590 compared with $8,792 for the note. In the second comparison, assume you are trading down. In the equity share, you pay no tax at the time of sale. With the note, even though you defer some of your gains tax, you still pay $11,971 at the time of sale. In addition to the tax savings, the equity share yields $4,436 extra after five years.

Cash at Sale—Equity Sharing vs. Seller Financing

Equity Share
Cash available for new home
   (Calculation F in Example A.5) $57,250

Sale at $150,000—Trading Up

Sale price	$150,000	
Less: Seller closing costs (6.5% of $150,000)	(9,750)	
Repayment of original mortgage	(75,000)	
Seller financing	(8,000)	
Cash proceeds		$57,250
Income tax on gain		(0)
Cash available for new home		$57,250

Sale at $150,000—Trading Down

Sale price	$150,000	
Less: Seller closing costs (6.5% of $150,000)	(9,750)	
Repayment of original mortgage	(75,000)	
Seller financing	(8,000)	
Cash proceeds		$57,250
Sale price	$150,000	
Less: Seller closing costs (6.5% of $150,000)	(9,750)	
Original purchase price	(100,000)	
Original closing cost	(2,000)	
Taxable gain	$ 38,320	

(Continued)

(Example Continued)

Percentage of sale price taken as cash ($142,000/$150,000)	94.67%	
Portion of gain taxable (94.67% of $38,320)	$ 36,276	
Less: Income tax on gain (33% of $36,276)		(11,971)
Cash available for new home		$45,279
Extra cash out from equity sharing		$11,971

Monthly After-Tax Return—Equity Sharing vs. Seller Financing

Equity Share (Calculation G)

Rental income calculation

Fair market rental (30% of $800)	$ 240	
Less: Good tenant discount (10%)	(24)	
Management discount	(100)	
Fair rental		$ 116
Less: Investor expenses (see Chapter Four)		(116)
Monthly negative cash flow		$ 0

Depreciation

Cost of building (75% of $100,000)	$ 75,000	
Original closing costs	2,000	
Equity share closing costs	1,500	
Total cost basis	$ 78,500	
Seller share (30% of $78,500)	23,550	
Monthly depreciation ($23,550/27.5%/12)	(71)	
Tax savings from depreciation (33% of $71)	24	
After-tax return (negative cash flow + tax savings)		$ 24
As annual percentage of $8,000 investment		3.60%

Seller Financing

Interest income		$ 53
Less: Income tax (33% of $53)		(17)
After-tax return		$ 36
As annual percentage of $8,000 investment		5.40%
Extra return from seller financing		$ 12

(Continued)

(Example Continued)
Return at Conclusion—Equity Sharing vs. Seller Financing

Equity Share

Appreciation (20% of $150,000)	$30,000
Less: Closing costs on purchase (2% of $150,000)	(3,000)
Costs of sale (6.5% of $180,000 sale price)	(11,700)
Net appreciation	$15,300
Less: Occupier split (70% of $15,300)	(10,710)
Your return	$ 4,590
Less: Tax on return	(0)
Principal	8,000
Total funds for reinvestment	$12,590

Sale at $150,000—Trading Up

Principal repayment	$ 8,000
Less: Tax on repayment	(0)
Value of extra $12/month invested at 5.5%	827
Less: Tax on interest ($827 − (60 × 12) = $107	
in interest; 33% of $107 = $35)	(35)
Total funds for reinvestment	$ 8,792

Sale at $150,000—Trading Down

Principal repayment		$ 8,000
Less: Tax on repayment		(0)
Taxable gain (from original sale)	$ 38,320	
Percentage of sale price taken as seller		
financing ($8,000/$150,000)	5.33%	
Portion of gain now taxable		
(5.33% of $38,320)	$ 1,933	
Less: Income tax on gain (33% of $1,933)		(638)
Value of extra $12/month invested at 5.5%		827
Less: Tax on interest		
($827 − (60 × 12) = $107 in interest;		
33% of $107 = $35)		(35)
Total funds for reinvestment		$ 8,154

Equity Sharing versus Holding, Refinancing, and Renting

Advantage 1: More cash out. Lenders consider equity share property owner-occupied and typically will lend 90 percent of value. By contrast, most lend only 75 percent on rental property. The extra 15 percent means $22,500 in extra cash on a $150,000 property. Even if you contribute $8,000 to the equity share, you still pocket $14,500 more from equity sharing than from refinancing and renting.

Advantage 2: No negative cash flow. When you refinance your old home to purchase your new one, the mortgage payments on the old home will rise and may well exceed rental income. Even if they don't,

---

Example A.7   Financial Comparison of Equity Sharing versus Holding, Refinancing, and Renting

Assume you are comparing the equity share of the previous examples with keeping your old home, refinancing with a 75 percent loan, and renting it out. At the time of sale, the equity share will give you an extra $22,000 in cash. Over the next five years, the equity share avoids an average of $270 per month in losses and provides a tax savings of $24, which makes you $294 better off. Assume you deposit the $294 in a 5.5 percent money market account. At the end of five years, your equity share investment in your old house, plus your $22,000 in extra cash from the sale invested in another equity share, plus your $294 in monthly savings, is worth a total of $66,629. By contrast, even if your old home appreciated 20 percent while you rented it out, your equity after five years would be only $28,225.

Cash at Sale—Equity Sharing vs. Holding, Refinancing, and Renting

Equity Share		
Cash available for new home		
(Calculation F in Example A.5)		$ 57,250
Hold, Refinance, and Rent		
New mortgage (75% of $150,000)	$112,500	
Less: Closing costs on new mortgage	(2,250)	
Repayment of original mortgage	(75,000)	
Cash available for new home		$ 35,250
Extra cash available from equity sharing		$ 22,000

Monthly After-Tax Return—Equity Sharing vs. Holding, Refinancing, and Renting

Equity Share		
After-tax return		
(Calculation G in Example A.6)		$ 24

(Continued)

(Example Continued)

Hold, Refinance, and Rent

Total monthly negative cash flow		
(Calculation E in Example A.4)		(523)
Less: Tax savings from negative cash flow		
(33% of $523)		173
Depreciation (see Chapter Four)		
Cost of building (75% of $100,000)	$ 75,000	
Original closing costs	2,000	
Refinance closing costs	2,250	
Total cost basis	$ 79,250	
Monthly depreciation ($79,250/27.5/12)	(240)	
Less: Tax savings from depreciation (33% of $240)		80
After-tax cost (negative cash flow + tax savings)	$	(270)
Extra funds from equity sharing	$	294

Return at Conclusion—Equity Sharing vs. Holding,
Refinancing, and Renting

Equity Share

Appreciation (20% of $150,000)	$ 30,000
Less: Closing costs on purchase (2% of $150,000)	(3,000)
Costs of sale (6.5% of $180,000 sale price)	(11,700)
Net appreciation	$ 15,300
Less: Occupier split (70% of $15,300)	(10,710)
Your return	$ 4,590
Less: Tax on return	(0)
Principal	8,000
Extra cash out from equity sharing (see above)	22,000
Return on extra cash out (11.5% × $22,000 × 5)*	12,650
Less: Tax on extra cash out	(0)
Value of $294/month invested at 5.5%	20,251
Less: Tax on interest ($20,251 − (60 × 294) = $2,611	
in interest; 33% of $2,611 = $862)	(862)
Total funds for reinvestment	$ 66,629

Hold, Refinance, and Rent

Sale price	$180,000
Less: Closing costs on refinance (2% of $112,500)	(2,250)
Costs of sale (6.5% of $180,000 sale price)	(11,700)
Mortgage balance	(106,445)
Negative cash flow ($523 × 60)	(31,380)
Total funds for reinvestment	$ 28,225

*Assumes amount is reinvested in another equity share that yields 11.5%.

you risk that interest rates (on an adjustable mortgage), property taxes, insurance, utilities, and other regular expenses will rise faster than rents. By contrast, you will have no monthly expenses in the equity share.

Advantage 3: Less management and no management fees. See comparison of equity sharing to rental property.

Advantage 4: Less risk of vacancy. See comparison of equity sharing to rental property.

Advantage 5: Lower maintenance costs. See comparison of equity sharing to rental property.

Disadvantage 1: Risk of default. See comparison of equity sharing to rental property.

Disadvantage 2: Loss of control. See comparison of equity sharing to certificate of deposit.

PARENT/RELATIVE ANALYSIS—ADVANTAGES AND DISADVANTAGES

If you are the parent or relative of a would-be home buyer, equity sharing has a dual purpose: (1) to help your relative purchase his first home and (2) to provide you with a high-quality, low-risk investment. In earlier sections of this appendix, we examined the advantages of equity sharing over low-yielding investments such as certificates of deposits, treasury bonds, and money market funds. Reinvesting a portion of your savings in an equity share provides an excellent way to add variety and diversity to your investments. You may not care about the investment benefits of equity sharing; traditionally, many parents and relatives have provided down payment assistance either as a loan that was subsequently forgiven or as a gift. This section will compare equity sharing to these arrangements.

It may also be possible to equity share without tapping into your savings. If you are among the many older people who have owned their homes for many years and have little or no remaining mortgage, your home equity represents substantial savings that you may never have realized you had. Through refinancing your home, you can use a portion of this savings to equity share. If you make the monthly payments on the refinanced mortgage, the interest portion of your payment is tax-deductible. If you cannot afford to make these payments, perhaps your son, daughter, or other relative can afford to make them for you as part of the equity share. At the time of the buyout or sale of the equity share property, you can use the proceeds to repay the refinanced mortgage. The advantages and disadvantages of this arrangement are discussed later in this section.

Equity Sharing versus Lending with Debt Forgiveness or Giving

Advantage 1: Avoids gift tax. Gift tax is payable on all gifts over $10,000 made in a single year. If you provide down payment funds over $10,000 as a gift, either you or the recipient will need to pay these taxes. If you loan rather than give the down payment, the mortgage lender will not consider the loaned money to be part of the down payment. This means that if the lender requires a 10 percent down payment, the money you loan will not be counted toward that 10 percent. Moreover, if you later forgive the debt, it will become a gift in the year it is forgiven, and gift tax will be payable at that time. Equity sharing does not trigger gift tax and is counted as down payment by most lenders.

Advantage 2: Adds qualification strength. Through equity sharing, your financial strength and creditworthiness will help your son, daughter, or other relative qualify for a bigger and better mortgage.

Advantage 3: Can be used as a tax-deferred exchange from other investments. If you already have real estate investments, you can sell them and reinvest in an equity share without paying taxes. By contrast, a gift or loan would not allow you to defer taxes.

Advantage 4: Tax shelter. See comparison of equity sharing to certificate of deposit.

Disadvantage 1: More complicated. Equity sharing is substantially more complex than giving or making a loan.

Refinancing to Equity Share

Advantage 1: Puts savings to work. Having a very small mortgage or no mortgage on your home is tantamount to having a very large savings invested in your home. But the savings provides no benefit to you. Your home is appreciating at the same rate whether you have a large or a small amount invested there. Refinancing to equity share puts the money to work earning return and helping your son, daughter, or other relative purchase a first home.

Advantage 2: Two sources of appreciation. You are already deriving all the benefit you can from the appreciation of your home. Equity sharing will allow you to benefit from the appreciation of another property as well.

Advantage 3: Tax deductions. If your mortgage is older, most of your monthly payment is now principal rather than interest and is therefore not tax-deductible. This factor, coupled with the small size of the mortgage relative to the property value, means that you are getting a much smaller mortgage interest tax deduction than you are entitled to. If you have no use for additional money, it does not make sense to refinance and increase your monthly payment just so you can get a larger deduction. But if you have a worthwhile use for the money, such as equity sharing with a son, daughter, or other relative,

---

Example A.8   Financial Analysis of Refinancing to Equity Share

Assume you purchased your home 25 years ago for $50,000 with a 7.25 percent fixed mortgage of $40,000. The house is now worth $150,000 and you owe $13,699. Assume the house appreciates 20 percent over the next five years. You work, and you pay 33 percent of your income in taxes. In the equity share, you will refinance with a new 7.25 percent fixed loan of $23,000, enough to repay your old mortgage, invest $8,000 in the equity share, and pay $1,000 in loan closing costs. Your after-tax monthly cost will drop $170 because the payments on your new $23,000 mortgage are lower than the payments on your old $40,000 mortgage, and because more of the payments are going toward tax-deductible interest. Assume you save this money in a 5.5 percent money market account. At the end of five years, your equity share interest, plus the $170 monthly savings, plus the 20 percent appreciation on your home will be worth a total of $50,852. By contrast, if you did not equity share, you would have gained only the 20 percent appreciation on your home, worth $28,050. Moreover, the money you earn from the equity share, together with your monthly savings, would be enough to completely retire your new mortgage and still leave you with $2,095 cash.

Monthly Cost—Refinancing to Equity Share

Current Monthly Cost (without Refinance or Equity Share)

Mortgage payment	$ 273
Property tax	50
Insurance	25
Total PITI	$ 348
Less: Tax savings (33% of $83 mortgage *interest*)	(27)
Tax savings (33% of $50 property taxes)	(17)
After-tax monthly payment	$ 304

(Continued)

(Example Continued)
Monthly Cost with Equity Share—Parent Makes Payments

Mortgage payment	$ 157
Property tax	50
Insurance	25
Total PITI	$ 232
Less: Tax savings (33% of $296 mortgage *interest*)	(46)
Tax savings (33% of $50 property taxes)	(17)
Tax savings from equity share (Calculation C in Example A.3)	(35)
After-tax monthly payment	$ 134
Monthly savings with equity share/refinance	$ 170

Investment Return—Refinancing to Equity Share

Return without Equity Sharing (Calculation H)

Appreciation of your home (20% of $150,000)	$30,000
Less: Cost of sale (6.5% of $30,000)	(1,950)
Net appreciation	$28,050
As annual percentage of equity of $136,301	4.1%

Return with Equity Sharing

Appreciation on equity share property (20% of $150,000)	$30,000
Less: Closing costs on purchase (2% of $150,000)	(3,000)
Costs of sale (6.5% of $180,000 sale price)	(11,700)
Net appreciation	$15,300
Less: Occupier split (70% of $15,300)	(10,710)
Your return	$ 4,590
Less: Tax on return	(0)
Principal	8,000
Less: Repayment of $1,000 closing costs for refinance loan	(1,000)
Value of $170/month invested at 5.5%	11,710
Less: Tax on interest ($11,710 − (60 × 170) = $1,510 in interest; 33% of $1,510 = $498)	(498)
Net appreciation from your home (Calculation H)	28,050
Net appreciation	$50,582
As annual percentage of equity of $136,301	7.5%

Repaying Your Mortgage

Proceeds from equity share	$12,590
Value of $170/month invested at 5.5% less taxes	11,212
Total available	$23,802
Less: Balance of your new mortgage	(21,707)
Amount remaining after payoff	$ 2,095

it makes sense to refinance and use the home mortgage deduction to help accomplish your goal. The cost of the funds invested in the equity share will be partially offset by the tax savings created by the mortgage interest deduction. You will also have the additional tax deductions created by the equity share itself.

Advantage 4: Home buyer can make payments. If you cannot afford to make higher monthly payments and/or cannot take advantage of tax deductions because you are retired, another option is to have your equity sharing son, daughter, or other relative make the payments for you. The repayment of a small loan at home mortgage rates is usually not a significant additional burden for the occupier.

Disadvantage 1: Risk of loss. Any amount you borrow against your current home must eventually be repaid. If the equity share property loses a substantial portion of its value, some or all of the money you invested could be lost, and you could have difficulty repaying your home mortgage. You can reduce this risk by providing in the equity sharing agreement that any amount borrowed against your home will be the first contribution returned following buyout or sale.

EMPLOYER ANALYSIS—ADVANTAGES AND DISADVANTAGES

Many employers use some form of housing cost assistance as a perk, a recruiting tool, or part of a relocation package. More progressive companies are also using these programs to boost the local economy, demonstrate commitment to the community, or create incentives for employees to live close to work. Most programs involve lump-sum payments by the employer either directly to the employee (for moving expenses or closing costs) or to a lender in exchange for reduced-rate mortgages. This section compares equity sharing to such payment programs.

Equity Sharing versus Lump-Sum Payments

Advantage 1: Payment not taxable to employee. Most lump-sum payments are taxable income for the employee; an equity sharing contribution is not.

Advantage 2: Properties can be reused. When an employee is transferred, relocates, or leaves the company, the employer can buy him out and offer an equity share in the same property to another employee or prospective employee with dramatically reduced closing costs.

Advantage 3: Investment return for employer. Lump-sum payments provide no direct investment return for the employer; equity sharing can provide both investment return and continuing tax deductions.

Disadvantage 1: Payment not deductible in year made. Equity sharing contributions are not tax-deductible in the year made; lump-sum payments are.

REAL ESTATE AGENT ANALYSIS—ADVANTAGES AND DISADVANTAGES

Equity Sharing for Real Estate Agents

Advantage 1: Increases clients' buying power. Equity sharing provides additional down payment and loan qualification strength for your existing home buyer clients.

Advantage 2: Enables weaker prospects to enter market. Most agents have a file full of prospective clients who aren't in the market because they can't afford the type of home they want. Equity sharing turns these prospects into buyers.

Advantage 3: Attracts home buyer clients. Expertise and experience in equity sharing attracts new home buyer clients. Advertising your equity sharing know-how through word-of-mouth, print ads, or workshops is an effective way to generate sales.

Advantage 4: Attracts investor clients. Equity sharing attracts investors who had never considered real estate investment because they thought it involved too much investment, experience, risk, or management effort. You will be surprised how many investors you can generate from past clients, including parents looking for a way to help children purchase, or home owners who have accumulated equity that they want to put to work.

Advantage 5: Databasing. Once you start generating equity sharing clients—both occupiers and investors—you can start a database that will attract more new clients. This process works very quickly once you take the first few steps.

Advantage 6: Increases salability of listings. Equity sharing increases the number of qualified buyers for your listings. It also provides a new and effective marketing hook to get buyers and agents to your open houses.

Advantage 7: Attracts new listings. Equity sharing knowledge enhances your farming efforts and listing presentations. You can present it as an additional and unique marketing approach for the seller's property. If you are databasing, you can also promote your ability to generate a large number of buyers from your own database.

Disadvantage 1: Increases complexity. Equity sharing involves more parties and more issues than most other transactions. As a result, it is more time-consuming and risky.

Disadvantage 2: Increases liability. Having more parties involved in the transactions means that there are more interests to represent and a greater likelihood of conflicts. You must disclose potential conflicts and avoid favoring one client's interests over another's. Equity sharing also involves legal and accounting issues that are not present in other transactions. To avoid liability for giving incorrect advice or for practicing law or accounting without the proper license, be careful about what advice you give and what advice you defer to other professionals.

QUESTION THE NAYSAYERS

Rarely does a day pass when I don't hear about some real estate agent, attorney, accountant, financial planner, radio personality, or cocktail party companion who thinks equity sharing should be avoided like the plague. I always press for the details underlying these opinions, and usually find they fall into one of three categories: (1) a misunderstanding of equity sharing risks, (2) an unsupported statistic about equity sharing defaults, or (3) a secondhand account of an equity sharing disaster.

Misunderstandings of equity sharing risks are common because the practice is relatively new and is evolving quickly. Few people, including real estate professionals, understand how modern equity sharing works. A ten-minute discussion can convince even the most ardent critic that his concerns are unfounded and that there is a logical solution to the issue or danger he felt was insurmountable.

Unsupported default "statistics" come from offhand comments by a few pundits in speeches and articles. There are equity sharing defaults just as there are mortgage foreclosures, credit card delinquencies, and people who take forever to pay legal bills. But in representing over 350 co-ownership clients over seven years, I have heard of only three defaults. Based on my own experience and that of other professionals who handle equity sharing transactions, the incidence of default is actually lower than the incidence of ordinary mortgage foreclosures.

Horror stories involve equity sharing without competent representation and a complete agreement. A disaster outside the equity share, such as illness, marital breakdown, or job loss, affected all of the victim's personal and business relationships, and the parties had not considered this possibility at the outset. These incidents say little about equity sharing, and much about bad breaks and the value of contingency planning.

The true root of all the naysaying is ignorance and fear of anything new. Few professionals are anxious to learn a new discipline, and they correctly assume that if it catches on, they will lose business to competitors who have mastered it. Consequently, their initial reaction is defensive; they point out problems rather than develop solutions. Not long ago, similar misinformation, unfounded statistics, and secondhand horror stories circulated about condominiums; today, there are over 12,000 condominium associations in California alone. The moral of this story is not to ignore the naysayers; their criticisms and concerns may be well-founded. Instead, question them, understand potential problems, find out what solutions are available, and weigh all the risks and benefits for yourself.

Appendix B

Lenders and Loans

Most first-time buyers find mortgages hopelessly complicated and arbitrary, and they are absolutely right. But a basic understanding of the players and the plays can make the loan qualification process considerably less frustrating. Begin by thinking of home loans as products like cars, with specific features, drawbacks, and prices. Think of lenders as loan dealerships that offer a variety of loan products and make money from selling you a loan. Now you are ready to enter the twilight zone of mortgage lending.

LOAN DEALERS

There are many different types of loan dealers, but they all fall into two categories: (1) loan originators and (2) loan distributors. Loan originators, including banks, savings and loan associations, and credit unions, actually lend their own money. Loan distributors, called mortgage brokers, act as middlemen between loan originators and borrowers. When you go directly to loan originators for a loan, they will feature only their own loan products, but the information you get about your ability to qualify for those loan products is almost always right. When you go to a loan distributor, he can help you shop among a variety of loan products from different originators, but what you see may not be what you get. Every borrower's worst nightmare, and an all-too-common occurrence in real life, is to be told at the last minute that the lender rejected your loan application, or that the loan terms have suddenly changed. To guard against this risk, always submit at least one loan application to a loan originator.

All loan dealers charge fees for their services. When loan dealers advertise "no fee" or "no points" loans, they mean the fees are hidden as extra interest charges. Up-front fees are often called **loan points** and are based on a percentage of the loan amount. A fee of one point is one percent of the loan amount. Loan dealer fees can also be called **appraisal fees** and **application fees**, in which case they are usually flat fees rather than percentages. When a loan distributor is involved, fees are split between the loan distributor and the loan originator. If possible, avoid paying any fees before your loan is approved in writing. If you must pay an advance fee, get a written promise from the dealer that the fee will be returned if he does not deliver the promised loan.

THE RISK SEESAW

Loan shopping is complicated because there are so many different features to compare. To be a smart shopper, you need to understand how the features fit together from the lender's perspective. You then have the foundation to evaluate which loan is the best deal for you. Each loan has its own set of **terms** and **underwriting guidelines**. They are like two ends of a seesaw: the riskier the terms for the lender, the tougher the underwriting guidelines.

The risk seesaw is important to you because tough underwriting guidelines will often lower your maximum mortgage amount. Your best loan will combine most of the terms you want with underwriting guidelines that allow you to qualify for the mortgage amount you need.

Here is a list of the types of loan terms you should compare, along with a description of how they affect lender risk:

- *Interest.* The mortgage **interest rate** is the amount you pay the lender for the use of its money. An interest rate can be **fixed**, meaning it stays the same until the loan is repaid, or **adjustable**, meaning it floats up and down with the market. The next section compares fixed and adjustable rates from your perspective; for now, we focus on lender risk. Lenders pay for the money they lend, and they lose money if the interest they receive is less than the interest they pay. The interest a lender pays is not fixed, so when it makes a fixed-rate loan it take the risk that the interest it pays will rise above the interest it receives. This risk is lower with adjustable-rate loans. The more freely and often a lender can adjust an interest rate, the lower the risk that the interest it pays will ever exceed the interest it receives.

- *Loan-to-value ratio.* The **loan-to-value ratio (LTV)** is the relationship of the loan amount to the property value expressed as a percentage:

$$\text{LTV\%} = \frac{\text{Loan amount}}{\text{Property value}}$$

Each loan has a maximum LTV. The higher the maximum LTV, the lower the minimum down payment. If you have a relatively small down payment, you will need a loan with a high maximum LTV. But higher maximum LTV means higher lender risk. The risk is that the property value will fall close to or below the loan amount. When that happens, a foreclosure sale may not yield enough to repay the loan balance and foreclosure costs.

- *Fees.* Try to pay the lowest possible fees, especially if you have limited down payment funds. Every dollar of loan fees means a dollar less for down payment. But higher fees mean the lender makes money sooner and can afford to take greater risks on other loan terms.

- *Term.* The loan **term** is the number of years before the loan must be fully repaid. You want the longest possible term so that you will never be forced to repay the loan before you are financially ready. Remember that you can always repay a 30-year mortgage on a 15-year schedule, but you can never repay a 15-year loan on a 30-year schedule. A longer term means more lender risk because there is more time for bad things to happen like falling property values, rising interest rates, or borrower insolvency.

- *Loan amount.* **Maximum loan amount** is the largest sum the bank will lend on a particular loan product. Lenders risk less when they loan less.

- *Prepayment.* **Prepayment** is repaying the loan before it is due. Some loans have a **prepayment penalty**, an extra charge imposed on a borrower if he makes a prepayment. You probably won't expect a prepayment penalty to matter because you won't expect to prepay. But some change in your life may cause you to need to sell your home, or falling interest rates may make refinancing attractive. Having a prepayment penalty may then become a very expensive mistake. Lenders charge prepayment penalties when they need to collect a certain amount of interest before they break even on loan processing costs and start making a profit. This is often true with "no fee" loans, where the lender has buried most or all of its processing costs and profits in the interest. The more free the borrower is to repay the loan, the higher the chance that the lender will lose money because the borrower will repay (by selling the property or refinancing) before the lender recovers its costs and starts making a profit. The greater the restrictions or fees on prepayment, the lower the risk.

• *Assumability.* In a loan **assumption**, a new borrower substitutes himself for the original borrower. Some loans allow assumption, provided the new borrower is qualified and pays an assumption fee. Assumability is a valuable feature because it can yield a higher price when you sell your property. This will occur in two situations: (1) when interest rates have risen and your loan has a lower rate than any new loan your buyer can get, and (2) when property values have fallen and your loan has a higher LTV than any new loan your buyer can get. These same situations create risk for the lender, who may be stuck continuing a loan with a below-market interest rate or a high LTV for longer than it would have if the loan were not assumable.

• *Private mortgage insurance.* **Private mortgage insurance (PMI)** is an insurance policy for the lender against your default. If you don't make your payments, the lender collects on the PMI. You pay the premiums for PMI, which can be as high as 1 to 2 percent of the loan amount per year and are not tax-deductible. Loans with the best terms are the most likely to require PMI.

Use this list as a guide to question lenders about the loans they offer. Make sure you get all the information about each loan so that you can truly compare. You will find that lenders create loan products by combining some risky terms with other less risky terms. For example, loans with higher-risk LTV ratios may only be available in less risky smaller amounts or may require risk-reducing PMI; high-risk "no point" loans may only be available with low-risk adjustable interest rates and prepayment penalties; fixed-rate loans may not be assumable. It is likely that you will sacrifice some terms you would like to have but can live without for others that are more beneficial to you. The important thing is to understand what you are getting and what you are giving up.

Now let's examine the other end of the seesaw: underwriting guidelines. Loan terms determine the risk of the loan; underwriting guidelines determine the risk of the borrower. A lender taking more risk with loan terms will accept less risk with the borrower.

For each set of terms, a lender has underwriting guidelines that establish standards for borrower risk.

There are two types of underwriting guidelines: (1) creditworthiness and (2) debt-to-income ratio (DTI). **Creditworthiness** is an assessment of the borrower's stability and responsibility. Typical creditworthiness standards dictate a maximum number of blemishes on a credit report, demand an indisputable verification of earnings, or require a long job history with a big employer. If you are strong on creditworthiness, you need not worry about these standards; but if you have a bad credit report, are self-employed and show little income on your tax return, or recently changed jobs, you will be limited to loans with less stringent creditworthiness guidelines.

Debt-to-income ratio is an assessment of the borrower's income strength. It is the percentage that expresses the relationship between PITI and gross monthly income:

$$DTI\% = \frac{PITI}{Gross\ monthly\ income}$$

In other words, DTI is the percentage of your monthly income that you spend on house payments. The underwriting guidelines for a particular loan establish a maximum DTI for that loan. If you are trying to qualify for the largest possible loan, look for the one with the lowest interest rate and the highest maximum DTI. A borrower who earns $25,000 will qualify for $69,000 on a 7.25 percent fixed-rate mortgage with a 28 percent maximum DTI; the same borrower will qualify for $105,000 on a 6 percent adjustable-rate loan with a 35 percent maximum DTI.

Now that you understand the risk seesaw, you are ready to tackle the most fundamental decision in loan shopping: choosing between an adjustable or fixed interest rate loan.

HOW ADJUSTABLES WORK

To understand and evaluate adjustable-rate mortgages, you need to learn more terminology. The **interest rate** is the amount of interest you are paying on the mortgage on any given day. With an adjustable-rate mortgage, the interest rate moves up or down according to an **index**. The index is always some published benchmark that is beyond the control of the lender. Think of an index as if it is the air temperature in a particular city. In Boston, the air temperature changes often, moves quickly when it changes, and has a wide differential between its highs and its lows. But in San Diego, the temperature never changes very much or very fast. Some indexes are more **volatile**, like Boston temperatures, and some are less volatile, like San Diego temperatures. Your interest rate is like a thermometer; it rises with the index. When you evaluate an adjustable loan, you need to determine the volatility of its index. The lender can provide historical charts to help you.

The **margin** is the amount the lender adds to the index to determine the interest rate. The margin is only important when comparing two adjustable loans with the same index: you will pay less interest on the one with the lower margin. The **change date** is the day when the interest rate is adjusted. An adjustable mortgage may have change dates once a month, once a year, or according to some other schedule. The fewer the change dates, the better the loan. **Caps** are limits on the amount the interest rate can change. Most adjustable loans have at least two types of caps: (1) a cap on the amount the interest rate can change on each change date, and (2) a cap on the amount it can change during the entire life of the loan. Like mercury reaching the top of a thermometer, the interest rate stops following the index whenever it bumps into a cap.

Here's how an adjustable loan works. It usually begins with an artificially low interest rate, often called a **start rate** or a **teaser rate**. We say the rate is artificially low because it is less than the index plus the margin. For example, a loan with a margin of 2 percent and an index that happens to be 4.5 percent on June 15, 1994, should have an interest rate of 6.5 percent on that date; but people who borrow their mortgage on that day might start with a teaser rate of 4.5 percent. The teaser rate lasts until the first change date, when the mortgage moves up to the index plus the margin unless it bumps into a cap. Regardless of the cap, the interest rate catches up to the index-plus-margin by the second or third change date. Then, on each change date, it moves up or down with the index unless it bumps into a cap.

ADJUSTABLE VERSUS FIXED

Adjustable-rate loans offer two major advantages over fixed-rate loans: (1) lower short-term costs and (2) larger loan amounts. In the first few years, you pay less interest on an adjustable loan even if the interest rate moves up as fast as it can. Your interest savings comes from lower fees, a teaser rate, and, after the teaser rate ends, an index-plus-margin interest rate that is still lower than the rate on fixed loans. To see this cost savings in action, compare total payments over three years for a fixed and an adjustable loan, assuming the adjustable goes up as fast as it can (see Example B.1).

In Example B.1, which uses loans available as I write, the adjustable saves *at least* $12,500 over the first three years. In practice, the adjustable saves more because the index-plus-margin rate is unlikely to

---

Example B.1   Cost Savings of Adjustable Mortgage

Loan 1: $200,000 loan at 7.5 percent fixed with fees of $4,250.

Loan fees	$ 4,250
Interest payments: 36 at 7.5%	45,000
Total payments	$49,250

Loan 2: $200,000 loan starting at 4.5 percent that has an adjustment cap of ½ percent every 6 months, and fees of $2,250. (The index-plus-margin rate is 5.75 percent at the start of the loan.)

Loan fees	$ 2,250
6 months' interest payments at 4.5%	4,500
6 months' interest payments at 5.0%	5,000
6 months' interest payments at 5.5%	5,500
6 months' interest payments at 6.0%	6,000
6 months' interest payments at 6.5%	6,500
6 months' interest payments at 7.0%	7,000
Total payments	$36,750

---

move up 1.25 percent in three years. The short-term cost savings usually lasts at least three years.

Adjustables offer larger loan amounts because of the risk seesaw. Lower lender risk translates into higher LTV and higher DTI. You would need $65,000 income to qualify for the $200,000 fixed-rate Loan 1 in Example B.1, but only $50,000 to qualify for the $200,000 adjustable-rate Loan 2 in Example B.2.

Fixed-rate loans offer long-term security. The interest rate on Loan 2 could go up as high as 11 percent after 6½ years; Loan 1 will always be 7.5 percent.

How should you choose? Take this true/false test.

T F You qualify for the home you want with a fixed-rate loan.
T F You can afford the extra fees of a fixed-rate loan.
T F You plan to keep your home for at least four years.
T F You think interest rates will rise before you sell.

If any of these statements were false, choose an adjustable- over a fixed-rate loan.

In today's mortgage marketplace, there are choices beyond the plain old fixed and the plain old adjustable. People who want the security of a fixed but the rates, fees, and underwriting guidelines of an adjustable, can choose from several hybrid loan products that are *less risky for the lender:*

- *Less term risk:* A 15-year fixed with equal monthly payments high enough to pay off the whole loan in 15 years. You will need to be able to qualify to make higher monthly payments.
- *Less term risk:* A 30-year fixed due in seven years. The payments are the same as on a normal 30-year fixed, but you need to pay the entire remaining balance (a **balloon payment**) at the end of the seventh year. Skip this unless you are sure you will move or refinance within seven years.
- *Less interest risk:* A fixed loan that converts to an adjustable loan after five years. You have the same long-term risks as with any adjustable, but your initial rate lasts three to five years. Choose this if you plan to keep the loan for three to five years but expect interest rates to rise rapidly during that time.

People who need the rates, fees, and underwriting guidelines of an adjustable but crave the security of a fixed also have a hybrid, an adjustable that can be converted to a fixed. Unfortunately, the fixed rate to which you convert is higher than the prevailing fixed rate at the time of conversion, so this option may be no better than refinancing with a new fixed when you think rates are starting to rise. But the conversion feature would prove useful if the property had dropped in value, you had lost your job, or some other disaster struck, and you could not qualify to refinance in response to the rising rates.

SHOPPING FOR LOANS

Now that you understand the basics, it's time to shop. Here's how to do it.

Step 1: Get some general help from a big local lender. Make an appointment with a loan agent from a big local lender. Bring in your pay stubs or tax returns and have the agent prequalify you for several loan products, including at least one fixed with tough underwriting guidelines and one adjustable with easy underwriting guidelines. This process will define the high and low limits of your loan qualification strength.

Step 2: Set a shopping strategy. Based on your visit with the big lender, can you qualify for a big enough fixed loan to buy the kind of home you want? If the answer is no, confine your shopping to adjustables. If the answer is yes, or if you are on the border, look back at the comparison of adjustable versus fixed, in the previous section, and decide which one you want.

Step 3: Gather information. Contact as many loan originators as time allows, and maybe one loan distributor. Tell each whether you are looking for a fixed or an adjustable, and make a list of the terms and guidelines for each loan in your category.

Step 4: Number crunch. Compare the loans. This will be much simpler with fixeds than with adjustables. If you are shopping for an adjustable, add up all the fees and interest for the first five years, assuming a fast rising interest rate, a slow rising interest rate, and a stagnant interest rate. Remember to consider the volatility of the index (Is it like weather in Boston or San Diego?) when you run the numbers with the fast rising rate. Rank your loan choices from best to worst.

Step 5: Prequalify with your top three choices. The terms that are best for you will probably be the riskiest for the bank. This means that your favorite loans will probably have the toughest underwriting guidelines. Prequalifying for your top three choices gives you a maximum mortgage size for each loan. Get a letter confirming the prequalification so that you can show it to the seller when you make an offer.

SELLER FINANCING

If you can't quite satisfy the underwriting guidelines for the type or size of loan you want, one solution might be **seller financing**, a loan made by the seller to the buyer. Like other mortgages, it is secured by a lien on the property, but unlike most, it is usually due in three to seven years instead of 30 to 40. Seller financing is generally used together with an institutional mortgage. A buyer makes a down payment of 5 to 10 percent, borrows 75 to 80 percent from a bank, and another 5 to 15 percent from the seller. (See Example B.2.)

Suppose you have a 5 to 10 percent down payment but cannot meet the strict underwriting guidelines for a 90 to 95 percent LTV loan. You may still be able to satisfy the less stringent requirements for an 80 percent LTV loan and use seller financing to fill the gap.

Here are some other good reasons to take advantage of seller financing:

- *Lowers loan fees.* Seller financing lowers both the rate and the amount of loan fees. The risk seesaw makes loan fee rates lower

Example B.2   Typical Seller Financing Arrangements

"Eighty-Ten-Ten"		
Bank mortgage	$120,000	80%
Seller financing	15,000	10%
Buyer down payment	15,000	10%
Total price	$150,000	100%
"Eighty-Fifteen-Five"		
Bank mortgage	$120,000	80%
Seller financing	22,500	15%
Buyer down payment	7,500	5%
Total price	$150,000	100%

on 80 percent LTV loans than on 90 percent LTV loans. Often, the fees drop from 2 percent of the loan amount to only 1 percent. And every dollar borrowed from the seller is a dollar not borrowed from another lender and therefore a dollar on which no loan fee is paid. Suppose you need to borrow 90 percent of $150,000. If you borrow all $135,000 from a bank, you are likely to pay a fee of 2 percent or $2,700. But if you borrow $15,000 from the seller and $120,000 from the bank, you are likely to pay a fee of 1 percent or $1,200. You save a total of $1,500 in loan fees: $1,200 because of the lower fee rate and $300 because of the lower loan amount.

- *Eliminates PMI.* The risk seesaw makes lenders less likely to require PMI on an 80 percent LTV loan than on a 90 to 95 percent LTV loan. Eliminating PMI will save you at least 1 percent of the loan amount per year, or $113 per month on that $135,000 loan.
- *Improves loan terms.* The risk seesaw makes loan terms better on an 80 percent LTV loan than on a 90 to 95 percent LTV loan. You save by paying a lower interest rate.
- *Temporarily defers seller taxes.* Until the loan is repaid, sellers do not need to pay income taxes on the portion of the sale price that they finance.

The drawback of seller financing is its short term, usually three to five years with a balloon payment required at the end. This means you will need to refinance within that period to repay the seller.

Appendix C

Cotenant Equity When Property Value Declines

C alculating cotenant equity is simple when equity share property substantially appreciates, but complicated when it does not. Co-owners must then determine how to allocate loss, and how much of each owner's capital contribution is returned. (See Example C.1.)

ALLOCATING LOSS BY TOTAL CAPITAL CONTRIBUTIONS

The simplest approach to allocating loss is to use total capital contributions rather than ownership percentages (Examples C.2 and C.3).

ALLOCATING LOSS BY CONTRIBUTION LAYERS

Most equity sharing agreements prioritize different types or "layers" of capital contributions, and provide that some contributions are returned before others. The purpose of prioritizing is to create incentives. An owner has a higher incentive to make a contribution if he

Example C.1   Investment Loss

Assume the facts from the sample transaction at the beginning of Chapter Three, and suppose that the value of 3321 Elm Street increases to $210,000.

Value	$210,000	
Less: Disposition expenses (6.5%)	(13,650)	
Mortgage balance	(175,000)	
Total equity		$21,350
Initial capital contribution	$ 25,000	
Monthly capital contribution	594	
Additional capital contribution	5,000	
Less: Total capital contributions		(30,594)
Loss		$ (9,244)

The 3321 Elm Street owners have invested $30,594 in the equity share, but have equity of only $21,350. Even though the property value has increased slightly, they have lost $9,244, about 30 percent of their investment.

Example C.2   Contribution-Based Allocation

The 3321 Elm Street owner contributions are 59 percent for the Smiths, and 41 percent for Laura. If the remaining equity is split according to capital contributions, each owner will lose 30% of his investment.

	Smiths	Davidson	Total
Down payment	$14,500	$10,500	$25,000
Monthly credit	594	0	594
Future/Unforeseen	3,000	2,000	5,000
Total	$18,094	$12,500	$30,594
Percentage	59%	41%	100%
Equity split (59/41)	$12,597	$ 8,753	$21,350
Less: Investment	(18,094)	(12,500)	(30,594)
Loss	$(5,497)	$(3,747)	$(9,244)
Percent of investment	30%	30%	30%

Example C.3   Problems with Ownership Percentage Allocation

The 3321 Elm Street ownership percentages are 55/45. If these percentages (rather than the 59/41 capital contribution percentages) were used to divide the equity, the Smiths would receive $11,742 and Laura would receive $9,608. This would mean that the Smiths would lose $6,532 or 35 percent of their investment, and Laura would lose $2,892 or 23 percent of her investment.

	Smiths	Davidson	Total
Equity split (55/45)	$11,742	$ 9,608	$21,350
Less: Investment	(18,094)	(12,500)	(30,594)
Loss	$ (6,532)	$ (2,892)	$ (9,244)
Percent of investment	35%	23%	30%

---

knows that there is a high probability of getting the money back. This incentive may become important if the real estate market is doing poorly and the owners feel their original investment may be lost. Under these circumstances, an owner might refuse to contribute additional money unless he knows it will be returned.

The model agreement in Chapter Ten has three categories or "layers" of capital contributions prioritized in the following order: (1) "Additional," (2) "Monthly," and (3) "Initial." The first money reimbursed is additional capital contributions. If there is not enough money to return all additional capital contributions, each owner gets a proportional share:

$$\frac{\text{Additional capital contributions by Owner A}}{\text{Total additional capital contributions}}$$

So long as there is still equity to distribute, this same process is repeated for each "layer" of capital contributions.

To illustrate the layered contribution-based allocation, assume 3321 Elm Street is worth $210,000.

Step 1: Calculate total equity.

Appraised value	$210,000
Less: Disposition expenses (6.5%)	(13,650)
Mortgage balance	(175,000)
Total equity	$ 21,350

Step 2: Compare total equity to additional capital contributions.

	Amount	Percent
Smith additional capital contribution	$3,000	60%
Davidson additional capital contribution	2,000	40%
Total additional capital contributions	$5,000	100%
Total equity (from Step 1)	$21,350	

If the total equity were less than $5,000, we could not credit the owners with all of their additional capital contributions. Instead, the Smiths would get 60 percent of the total equity and Laura would get 40 percent. But, in this illustration, there is enough money to credit each owner with all of his additional capital contributions. This means we move on to the next step.

Step 3: Subtract additional capital contributions from total equity.

Total equity (from Step 1)	$21,350
Less: Total additional capital contributions	(5,000)
Equity balance	$16,350

Because we have a remaining balance, we go to the next "layer" of capital contribution, the monthly capital contribution.

Step 4: Compare equity balance to monthly capital contributions.

	Amount	Percent
Smith monthly capital contribution	$594	100%
Davidson monthly capital contribution	0	0%
Total monthly capital contributions	$594	100%
Equity balance (from Step 3)	$16,350	

If the equity balance were $300 instead of $16,350, we could not credit the Smiths with all of their monthly capital contributions. Instead, the Smiths would get only the $300. But, in this example, there is enough money to credit the Smiths with their entire Monthly Capital Contribution of $594. This means we move on to the next step.

Step 5: Subtract monthly capital contributions from equity balance.

Equity balance (from Step 3)	$16,350
Less: Total monthly capital contributions	(594)
Equity balance	$15,756

Because we have a remaining balance, we go to the next "layer" of capital contribution, the initial capital contribution.

Step 6: Compare equity balance to initial capital contributions.

	Amount	Percent
Smith initial capital contribution	$14,500	58%
Davidson monthly capital contribution	10,500	42%
Total monthly capital contributions	$25,000	100%
Equity balance (from Step 5)	$15,756	

If the equity balance from Step 5 had been more than $25,000, each owner would have been credited with his full initial capital contribution. Any remaining balance at that point would have been profit, allocated according to the 55/45 ownership percentages. Here, the remaining equity balance is not enough to credit both owners with the full amount of their initial capital contribution. Under these circumstances, the Smiths get 58 percent of the equity balance and Laura gets 42 percent.

Step 7: Divide equity balance.

Smith share (58% of $15,756)	$9,138
Davidson share (42% of $15,756)	$6,618

The last step is to add up all of the credits for each owner to arrive at cotenant equity.

Step 8: Calculate cotenant equity.

	Smiths	Davidson	Total
Additional capital contributions	$ 3,000	$ 2,000	$ 5,000
Monthly capital contributions	594		594
Initial capital contributions	9,138	6,618	15,756
Total cotentant equity	$12,732	$ 8,618	$21,350

This means the Smiths could buy Laura's share for $8,618, and Laura could buy the Smiths' share for $12,732. These would also be the amounts of proceeds each owner would receive if the property sold for $210,000 and the costs of sale were exactly 6.5 percent.

CREATING SPECIAL INCENTIVES

A particular owner's contribution can be given special priority so that it is returned before the other owner's contribution. This type of incentive is sometimes offered to persuade an investor to equity share. It is frequently used where the investor is a parent, relative, or friend who is borrowing his capital contribution by refinancing his own home, and needs to be confident that he will receive from the equity share at least enough to repay the refinanced amount.

As an illustration of owner priority, assume 3321 Elm Street is worth $210,000, and the owners had agreed that Laura's contributions would have priority.

Step 1: Calculate total equity.

Appraised value	$210,000
Less: Disposition expenses (6.5%)	(13,650)
Mortgage balance	(175,000)
Total equity	$ 21,350

Step 2: Calculate investor contributions.

Davidson additional capital contributions	$ 2,000
Davidson monthly capital contributions	0
Davidson initial capital contributions	10,500
Total Davidson contributions	$12,500

Step 3: Calculate cotenant equity.

Total equity	$21,350
Less: Total Davidson contributions	(12,500)
Remaining equity for Smiths	$ 8,850

Similarly, giving special priority to the investor's capital contribution to a particular improvement might be used to provide additional incentive for the investor to contribute to that improvement.

Suppose that in the fourth year of the equity share, 3321 Elm Street is worth $180,000. The Smiths feel that a bedroom addition would add at least $50,000 to the property value, and that George could build it on weekends if Laura provides $10,000 for materials. Laura feels her money is already lost and is reluctant to invest more. The Smiths offer to return her bedroom contribution before any other proceeds. In that way, even if 3321 Elm Street sells for only $190,000 with the new bedroom, Laura will still get her $10,000 returned. She agrees because, in her mind, she will get the money back even in the "worst case" scenario.

Assume the Smiths' contribution of labor to the bedroom is valued at $10,000 but does not get special priority. After the bedroom is added, 3321 Elm Street is worth $210,000.

Step 1: Calculate total equity.

Appraised value	$210,000
Less: Disposition expenses (6.5%)	(13,650)
Mortgage balance	(175,000)
Total equity	$ 21,350

Step 2: Subtract priority contribution.

Total equity	$21,350
Less: Priority contribution	10,000
Equity balance	$11,350

Step 3: Compare equity balance to additional capital contributions.

	Amount	*Percent*
Smith additional capital contribution	$13,000	87%
Davidson additional capital contribution	2,000	13%
Total additional capital contributions	$15,000	100%
Equity balance (from Step 2)	$11,350	

Note that the Smiths' additional capital contribution includes their $10,000 labor contribution to the new bedroom. Laura's contribution is not included because it was given a priority return in Step 2. The equity is not sufficient to return all of the additional capital contributions. Under these circumstances, the Smiths get 87 percent of the equity balance and Laura gets 13 percent.

Step 4: Divide equity balance.

Smith share (87% of $11,350)	$9,875
Davidson share (13% of $11,350)	$1,475

Step 5: Calculate cotenant equity.

	Smiths	*Davidson*	*Total*
Priority contribution	$ 0	$10,000	$10,000
Additional capital contributions	9,875	1,475	11,350
Monthly capital contributions	0	0	0
Initial capital contributions	0	0	0
Total cotenant equity	$9,875	$11,475	$21,350

SUBTRACTING DISPOSITION EXPENSE

Note that in calculations of cotenant equity throughout this book, we subtract disposition expense from the sale proceeds prior to calculating equity. It is essential to subtract projected costs of sale, even if the equity share ends in a buyout rather than a sale. If you don't, a loss can look like a profit, and an owner who is bought out may get more money than he deserves. Example C.4 illustrates this problem.

Example C.4   Failure to Subtract Disposition Expense on Buyout

Suppose that, in the layered contribution-based allocation, disposition expense had not been deducted. Without this adjustment, total equity would have been $35,000 instead of $21,350, and the loss would have looked like a profit.

Appraised value	$210,000	
Less: Cost of sale	(0)	
Loan balance	(175,000)	
Total equity		$35,000
Total Smith contribution	(18,094)	
Total Davidson contribution	(12,500)	
Less: Total owner contribution		(30,594)
Profit to split		$ 4,406

The price for the Smiths to buy Laura out would have been:

Davidson additional capital contributions	$ 2,000
Davidson monthly capital contributions	0
Davidson initial capital contributions	10,500
Davidson profit (45% of $4,406)	1,983
Davidson cotenant equity	$ 14,483

Laura receives $14,483, a profit of $1,983. Now suppose the Smiths sell soon afterward:

Sale price	$210,000
Less: Cost of sale	(13,650)
Amount paid to Laura	(14,483)
Loan balance	(175,000)
Net proceeds	$ 6,867

The Smiths would lose $11,227, over 62 percent of their investment, even though Laura made a profit. Subtracting the disposition expense avoids this inequity.

Appendix D

Alternatives to Buyout and Sale

Occasionally, an occupier cannot afford an investor buyout but doesn't want to sell. This appendix explores other dispositions of the property at the end of the equity share term.

PARTIAL BUYOUT

In a partial buyout, the occupier buys a portion of the investor's share for a price based on the investor's equity, and the ownership percentages are modified to reflect the investor's smaller stake. Essentially, the owners start a "new" equity share upon the partial buyout.

Suppose the 3321 Elm Street owners agree to a 50 percent partial buyout by the Smiths after five years. Assuming the property is worth $250,000, Laura's cotenant equity is $25,170. In a 50 percent buyout, she would receive half of this amount, or $12,585. The owners would then calculate new ownership percentages based on Laura's lower stake in the equity share.

Step 1: Calculate total equity.

Appraised value	$250,000
Less: Disposition expenses (6.5%)	(16,250)
Mortgage balance	(175,000)
Total equity	$ 58,750

Step 2: Calculate capital contributions.

Initial capital contributions	$25,000
Monthly capital contribution	594
Additional capital contribution	5,000
Total capital contributions	$30,594

Step 3: Calculate total profit to date.

Total equity	$58,750
Less: Total capital contributions	(30,594)
Total profit	$28,156

Step 4: Calculate Davidson cotenant equity.

Davidson initial capital contributions	$10,500
Davidson monthly capital contribution	0
Davidson additional capital contribution	2,000
Davidson profit share (45% × $28,156)	12,670
Total Davidson cotenant equity	$25,170

Step 5: Calculate Smith cotenant equity.

Smith initial capital contributions	$14,500
Smith monthly capital contribution	594
Smith additional capital contribution	3,000
Smith profit share (55% × $28,156)	15,486
Total cotenant equity	$33,580

We assume at this point that the Smiths pay Laura $12,585, which is half of her cotenant equity.

Step 6: Calculate initial capital contributions to "new" equity share.

Davidson initial capital contribution	
Remaining cotenant equity	$12,585
New contributions	0
Total	$12,585
Smith initial capital contribution	
Remaining cotenant equity	$33,580
New contributions (paid to Laura)	12,585
Total	$46,165

If the agreement provided for pure "contribution-based" ownership percentages, the new ownership percentages would be:

$$\text{Smith:} \quad \$46,125/\$58,750 = 79\%$$
$$\text{Investor:} \quad \$12,585/\$58,750 = 21\%$$

In practice, the new ownership percentages would probably be modified to reflect other factors, as discussed in Chapter Five.

Partial buyouts are frequently used when the occupier is unable to buy out the investor and the investor is unable or unwilling to continue the equity share without recovering some of his investment. In this situation, the type of partial buyout illustrated above enables the occupier to keep the property even though he could not afford to fully buy out the investor.

A slightly modified version of the partial buyout can be used where the investor needs to recover *all* of his investment at the end of the original term. The occupier and the investor together refinance the property to borrow a large enough sum to pay the investor the full amount of his cotenant equity. The combined financial strength of the occupier and the investor allows the owners to borrow more than the occupier could borrow alone. After the refinancing, the equity share continues in a modified form to reflect the investor's continued involvement as a signer on the loan.

Had this occurred in the above example, Laura would have received all of her equity ($25,170) and had no initial capital contribution to the "new" equity share. But because she would be named as a borrower on the 3321 Elm Street loan, she would still be on title as an owner, still be a party to the equity sharing agreement, and still be entitled to some share of appreciation.

If the investor agrees to accept one or both of these types of partial buyout at the time the equity sharing agreement is prepared, these options can be included in the original equity sharing agreement. Otherwise, the owners can explore the options, if necessary, at the end of the equity share term.

OTHER ALTERNATIVES TO BUYOUT AND SALE

Equity sharing owners have many post-term alternatives to buyout and sale. An equity sharing attorney can help you evaluate your options and structure a creative solution. These are some buyout alternatives:

- Extend the equity share term with the occupier in possession. This alternative works when neither owner needs to change his position. Make sure you amend your agreement to set a new sale/buyout date or to provide that either owner may trigger a sale/buyout at any time. Do not leave the agreement as it was or amend it to provide that you will continue the equity share until both owners agree to end it; either of these options might trap one of the owners in the arrangement when he wants to leave.

- Extend the equity share term with a tenant-in-possession. This alternative works when the occupier needs to move out but neither party wants to sell. Again, make sure you amend the agreement. It needs a new term end and a new allocation of income and expenses.
- Sell part of the property to a new occupier and convert the old occupier to an additional investor. This alternative works when the occupier needs to move and neither party wants to sell, but both owners need some of their investment. You will need a completely new agreement.
- Complete a partial buyout and convert the investor's remaining equity to a loan. This alternative works when the occupier cannot afford to fully buy out the investor but the investor is not confident about the potential for future appreciation.

Index